TRIUMPH
B O O K S

100 THINGS ISLANDERS FANS
SHOULD KNOW & DO BEFORE THEY DIE

100 THINGS
ISLANDERS FANS
SHOULD KNOW & DO
BEFORE THEY DIE

Arthur Staple

TRIUMPH
BOOKS

Copyright © 2021 by Arthur Staple

No part of this publication may be reproduced, stored in a retrieval system, or transmitted in any form by any means, electronic, mechanical, photocopying, or otherwise, without the prior written permission of the publisher, Triumph Books LLC, 814 North Franklin Street, Chicago, Illinois 60610.

Library of Congress Cataloging-in-Publication Data available upon request.

This book is available in quantity at special discounts for your group or organization. For further information, contact:

Triumph Books LLC
814 North Franklin Street
Chicago, Illinois 60610
(312) 337-0747
www.triumphbooks.com

Printed in U.S.A.
ISBN: 978-1-62937-899-2
Design by Patricia Frey
All photos courtesy of Getty Images

For Beth

Contents

Foreword

May 15, 1973. That's the day my life changed forever. That's the day Bill Torrey made me an Islander.

When I think back on all the history we made in my 15 years on the Island, it all goes back to that beginning. How huge a task it seemed when I got there, at 19 years old, coming to a team that had won only 12 games the season before and was still trying to establish itself in an area the Rangers owned quite literally, given that Roy Boe and his nearly two dozen minority partners in the Islanders owed the Rangers $4 million just to exist.

But Mr. Torrey had a vision. Less than a month after he drafted me, he hired Al Arbour to coach us. Al taught us all how to play a complete game, he reduced our goals against by 100 that first season, and he laid the foundation for how hard we would have to work to compete against the established NHL clubs.

We had fun building it up. I loved getting to play again with my brother, Jean. I loved having a group of players close to my age—guys such as Bobby Nystrom and Andre St. Laurent, and later Clark Gillies, Bobby Bourne, Bryan Trottier, and Mike Bossy. We all grew up together and grew together as players.

And I loved Long Island. When I heard "New York," I thought of the big city, which was exciting. But I came to find out the Island was a sportsman's paradise where I could head out to Montauk to fish. Or it was an easy train ride to the city to enjoy the nightlife.

We made names for ourselves in 1975, when J.P. Parise scored that goal 11 seconds into overtime to knock out the Rangers on their own ice in our first-ever playoff series. We also began making more Islanders fans, getting an even bigger slice of the Island to come over to our side because of what we were building.

And we *kept* building, even through the disappointments of 1978 and 1979. Bill and Al stood by us, naming me captain and keeping our group together, then adding Butch Goring, the last piece of the puzzle we needed to secure the Stanley Cup in 1980 (the first of our four consecutive Cup victories). The feel of Nassau Coliseum that year when Bobby Nystrom scored to beat the Flyers is something I'll never forget.

The last of our Cup victories is extra-special to me. When we beat the Oilers in 1983, I looked up to the stands to see my father. He was sick with cancer, and I knew he wouldn't live to see us try to win another one. But seeing him there at the Coliseum, with all our fans screaming around him, is a memory I'll always cherish.

We were an amazing team—the 32 of us who were Islanders those four years. I've always said we should have been the first team inducted into the Hockey Hall of Fame. It was an honor to be voted in myself in 1991, but we couldn't have won those Cups without every single player on the roster.

We played and won for each other and for you, our amazing fans, and this book is for you as well. It's a collection of great stories, great moments, and fun times—not just from my era but from the more recent years as well.

Some of the last 30 years of Islanders hockey have been hard on you. When I would come to the Coliseum during my time as a broadcaster with Ottawa and Florida, I would hear from so many of you who longed for the good old days. Well, the Isles haven't quite gotten back there yet, but watching them now—working as hard for Barry Trotz as we did for Al, carrying themselves as professionally and respectfully for Lou Lamoriello as we did for Bill—you can't help but be enthusiastic about what's to come.

And you fans who stuck by the Islanders during all those tough times and battles for a new arena finally have an amazing new place to call home. UBS Arena is the palace you deserve for all your years of unwavering support.

It's hard to believe it's been almost 50 years since I came to Long Island. I arrived as a teenager, a kid, and left as a man, a four-time Stanley Cup champion. I got to see the greatest honor of my career—my No. 5 going to the Coliseum rafters, followed deservedly by those of my friends and teammates: Boss, Billy Smith, Trots, Clark, Bobby Ny, John Tonelli, and Butchie, along with Bill's bow tie and Al's 1,500 banner for all the games he coached with us.

And you grew right along with us, making our building a place no one wanted to play. Thank you to all of you who got behind us all those years ago and to those new Islanders fans who want to read about our ups and downs and all the great (and some not-so-great!) stories about this franchise.

—Denis Potvin

1 Birth of the Islanders

It's fitting to look back 50 years and see that the Islanders were born out of the National Hockey League's desire to crush the World Hockey Association and born into immediate debt. Nothing about the Isles has ever been simple, or easy.

Roy Boe was the man who brought the idea of NHL hockey to Long Island. In 1971 he already had owned the Nets for two years, with lavish plans for the local team that played in the American Basketball Association. The Nassau Coliseum, a new sports arena, was opening in Uniondale the next year, and he wanted his basketball team there. The idea of a hockey team joining them there intrigued Boe and his dozens of partners in the Nets.

The NHL, meanwhile, was looking to freeze out the WHA, which had lifted a few big-name NHLers with the promise of larger salaries. The New York Raiders were the new local WHA team, and they were looking for a place to play; the NHL, under Clarence Campbell's direction, wanted to make sure the New York market was for their league only. So the NHL—then at 14 teams—awarded expansion franchises to Atlanta and Long Island on November 8, 1971. Boe had his hockey team to go with his basketball team—and an immediate load of red ink.

The NHL asked for a $6 million expansion fee. The Rangers, owners of territorial rights for 50 miles from Madison Square Garden, demanded a $4 million fee just for allowing the Islanders to exist. That alone could have created a rivalry that burned through every Islanders fan before the two teams had even played a game.

Boe and his partners had $2.3 million cash on hand. This was to be the story of Boe's tenure as principal Islanders owner, a six-year span that crashed and burned before the run of Stanley Cups began.

But the best move Boe ever made was hiring the guy the NHL suggested he hire: Bill Torrey. Torrey had run the California Golden Seals for three years, quitting after the 1970–71 season to get away from meddling new owner Charlie Finley.

The NHL recommended that both expansion clubs speak to Torrey, who recalled to the *New York Times* a conversation he had with Steelers owner Art Rooney, a good friend. "If you have a choice, take Long Island," Rooney said. "Atlanta's a great city, and it's a fun place to go, but you'll have to sell hockey. If you go to New York, all you'll have to do is worry about building a team, because the fans will come."

Torrey was the Islanders' first employee, hired in February 1972. He soon embarked on a nearly monthlong scouting trip in Canada, coming away with his first three scouts—Ed Chadwick, Henry Saraceno, and Earl Ingarfield, the last of whom would end up as the replacement coach for the last two months of the dismal 1972–73 inaugural season.

It was Torrey who insisted to Boe that there was only one way forward for the Islanders to succeed. Torrey told *Sports Illustrated* in 1982: "I told Boe, 'OK, you're going to go through the expansion draft and get 19 problem children. Either the guys can't play, they're too old, or they have personal problems. Second, your product is going to be constantly compared to the Rangers, who were then the second-best team in hockey." Also, we were in the East Division with Montreal, Boston, the Rangers and four other established teams. We were guaranteed last place. But there was a ray of hope if we were patient because everyone in hockey knew that the amateur draft for the next few years was loaded. What other choice did we have?"

By the time the 1972 NHL Draft came around and the Islanders made Billy Harris the franchise's first draft choice, the team had nearly 8,000 season-ticket holders. Attendance was never the problem in the early days, even during that first season of true awfulness, but Boe and his partners could never dig out of the financial hole that began when the Islanders began. Still, they had the right guy in charge. That laid the groundwork for what was to come, and quickly.

2 The Architect Builds

Bill Torrey's mantra to build from within was put to the test immediately with the expansion draft, held on June 6, 1972, four months after he was hired to run the Islanders. The rules were different back then, so he had no illusions that he'd come away with a ready-to-compete team.

There were a couple bright spots. The second goalie he chose was a feisty 21-year-old from the Kings, Billy Smith, who Torrey teamed with journeyman Gerry Desjardins that first season. Ed Westfall, who'd just won his second Stanley Cup with the Bruins, was Torrey's fifth pick—the Islanders and Atlanta Flames alternated selections. Torrey traded a 1973 second-round pick to the Canadiens for four players, including Glenn Resch, another promising young goalie.

The rival World Hockey Association was lurking, also with new franchises in need of players. They signed 8 of the Isles' 19 expansion draft picks, and Torrey believed the NHL contracts the players he'd drafted held were still valid.

"I called [NHL President] Clarence Campbell to find out what hold I would have on the players I drafted, all of whom were under contract to their previous clubs. He said he had no doubt

Torrey, all smiles, in 2010.

that the contracts would be upheld in the courts," Torrey told *Sports Illustrated* in 1982. "At the expansion draft the press asked him the same question, and Mr. Campbell replied, 'Let the buyer beware.' I ran up to him and said, 'What the hell do you mean, buyer beware?'"

At that 1972 draft, the Islanders were really born. Billy Harris went first overall to the Isles; their second- and third-round picks, Lorne Henning and Bob Nystrom, have their names on the Stanley Cup numerous times. And in the 10th round the Isles scooped up a scrappy kid from Alberta named Garry Howatt.

It was a foundation, even if the payoff wasn't immediate. And Torrey never stopped tinkering and planning for the future in those early years, disregarding the snickers of opposing fans and executives as the Isles tripped over their skates repeatedly in the first season.

Torrey's trades were mostly swapping small amounts of cash for players to fill out the Isles' roster or someone else's. But the first incredibly shrewd Torrey deal of many to come was late in the 1972–73 season, when the Isles were already on their way to one of the worst records in NHL history.

Torrey went to Flyers GM Keith Allen and asked what it would take to get Jean Potvin, Denis's older brother and a capable defenseman with a couple years of NHL experience. "The idea was to establish a rapport with Jean Potvin, invite his parents down to the Island and have Jean tell Denis that Bill Torrey and the Islanders were going to get this thing turned around, which would then lead to Denis choosing the Islanders," Jim Devellano wrote in his book *The Road to Hockeytown*. "Now Jean Potvin for Terry Crisp will not go down in the annals of NHL history as one of the most important deals ever made—they were both decent NHL players, but nothing more—but did that deal ever help the New York Islanders start to build their franchise. Year one was a write-off, we were just terrible, but now we had a star to build our team around. We had our first big building block, and it was thanks in part to that trade with the Flyers."

There were a couple others like that. Just prior to the 1974–75 season, Torrey swapped Bart Crashley and Larry Hornung, two of his expansion draft picks who had bolted for the WHA, to the Kansas City Scouts for a 20-year-old they'd just drafted three months earlier, a winger named Bob Bourne.

And those 1973, 1974, and 1975 drafts yielded more young talent. Dave Lewis and Andre St. Laurent went in the third and fourth rounds behind Denis Potvin in 1973, plus Bob Lorimer in the ninth round.

With the fourth pick in 1974, the Isles went with Clark Gillies, then they took a not-yet-18-year-old (permissible then but rare, with most players drafted at age 20) from a small town in Saskatchewan named Bryan Trottier with their second-round selection.

"I don't think a lot of teams knew about him," Torrey told *Sports Illustrated*. "He was only 17, and he played in Swift Current, which is off the beaten track. When I went up to see Bryan, the wind-chill factor was something like minus 83 degrees. I've never been colder in my life, or in a colder rink. Trots didn't do much the first two periods, but in the third period he scored two goals. I decided to stay over another day."

Boe's best decision was hiring Torrey, and given all his financial woes, it may have been his only good one.

Torrey made dozens of great moves. But his best by far was hiring the right coach after that awful first season.

3 Al Arbour Comes Aboard

After the 12–60–6 debut season that featured Torrey firing Phil Goyette, his first coach, and installing Earl Ingarfield, a scout, as his replacement, the Islanders immediately got back to scouting western Canada for a new head coach.

The search for the next Islanders coach started in the 1973 off-season. Torrey told Jim Devellano, his top amateur scout, that the GM had two veteran coaches in mind: Johnny Wilson, who'd just been fired as Red Wings coach, and John McLellan, who'd just been dismissed as the Maple Leafs' coach.

Devellano, who'd been a scout with the Blues for five years before joining the Islanders, suggested another former player who'd had a brief, dispiriting run as an NHL coach: Al Arbour. The three-time Stanley Cup champion as a player (with the Wings, Hawks, and Leafs) had finished his playing career with the expansion Blues, then stepped right into a coaching role that St. Louis ownership never quite saw as the right fit.

Arbour was scouting for the Atlanta Flames in their first season. And he definitely wasn't sure he wanted to get back into the coaching game with a second-year team that had just set an NHL record for futility.

"The first thing Al didn't like was our team," Torrey told *Sports Illustrated* in 1982. "He said, 'Hey Bill, I got gassed in St. Louis when they had a pretty good team, and I'm not making a move and taking this on.'"

Al's wife, Claire, wasn't too hot on moving to New York either. Like a lot of people back in the early 1970s who weren't from the area, the Arbours—who had four kids and lived in St. Louis—saw Long Island and New York City as one and the same.

Torrey drove Al around through some beautiful Island towns on his visit to interview. Still, the turning point may have been after Al left to take a family vacation to Florida in early June 1973, with the Canucks and Golden Seals also interested in his services. As it happened, the Arbours fell into a conversation with a couple from the Island down on the beach in Florida. That couple may have been the closer for Torrey, as they told Al and Claire about the Island's beaches, golf courses, and quieter life than one would find in tumultuous New York City.

Five days later, on June 10, Al Arbour was named the Islanders' coach. There will hardly be a chapter you read in this book that doesn't mention Arbour in some way, large or small—Torrey was the business brains behind the Islanders' success, but Arbour managed the personalities and skills of his players like few coaches who have ever worked in the NHL.

"Al Arbour is the Vince Lombardi of hockey," Pat LaFontaine said. "There's no one else like him."

"Scotty Bowman was an amazing coach, but he was a bit aloof with his players," Chico Resch said. "Al had that personal touch. In terms of a man coaching a pro team, someone who is tough but also lets you feel that this coach cares for you, there's never been someone like Al."

And he set the tone during his first training camp, back in Peterborough, Ontario, where the team's first had been a year earlier. Where that 1972 camp had been ragtag and wild, Arbour had his grip firmly on the reins. "Normally when you go to camp, you get all your equipment, go for a light skate, break things in," Bob Nystrom said. "We got out there, he made a little speech, and said we were going for a light practice. Two and a half hours later we were still out there."

That was just day one. And it set the tone for all that was to come.

4 Denis Potvin

The 1973 NHL Amateur Draft was held in Montreal on May 15. The entire hockey world knew who was going first: a strapping, skilled, feisty defenseman from Ottawa named Denis Potvin. And from about the second month of the 1972–73 season, the entire hockey world knew the Islanders were going to possess that No. 1 pick. So began the chase for Potvin.

Torrey swung the deal for Denis's brother, Jean, in March 1973. He hired Arbour in June. And at that 1973 draft in Montreal, the Canadiens' legendary GM, Sam Pollock, made offer after offer for the Isles' top pick—all rebuffed by Torrey. There was also the fledgling WHA, which was trying to poach any and all players from the NHL to establish some legitimacy.

"I really didn't want to go to the WHA," Denis Potvin said. "The Chicago Cougars owned my rights, and they were offering good money. But I'd spent the whole summer with my brother Jean, and he was certainly influential. The idea of playing with him was great for me."

Potvin added, "Of course, being a French-Canadian kid, Jean Beliveau was my idol. And to think of that Canadiens defense— Serge Savard, Larry Robinson, Guy Lapointe. It was formidable. With the Islanders, I knew I'd be playing from day one and we'd be building something. I'm glad Bill didn't trade that pick, even though I was a Canadiens fan growing up."

Potvin's first Islanders camp was also Arbour's, just a couple months later. And he got a rather rude welcome even before things got started. "We got up to Peterborough on Sunday before we were supposed to officially get going Monday, and a bunch of us got out on the ice, just in sweats and stuff," Chico Resch said. "The guys rush down on me, I kick my leg out, and this defenseman I didn't know falls backward over my pad, hits his head on the ice. He gets up, shakes it off. Well, someone skates up to me and says, 'Hey, you just about killed the franchise—that was Denis Potvin you tripped up.'"

Arbour's demanding training camp didn't faze Potvin, other than Arbour making sure to comment on his young defenseman's weight. "He put me on the scale first thing, and that routine didn't end even 15 years later," Denis said.

That 1973–74 team was starting to look more like a competitive outfit, and Potvin was the main attraction. Billy Smith and Gerry Desjardins looked a fair bit better than they had in year one, Bob Nystrom and Garry Howatt had earned permanent roster spots, Billy Harris and Ralph Stewart were the big forwards, and Ed Westfall was the captain.

It still wasn't a smooth-running unit, but the Isles had their first real star in the making. And he was busy making himself at home on the Island. "My brother was married, so even though we spent plenty of time together, I had a group of guys around my age who were basically inseparable," Denis said. "We lived in Westbury, right across from the Westbury Music Fair. Myself, Bobby, Lorne [Henning], and Andre St. Laurent were all in the same apartment complex. We went to practice together, to lunch together, we lived together. It was such an exciting time."

The 1973–74 season began—and it started immediately to look a bit like the prior one. The Isles began the year 0–3–4, and Potvin was still searching for his first goal.

He got it on October 27 at the Coliseum—two of them, in fact—in a 3–2 win over the rival Rangers. It was a night of firsts. Potvin's first goals, Arbour's first win behind the Islanders bench, and the first time the Islanders had beaten the Rangers.

"They were playing the body, not the man, something they didn't do last year," Rangers defenseman Brad Park said. "They're organized, they play with some system on the ice. They look like a hockey team."

It wasn't a good season by anyone's standards, with the Isles finishing 19–41–18. But the 26-point improvement meant something; so did cutting down their goals against by 100.

And it meant something to Potvin, who won the Calder Trophy as the league's top rookie and led the Isles with 54 points. "We knew we were building something," he said. "We certainly weren't close, but we were at the start of something we felt could be good."

5 Bryan Trottier

Nobody has played more games in an Islanders uniform than Bryan Trottier. And nobody, some would say, worked harder in the blue, orange, and white. "When you see your best player is your hardest worker," former teammate Bob Bourne said of Trottier, "how [can] you not try and match that?"

And yet Trottier's Islanders career got off to a strange start. He was a month shy of his 18th birthday when Bill Torrey drafted him 22nd overall in 1974 out of Swift Current in the Western Hockey League—that was young for draft picks back then.

But still Trottier would have earned lots of playing time on the 1974–75 Islanders. They didn't have a skilled center like Trottier. Torrey, however, had other ideas, and he sent Trottier back to junior hockey before that season began. "Everyone fought me on it," Torrey told *Sports Illustrated* in 1982. "His father, the press, Bryan. The only person I had on my side was his mother. He was certainly as good as the players we had, but I didn't want to bring him into the atmosphere. We were still getting knocked around a lot, and I wasn't going to bring a kid that age into New York and put him under the gun."

The 1974–75 Islanders had their breakthrough, upsetting the Rangers in the best-of-three first round, then rallying from three goals to none to beat the Penguins and nearly doing it again in the semifinals against the Flyers. By that spring, Trottier was on the taxi squad, skating with the extras and soaking up what his future team was doing. "[I was] sitting in the stands for the comeback against Pittsburgh, the comeback against Philly, feeling the energy in the Coliseum," Trottier said. "I couldn't wait to be a part of it."

He came back for training camp the next season the most determined rookie around. He was in with the extras, long shots, and rookies for training camp, watching guys pack their bags on a daily basis. "Until I was the only one left," he said. "Me, a bunch of Gatorade jugs, and bags of oranges. Finally [equipment manager] Jim Pickard came down and said, 'We're moving you to the weight room, kid. We need this room.'"

Nothing was assured with Al Arbour or Torrey, neither of whom talked much to their new young center. Trottier had made temporary living arrangements with Warren and Pat Amendola of Lloyd Harbor. (Warren Amendola owned Koho, the stick manufacturer, and happened to be at practice before the 1975–76 season when Trottier jokingly asked aloud where he could live for the year.) The Amendolas had three boys around Trottier's age. It was a billet-type situation but on the Island, and Trottier loved it. "They were the first people to take me in," said Trottier, who had the Amendolas help raise his No. 19 to the Coliseum rafters on October 20, 2001.

Trottier could have been an Islander a year earlier and no one would have batted an eye. But Torrey showed patience and Trottier responded—pretty much for the rest of his career. On the ice that first season, there was no doubt what kind of player the Islanders had. In his second NHL game—his Coliseum debut on October 11, 1975—Trottier had a hat trick and added two assists in a 7–0 win over the Kings. That night began a march to one of the best rookie seasons in NHL history, 95 points and yet another Calder Trophy for an Islander.

It was just the beginning. Away from the ice, the 19-year-old was the kid brother for the group. "Guys [snuck] me into bars on the Island my first couple years," he said. "One of the most fun times we had was doing celebrity bartending at the Oak Beach Inn on Jones Beach—I'm not old enough to get in there, and here I am probably serving state troopers from behind the bar."

The Islanders went from 30 points in 1972–73 to 56 points in 1973–74 to 88 points and a game from the Stanley Cup Finals in 1974–75 to 101 points in 1975–76. They had Billy Smith and Chico Resch hitting their prime in net—Resch, at age 27, was runner-up to Trottier for the Calder after getting only 25 games in net the year before.

Denis Potvin won his first Norris Trophy in 1976 at age 22, a runaway winner while leading the team in scoring with 98 points. He was second to Bobby Clarke for the Hart Memorial Trophy that year. Clark Gillies, Bob Bourne, Billy Harris, Bob Nystrom, Garry Howatt, and Denis's brother, Jean, comprised the young core, complemented by veterans such as Jude Drouin, J.P. Parise, Gerry Hart, Ed Westfall, and Bert Marshall.

The Islanders were on the brink after just four seasons of existence.

6 Mike Bossy

At the 1977 draft table in Montreal—back at the Mount Royal Hotel, where in 1973 Canadiens GM Sam Pollock walked Bill Torrey around the building a few times to try and coax the No. 1 pick away, to no avail—the Islanders brain trust was debating whom to select at No. 15. The choices were Dwight Foster—a solid, physical forward from Toronto—and Mike Bossy, a pure scorer who wasn't very physical from Montreal.

Torrey listened to his scouts, especially Henry Saraceno, who'd been with the Islanders since the beginning. Saraceno saw plenty of Bossy's games for Laval and made a strong case. The clincher was Al Arbour, who was also on hand. "If you can assure me that Bossy isn't scared, then take him," Arbour said, according to Jim Devellano in his book *The Road to Hockeytown*. "I can teach a player to check, but I can't teach a player to score, and we need goals." Foster had a fine, unspectacular NHL career; Bossy became a legend.

The legend started in Torrey's office before that 1977–78 training camp. As Bossy accepted a below-market rookie contract, he gave a remarkable answer to Torrey, who'd asked his new forward, "So, Mike, since you're not happy with this deal, how do you think you'll perform at the NHL level?"

Bossy told his new boss, "Well, I think I can score 50 goals this year."

How his new teammates saw him—well, that was a different story. "We'd read and heard so much about this kid, and here he was: scrawny, busted nose, busted teeth," said Bryan Trottier. "You could tell he was homesick. Then he got hurt in camp. I went by the trainer's room and saw him in there looking miserable, and

I said, 'Hey—you want a home-cooked meal?' He said, 'I'd love one.'"

A lifelong bond was formed. Bryan and his wife, Nickie, had Mike and his wife, Lucie, over for dinner and the Bossys ended up crashing for two weeks, until they found their own place.

Arbour saw the chemistry on the ice too, putting his top center and his new scoring winger together out of the gate. Trottier, Clark Gillies, and Billy Harris had been the Isles' top line in 1976–77, and it was a good one—Gillies led the team with 33 goals, Trottier had 30 goals and 72 points, and Harris went 24–43–67. But Bossy went into Harris's spot, the Trio Grande was born, and there were hardly any concerns about the Isles' No. 1 line for the next half a dozen years.

And those worries about Bossy's checking and defense? Arbour told his young forward not to fret during those first few practices in 1977–78.

Bossy said Arbour told him, "Mike, we brought you here to score goals. Can you score goals for us?"

"Well…"

"Mike, don't bother me about your defense ever again. If I have anything to say about your defense, I'll come and see you, OK?"

"When I first came to the Island, Al gave me confidence to play the game for the reason they drafted me, and that was to score goals," Bossy said in 2015. "He said just go out there and score goals. That's what I did."

His first came 9:24 into the season opener, a tap-in after Sabres goalie Don Edwards turned the puck over to Gillies behind the Buffalo net. Bossy did the first of many Running Man goal celebrations on that one.

He had 13 points (6 goals) in his first 10 games. The first of his franchise-record 39 hat tricks came on February 4, 1978, against the Capitals, giving Bossy 39 goals in 53 games to that point—not only a rookie record for the still-young Isles franchise but a record for goals *period*.

It was against those same Capitals on April 1, 1978, that Bossy made good on his confident boast to Torrey before camp began about getting 50 goals. He had been stuck on 49 goals for six games before tallying No. 50 on a power play to tie the Caps in the third period. Another power-play goal—Bossy's league-leading 24th— gave the Isles a much-needed 3–2 win with five seconds left in the third. "It's like 200 pounds off my back," Bossy said after the game. "And then to get the winner too. That was even better than No. 50 because, heaven knows, we sure need the points."

He finished the season with 53 goals, a rookie record that stood for 15 years. Trottier's 123 points earned him runner-up for the Hart Trophy. Gillies posted 35 goals and 85 points, both career highs. Potvin earned his second Norris Trophy. The high-flying Isles had arrived—in the regular season, at least.

7 Clark Gillies

As the biggest kid on the ice in the Saskatchewan youth hockey leagues, Clark Gillies had become accustomed to fighting. Not that it was his preference, but he did it mostly to keep the flies off his smaller, more skilled teammates.

It was his first coach in Regina, former NHLer Earl Ingarfield, who told Gillies he too could play in the NHL if he put his mind to it. "He took me aside one day and he said, 'I don't know if you realize it or not, but you have what it takes with your size and ability to play in the National Hockey League,'" Gillies said. "I said, 'Really? You think so?' He said, 'I know so! What you have to do is apply yourself and start believing in yourself.' That was the kick in the behind I needed to start taking the game a little more seriously."

Ingarfield went to work the next year as a scout for the expansion New York Islanders. Two years after that—and with Ingarfield having coached the final 30 games of the historically bad 1972–73 season before returning to scouting—Gillies was the Isles' first pick of the 1974 draft, fourth overall.

He looked the part of the 1970s NHL player: big, no helmet, full beard, and a real ability with his fists. But that 1974–75 rookie season for Gillies was more about showing the reason why the Islanders had taken him fourth overall. He scored 25 goals as a rookie and settled in on a team that made him feel comfortable. "We had a lot of guys I knew, guys I played against in juniors— Bobby [Nystrom], Dave Lewis, Garry Howatt, Bobby Bourne," he said. "It was far from home, sure, but it felt like home a bit too."

Gillies had 66 penalty minutes that first season, and it's a real misconception that he was a guy who fought as much as he played the game—he never had more than 100 PIMs in any of his 14 NHL seasons. "People want me to run around the ice hitting everything that moves," he said back in the dynasty days. "But that's not me. If a teammate needs me, I'm there—and the guys know it, and the opposition knows it. When it counts, I'm there, but I don't run all over looking to show how big or tough I am. The other teams know I can fight if I have to, but I would rather just play hockey."

"He was more easygoing than people think about him," Bryan Trottier said. "He was a huge presence on the ice, but it took a lot to make him mad."

The first time he did step forward was a memorable one. At the end of Game 5 of the 1975 semifinals, in which the Isles beat the Flyers 5–1 in Philadelphia to make it a 3–2 deficit in the series, the Broad Street Bullies tried to send a message. Dave Schultz, the reigning enforcer in the league, threw down with Gillies.

It didn't go well for Schultz. Gillies tagged Schultz so badly that big Andre "Moose" Dupont had to reach in and pull Gillies away. "I knew this was going to be a pretty scary situation," Gillies told *Newsday* in 2015. "I didn't know I was going to beat the crap out of him, but I had a hunch he was going to have to fight pretty hard to have me not beat the crap out of him. As everybody has talked about, that was a real turning point for this team."

And a turning point for Gillies, who showed as a 21-year-old that he wasn't to be messed with. Trottier arrived the next season, and with Gillies on the left side and Billy Harris on the right, the Islanders had themselves a true No. 1 line—one that only got better when Mike Bossy joined the team in 1977–78 and the Trio Grande was born.

But back as a rookie, Gillies just wanted to fit in. And like all the other dynasty stars, he credited his coach with the biggest help to his burgeoning career. "I've got to give all the credit in the world to Al," Gillies said. "He was a hard-nosed son of a bitch, but he really knew how to keep us in line. He knew when to push what buttons to really get you going. He was pretty patient with me as a rookie. I made a lot of mistakes, but I kept learning and learning and did my share from a rough-and-tough standpoint and ended up with 47 points. It was a real learning experience that first year."

8 Billy Smith, Money Player

This quote from Billy Smith after the last of the Islanders' four Stanley Cups sums him up pretty well: "I'm the first to admit that when it comes to the regular season, I fall asleep sometimes," Smith said after winning his first Conn Smythe Trophy as playoff MVP in 1983. "But I'll also be the first to say that when it comes to the money games, I'm there. And I haven't let them down yet."

For all his peculiarities, for all his aggression and his intensity, Smith was ultimately this: the best money goalie in the last 40 years of the NHL. He knew it, and his teammates knew it. "Something had to be on the line for Smitty," Chico Resch said. "Especially financially. That's when he played his best."

Smith had just gotten his feet wet in the NHL with the Kings, appearing in five games for L.A. in 1971–72, when Bill Torrey scooped up the then-21-year-old in the expansion draft. Smith was the only one of the dynasty core who endured the awfulness of 1972–73, splitting the season fairly evenly with veteran Gerry Desjardins—Smith recorded seven wins to Desjardins's five, and Smith set a record at the time with 42 penalty minutes, good for seventh on the team and initiating his reputation as Battlin' Billy.

"We used to face 50, 60 shots some games, but I had no complaints," Smith told *Sports Illustrated* in 1982. "I was fighting and enjoying it. The fans liked it; they knew they were getting their money's worth. There was no pressure. How can you put pressure on a team that's completely awful? That's one problem with playing on a winner—you can't go out and just hammer somebody because it might cost you the game. I used to have goals scored on me while I was looking the other way, trying to hit someone with my stick. So what? We were the biggest joke going, and even the players knew it. You'd go into a game knowing it was going to be a bombing. The idea was lose, but lose honorably."

That was another side of Smith that came out quickly: He was candid, truly a no-BS guy.

He didn't get a chance to show his talent in important games for a few years. Resch started Games 1 and 2 of the Isles' first playoff series against the Rangers in 1975, but the 8–3 shelling by the Rangers in Game 2 at the Coliseum convinced Al Arbour to put Smith in for his first playoff action in the deciding Game 3 at the Garden. Easy to say in hindsight, but it was the right call. Smith made 37 saves, J.P. Parise made history 11 seconds into overtime, and the Isles had a glimpse of what Smith could be.

It still took a bit. Smith and Resch still handled the goalie duties evenly for the next four years, playoffs included, until the 1980 postseason came around.

Before that fateful run began, the players gathered together prior to Game 1 of the best-of-five opening round against the Kings. There was, Resch remembered, a lot of talk of family, of playing for one another and supporting one another. "The Pittsburgh Pirates had just won the World Series in 1979 and their theme was 'We Are Family,' the old song," Resch said. "So it's very friendly and warm, nice flowery stuff. And Billy stood up and said, 'That's all fine, but I have my family. This is about getting cut for one another—I bleed for you, you bleed for me. That team over there is trying to take money out of our pockets, and there's no way I'm gonna let them do that.'

"And those playoff bonuses were a big deal to us then, because we didn't make the money the guys do today, of course. And Smitty always made a point to remind us. I love him for that."

Smith won Game 1 and Resch was pulled from Game 2 against the Kings in the Coliseum after giving up six goals in less than two periods. Smith would start every game except one from there until

Bob Nystrom's Cup winner, and the legend was born. "Smitty loved going into places like Philly, Boston, the Garden, where he knew he'd be hated," Bryan Trottier said. "He played better. He needed that extra push; it really drove him."

After the first Cup, Smith's temperamental ways earned him some leeway from Arbour. No more game-day skates. His own room off the side of the Coliseum locker room. Few practices during the playoffs.

Arbour knew that Smith would come to play every night in the playoffs. Through the first three Stanley Cups—1980, 1981, and 1982, with the very capable Rollie Melanson having replaced Resch as Smith's sidekick—Smith was basically unbeatable; he compiled a 44–10 record in those three postseasons.

And then came 1983. Smith was 31 by then, hardly ancient but the second-oldest player on the team, a year younger than Butch Goring. Melanson got the majority of the regular-season starts and performed better than Smith did. It was Melanson who came on and won Games 3 and 4 of the first-round win over the Capitals after Smith stumbled in Game 2. But after beating the Rangers in the quarterfinals in six games, the net again belonged to Billy.

In the Cup Finals against the Oilers, Smith cemented his status as not only the best goalie of his era but the feistiest. He took two mighty whacks at Glenn Anderson in Game 1 and then Wayne Gretzky late in Game 2, the latter sending Gretzky crumpling to the ice and drawing Smith a major penalty for slashing.

The Edmonton newspaper put Smith's masked face on the front page and labeled him Public Enemy No. 1. Oilers coach/ GM Glen Sather called for a suspension and got an audience with league discipline czar Brian O'Neill to plead his case. "People say he's cleaned up his act," Sather said after Game 1, "but to me he plays like a maniac."

Smith was also fully in the Oilers' heads. His 35-save Game 1 shutout completely baffled the high-flying Oilers, who had scored

73 goals through their first three playoff rounds, in which they lost just once. Smith followed with 30 saves in Game 2 and a direct attack on Gretzky, the best player in the universe. It was too much for the young, rising Oilers to bear.

Back at the Coliseum, Smith further stymied the Oilers with 33 saves in Game 3, and then in Game 4—with the Isles holding on to a 3–2 lead in the third—Smith sent himself sprawling after a whack from Anderson that drew a five-minute major penalty and squashed any possible Oilers rally. "I was hurt about as much as Gretzky was hurt in the second game," he said. "I just want to say to all you people right now, when I hit Gretzky, he lay down and he cried to the referee, so I just took a chapter out of his book. I put myself on my back and I squirmed and kicked and I played dead just like he did, and so they got five minutes just like I did in Edmonton. I found out from Gretzky that unless you put on a show, you don't get the five minutes. I just wanted to show that two can play that game."

Just a reminder: This was after he'd won his fourth Cup and his first Conn Smythe Trophy. The intensity simply never abated. Even after the dynasty had ended and Smith was a grizzled veteran, he still fought for every inch. "After I started to play a little more, Billy would have none of it," said Kelly Hrudey, who replaced Melanson in 1984–85 and shared goalie duties with Smith for five seasons. "If it looked as though I might get a start in front of Billy, he'd charge into the coach's office and demand to play. And I'd let him do it. One time when I had more confidence, I charged in behind him and I said, 'I'm playing better and I deserve to play.' And there was no disrespect shown.

"I learned so much from Billy about fighting for your job, for your space. I loved that relationship we had."

9 Mr. Islander, Bob Nystrom

He was there from the beginning, one of the 14 members of Bill Torrey's first draft class in 1972. He arrived on the Island for good for the 1973–74 season and barely left after that. He married a Long Island girl and settled in. "I just fell in love with the place," Bob Nystrom said of the Island.

And it loved him back. There's a reason that the team award for "leadership, hustle and dedication" was christened the Bob Nystrom Award 30 years ago—no member of the Isles' early teams, their Stanley Cup teams, personified what it meant to be an Islander more than Nystrom.

After spending most of that awful 1972–73 expansion season with the AHL's New Haven Nighthawks, Nystrom worked in as a regular the next season on what came to be known as the Commotion Line—a lunch-pail line with Nystrom on the right, Garry Howatt on the left, and Andre St. Laurent in the middle.

Nystrom had skill, but his skating was lacking. Ever since he'd joined the Islanders, Torrey had Nystrom working on his skating with an instructor on the Island, Laura Stamm, not only one of the first skating teachers for pro hockey players but without a doubt the first such instructor who was female.

"I told him I'd never tell anybody," Stamm told the *New York Times* in 1995. "Instead, he was the one who told everybody. He made me well-known. I've got schools all over the world now."

Nystrom grew into what you'd now call a middle-six winger's role. He would never have the flash and dash of Trottier or Bossy, never combine the ability to fight with the ability to score goals like Gillies. But he had a complete game.

And, from even before the goal that put him and the Islanders on the map in 1980, Nystrom had developed a knack for scoring big ones. Only six NHL players all time have more playoff overtime winners than Nystrom, who leads the Isles with four.

He started that tally with a Game 5 winner against the Leafs in the 1978 quarterfinals, then a Game 4 winner at Madison Square Garden in the 1979 semis against the Rangers. Those series ended in heartbreak.

But he saved his bigger moments for 1980. Game 2 of the semifinals in Buffalo, early in double OT, Nystrom snuck out of the corner to bang in a rebound of Bob Lorimer's point shot, and the Isles grabbed a 2–0 series lead on their way to their first Cup Final. Then, of course, came 7:11 of OT in Game 6 at the Coliseum—the moment of the most famous goal in Islanders history. "Bobby made me a champion," Trottier said. "How can you ever forget that?"

It's not only the biggest goal in Islanders history; it really stands out in the modern history of the NHL. Jacques Lemaire had won the 1977 Cup for the Canadiens on an OT winner, a sweep over the Bruins, but Nystrom's goal came as sports on television—hockey especially, after the Miracle on Ice a few months earlier—had risen to greater prominence.

"I've certainly reaped the rewards of people remembering it all the time," he said. "It was a really big moment in my life and just my way of paying back all the guys for all they'd done for me. I did my part to give the guys something they'd all dreamed about all their lives. That will always be special."

Much the way Arbour would years later be given one more game to coach so he could get to a nice, even 1,500 games behind the Islanders bench, Nystrom got one last spin at the very end of his career. He'd suffered a serious eye injury in January 1986 during practice, and his season and career were essentially over; the doctors who treated him said as much. But while he served out the rest of that season and two more as Arbour's assistant, the coach asked Nystrom to suit up for the regular-season finale against the Devils. He could take one more shift and finish his playing career on a round 900 games, only the second Islander to reach that mark at the time—Potvin had done it earlier in that 1985–86 season.

So there he was, blond hair a little less flowing than in his heyday, taking the opening shift alongside Trottier and Gillies.

Bob Nystrom skates against the Philadelphia Flyers during the 1980 NHL Stanley Cup Finals.

After seven seconds he came off, never to play again. "I guess you could say I did it my way," he said after that game.

He was always a fixture at charity softball games and other community events on the Island, something that's never changed in nearly five decades. The flowing hair may be long gone now, but you rarely see Nystrom without a smile on his face. "We felt a part of the community then," Nystrom said. "Al would say to us, 'These people are paying your salary. You have to get out there in the community and do things.'"

It was another lesson from Arbour that he's never forgotten that drove him to be the clutch scorer and performer he was. "Al would always instill in us this attitude of, 'What's the worst that can happen? You'll lose, the sun will come up tomorrow, everything will be fine,'" he said. "'But who would you rather be—the guy sitting back on his heels worried about making a mistake or the guy on his toes attacking to try and win it?' It's stayed with me my whole life. That's always in my mind: You may lose, but wouldn't you rather play full-out?"

10 11 Seconds: Isles-Rangers, 1975

It was just a matter of history for the Islanders in their first few years of existence: They had none, and the nearby Rangers had decades' worth. The feeling of being the new kid on the block was exacerbated by the $4 million in territorial rights that original Isles owner Roy Boe had to pay to the Rangers simply to exist, and it was only made worse by the presence of all those Rangers fans at the Coliseum every time the teams met during the first three seasons, from 1972 to 1975.

"I remember sitting on the bench in the Coliseum my rookie year, I think it was our first game against the Rangers that season," Clark Gillies said. "I was playing with Billy Harris and Eddie Westfall. The Rangers scored and the roof just about came off the place. I turned to Eddie and said, 'This is kind of bullshit.' Eddie turned to me and said, 'Get used to it, kid—we're not selling a ton of tickets and there's Rangers fans on the Island.'

"But I said, 'That's bullshit.' I felt it had to change. And eventually it did but not just then."

The 1974–75 Islanders were on the rise. They had Arbour behind the bench for his second season, having led the team to a 26-point improvement over the 1972–73 mess to a somewhat more respectable 19–41–18 record in 1973–74.

And by the next season, Gillies and Bob Bourne were in the fold. Potvin was coming off a Calder Trophy, Nystrom and Howatt were fixtures in the lineup, and the Islanders' identity was taking shape with some young, tenacious guys such as Andre St. Laurent and Gerry Hart. Smith and Resch were entrenched in net as the goalie tandem. It looked like a real NHL team, and it took Torrey just three seasons to make it a reality.

But the one thing those young Islanders could not do was beat the Rangers. Heading into the final 10 days of the 1974–75 season, they'd done it exactly once in 15 tries—Arbour's first win behind the bench, a 3–2 victory on October 27, 1973, at the Coliseum. One win wedged in between 13 losses and a tie spanning nearly three full seasons.

They had the Rangers twice in the final five games of the regular season, with the possibility of facing them in the playoffs looming. The Isles won both—first at the Coliseum on March 29, then at Madison Square Garden in the regular-season finale on April 6, both by scores of 6–4.

Resch was strong in both games, prompting Arbour to give him the nod over Smith to start the best-of-three series at the

Garden two nights later. "I think those wins gave [the Rangers] a little scare," Resch said. "We had just about the same record as them [both finished with 88 points; the Rangers got home ice due to more wins], but they really felt they were better than us. But those games, especially the one at the Garden, really gave us confidence."

They skated a bit taller after taking Game 1 in the Garden. Gillies capped a three-goal third period with the winner at 13:30 in a 3–2 victory that put the veteran Rangers on their heels. "It was a huge benefit to us for it to be best-of-three," Potvin said. "You win that first one and the pressure's all on them."

The Rangers didn't show it in Game 2, putting three by Resch before the game was barely seven minutes old. Arbour mercifully pulled Resch at 6–1 in the second, and the game finished at 8–3 and with 170 penalty minutes.

Clark Gillies skates with the Cup in celebration of the team's Stanley Cup victory against the Philadelphia Flyers.

The turnaround for Game 3 was quick: the next night, back in the Garden. And the young guys were ready, this time with Smith in net. The Rangers attacked most of the first two periods, Smith turned everything aside, and the Isles got out to a 3–0 lead on another goal from Gillies and two from Potvin in the second.

The Rangers changed goalies, from Gilles Villemure to Eddie Giacomin, looking for a spark. Giacomin tried to do it himself, pummeling Howatt after a collision at the crease late in the second. That seemed to wake up the Rangers, and they steadily clawed back in the third, tying it on goals 14 seconds apart by Billy Fairbairn and Steve Vickers inside of seven minutes to go.

But between the third period and overtime, there were no hanging heads, probably thanks to two veterans who Torrey snapped up midway through the season from Minnesota. J.P. Parise and Jude Drouin were the sort of skilled guys who had been around the league long enough to give the young Islanders a boost in the second half of the season. "Those guys were huge for us— that was Bill's Butch Goring trade but five years earlier," Potvin said. "We blew a lead in that game, but we weren't intimidated. It didn't feel like anything could intimidate us by then."

They dropped the puck for overtime, and 11 seconds later, it was done. The Islanders dumped the puck in off the draw, Westfall pressured below the goal line, and Drouin threw a pass from the wall right onto Parise's stick at the doorstep.

The rivalry was born that night as the upstart kids from the Island, three years old, took down the big boys from the big city. "That was a real start for us—it really created a group of people that switched over to us," Nystrom said. "We were able to say we were as good as anyone after that."

11 1980: The Road to the First Cup

The furious finish to the regular season gave the Islanders a decent No. 5 seed in the 1980 playoffs, which featured a new wrinkle with the arrival of four teams from the defunct WHA: 16 of the now-21 NHL teams made the playoffs, up from 12 in previous years. And no team received a bye; everyone jumped in at the start.

The Islanders drew the 12th-seeded Kings—a remarkable coincidence to be facing Butch Goring's old club and the place where longtime teammates Dave Lewis and Billy Harris had been traded for him a month earlier. For a team whose recent playoff disappointments were close in mind, this was a stress-inducing opening round.

"We found an identity there," Bryan Trottier said. "We're facing two good friends, and Butchie doesn't want to lose to these guys."

The Islanders steamrolled the Kings in Game 1, an 8–1 win in which Trottier completed a hat trick before the end of the second period. But in Game 2 at the Coliseum, with Chico Resch in net after Billy Smith played the opener, the Islanders couldn't get out of their own way. It was 6–0 midway through the second before Al Arbour mercifully pulled Resch, but the game ended with a 6–3 final score that did change Arbour's thinking. "Chico just didn't have it," Goring said, "and I think Al really decided to go with Smitty the rest of the way right there."

The rest of the way might not have been too long. The Islanders trailed 3–1 entering the third period of Game 3 in Los Angeles, and the ghosts of failures past must have made that visitors' locker room deathly silent. The Isles were also without Mike Bossy, who'd hurt his hand in Game 2.

"Everybody was just incredibly nervous and uneasy in there," Goring said. "I had to believe they were all thinking, *Here we go again*. I was sitting next to Clark [Gillies], and we both just said, 'We gotta get this done. We gotta find a way to make it happen.'"

Gillies brought the Islanders within a goal, then Goring tied it three minutes later. The game went to overtime, and yet another of the new guys from March, Ken Morrow, won it with a lucky bounce. His slap shot from the point was headed "about 10 feet wide," he said, when it banked off a Kings player's leg and went in, giving the Isles a 2–1 series lead.

The 6–0 whitewash in Game 4 showed the Islanders had started to put their nerves to bed. Next up in the quarterfinals was a perennial challenger the Isles hadn't seen in the postseason yet: the Boston Bruins.

It was sure that the Big, Bad Bruins were going to try and take a page out of the playbook that the Rangers and Leafs had employed the prior two playoff years: Be physical and take the Islanders' top skill guys out of the game. They were also willing to cross the line into goon-squad tactics to do it, with a roster of fighters that went pretty deep.

Arbour had to shuffle his lines because Bossy was out (he missed the final two games of the Kings series and the first three games against the Bruins). He'd already split up the Trio Grande during the regular season and put Bourne with Trottier and Bossy; when Goring arrived, the second line became Gillies, Goring, and Duane Sutter, the rookie brought in from juniors in late November.

The balance without Bossy was key. The Islanders went into Boston Garden and escaped with a pair of overtime wins: Game 1 ended on a Gillies rush up the left side and slapper past Gerry Cheevers just 62 seconds into OT. Then a wild Game 2 followed, in which eight players were tossed for a bench-clearing brawl at the end of the first period—including some punk Bruins defenseman named Mike Milbury. The game ended with another quick finish when Bourne picked off a bad pass and hammered a long shot home 1:24 into OT. "We showed we could handle whatever they wanted to bring and we could beat them without Boss," Gillies said. "It really set the tone for us."

A 5–3 win in Game 3—with the new top line of Trottier, Bourne, and Nystrom contributing three points—put the Islanders in charge. The Bruins eked out a Game 4 OT win, but the Islanders closed it out in Boston in Game 5, a 4–2 win on three third-period goals—with Bossy picking up two assists in his second game back.

The Islanders were back in the semifinals for the fifth time in six years. The Sabres, a team the Isles had rarely had trouble with over the years, were there. And the Isles jumped on top 3–0 in that series too, finally taking command of a semifinals series.

The 4–1 Game 1 win was fueled by an emerging key piece—John Tonelli had two goals, giving him six in the playoffs. "Johnny had so many big goals for us," Nystrom said, "and that's where it started. A lot of the time it was me, him, and Wayne Merrick, and we worked for our goals. No one worked harder than JT."

Nystrom scored the first big OT goal of that spring in Game 2, depositing Bob Lorimer's point shot past Bob Sauve at 1:20 of double overtime. Back on the Island at the raucous Coliseum, Game 3 was a rout—Trottier scored twice in the second to snap a 2–2 tie on the way to a 7–4 win.

The Isles were a win away from their first Finals—and got a little ahead of themselves. They blew an early 3–1 lead in Game 4, a 7–4 loss that saw Resch replace a beleaguered Smith. Arbour gambled on Chico to close out Game 5, but he was outdueled by Sauve in a 2–0 Sabres win.

Back to the Coliseum for Game 6. And the Islanders were quickly in the hole 2–0 on a pair of goals by Gilbert Perreault before the game was even seven minutes old. ("We sometimes got ahead of ourselves back in those days," Resch said.) But Tonelli converted a feed from Sutter to make it 2–1. Bossy scored on a power play early in the second to tie it. And then one of the many unsung heroes of the dynasty run popped up—Lorimer jumped off the point to convert a Goring pass for a lead the Isles wouldn't relinquish. A 5–2 final score sent the Islanders to their first Finals and a date with the Flyers, who were the top team in the league during the season and had finished 25 points ahead of the Isles.

But the Islanders, thanks to Arbour, were holding on to the lessons from five years of falling short. "Once we got over the hump of the first couple rounds, we just never seemed to be afraid," Goring said. "The hangover from those losses was gone."

Denis Potvin secured Game 1 in Philly on an overtime power-play goal—a feed from Tonelli behind the net—and the Islanders were off. The Flyers bombarded Smith in Game 2, but the Islanders returned the favor in Game 3, the first Finals game of many at the Coli. The 6–2 stomping featured five Islanders power-play goals on five opportunities. It was an amazing night for a power play that had been incredible in the 1978–79 season (31.1 percent) but disappeared in the 1979 semis against the Rangers. The Islanders were eighth in the league on the power play in the 1979–80 season, and now, at the best possible time, it was back to unstoppable.

"We knew at any time it could turn into a bit of a goon show with Philly," said Potvin, who had two goals and two assists in Game 3. "We had a first unit with Gillies, Trottier, and Bossy. A second unit with Bourne, Tonelli, and Goring. I was out there with both. [Stefan] Persson was there too. We knew we could make them pay."

Game 4 was another strong performance, a 5–2 win that brought the Islanders within a game of the Cup.

The Flyers fought back hard in Game 5, a 6–3 Islanders loss. The nerves were rising again. But being back home, in the place that would come to be known as Fort Neverlose, was inspiring. "We were still carrying some of the baggage from 1978 and '79 into that Game 6," Nystrom said. "And we went out for warm-ups for

Game 6, and I've never heard a building that loud. They started when we walked out of the tunnel, and it didn't stop the entire warm-up. We all got a huge boost from that."

The Islanders took a 4–2 lead into the third period—they got the benefit of one of the all-time missed calls when Hall of Fame linesman Leon Stickle missed the puck exiting the Flyers zone before Goring picked up a Gillies drop pass and fed Sutter for a goal that made it 2–1—and as had happened before, the Isles got out over their skis a bit. "Why they do it I'll never know," Arbour said afterward, "but they always do." The Flyers tied it before the third period was seven minutes old. "Panic? I was scared skinny," Smith said later.

The Islanders got to overtime, where they had won five of the six games that reached extra time in the playoffs. You know the drill well by now: Lorne Henning curled in center ice and snapped a pass to Tonelli as Nystrom, once the kid who needed a skating instructor to get him going, streaked toward the net. Tonelli passed, Nystrom reached his stick out, and the puck sailed over Pete Peeters.

And then, elation. Trottier won the Conn Smythe Trophy, though this was a true complete effort. And fitting that Henning and Nystrom, two of the four original Islanders who attended that gong show 1972 training camp, had hands in the winner.

"I jumped over the boards into Trots's arms. I was exhausted," said Morrow, who had played more than 100 games between U.S. hockey and the Islanders that season. "It was just relief."

"You never forget the first one," Potvin said. "It was so special to finally reach that goal."

And they were hungry enough not to be satisfied.

12 1981: Back-to-Back

The off-season after the first Cup was a delirious ride for the Islanders. It was back to business pretty quickly for Bill Torrey and Al Arbour, who wanted to make sure the team that had finally climbed to the top of the NHL was prepared to do it again.

The 1980 draft yielded some familiar names once again for Torrey and Jim Devellano, the Islanders' head scout. After taking Duane Sutter 17th overall in 1979 and seeing the impact he had on the championship run, the Islanders took another Sutter at No. 17 in 1980—Duane's next-youngest brother, Brent.

They selected Kelly Hrudey in the second round and Greg Gilbert in the fourth. A year after taking another goalie, Roland Melanson, it was clear the Islanders were already planning ahead in net—Chico Resch was 31 and a pending free agent, and the run to the Cup the year before had showed that Billy Smith was the true No. 1 goalie, even if the regular-season splits didn't show it.

The fire was clearly still there for the Islanders. An uneven first month of the season left them at 4–5–3, but a 6–4 win over the Red Wings at the Coliseum on November 4, 1980, proved pivotal for two reasons: It sent the Islanders off on a franchise-record 15-game unbeaten streak (13–0–2) that vaulted them to the top of the league standings, and it was Melanson's NHL debut.

The 20-year-old goalie went 4–0–1 after being called up from the IHL to replace Resch, who had a minor knee injury. But that audition, coupled with Resch's apparent desire to leave in free agency at the end of the year, planted the seed in Arbour's and Torrey's minds that there were options available if the Islanders needed to deal Resch for a reinforcement later in the year.

The rest of the regular season was a show of force. Mike Bossy scored 50 goals in 50 games, only the second player ever to achieve that feat, and finished with 68 for the year, 28 of them on the power play. Bob Bourne had a career year with 35 goals, and Anders Kallur, the key free-agent addition out of Sweden the year before, scored 36; those two combined for 13 shorthanded goals among the league-high 19 the Isles had.

And then on March 10—the one-year anniversary of the Butch Goring deal—Torrey struck again. Gord Lane broke his thumb the night before and the Islanders needed a defenseman. Torrey sent Resch, the beloved goalie, along with young center Steve Tambellini to the Colorado Rockies for Mike McEwen, an offensively inclined defenseman with a big shot.

The deal went down at 2:00 PM Eastern even though the deadline was considered noon (since it was still noon in Denver, the deal was legal), so the players and Arbour had relaxed a bit as they boarded a bus to the airport for a flight to Winnipeg.

Torrey called, and assistant coach Lorne Henning had to pull Resch and Tambellini off the bus, much to their teammates' surprise. As with the Goring trade, there were some emotions seeing Chico go. "This is the distasteful part of the business," Arbour said. "I've been here eight years, and Chico seven. He seemed part of the organization."

"He was an integral part in making this team great," Torrey said of Resch. "He was a key player in bringing credibility to the Islanders."

McEwen, who'd been a Ranger when they upset the Islanders in 1979, came in and struggled to find a place down the stretch. But the jolt of losing Resch snapped the Islanders awake; they ran off a 9–1–3 run to finish with 110 points, tops in the league. "That was Bill," Potvin said. "He had such a good feel for the group. Losing guys like Billy Harris and Dave Lewis and Chico stung, but you knew, especially after 1980, that Bill cared only about one thing: winning."

First up in the 1981 playoffs: the 1–16 matchup with the Maple Leafs. There was no hangover from 1978; the Isles drilled Toronto in three straight, outscoring the Leafs 20–4.

Next up in the quarterfinals: the 14-seed from Edmonton. The Oilers were just an upstart group then. Wayne Gretzky was already a star, leading the league with 164 points, but the legends we remember (Gretzky, Jari Kurri, Mark Messier, Paul Coffey, Glenn Anderson) were all kids, like the Islanders had been in 1975.

But the Oilers had just swept the vaunted Canadiens in the opening round and had to be taken seriously. The Islanders were all business, dismantling the Oilers 8–2 and 6–3 in the first two games at the Coliseum. Potvin had a hat trick, all three goals on the power play, in the second game.

The teams traded the next three games, with the Isles pulling out a 5–4 overtime win in Game 4 in Edmonton on Ken Morrow's second OT winner in as many playoffs. Back in Edmonton for Game 6, the Islanders put the kids to bed with a 5–2 win, capped by a power-play goal from McEwen. (In nine playoff games, he had three goals after not scoring one in the 13 regular-season games he played after the trade.)

In the semis, more history to erase: the Rangers. They were the No. 13 seed in the playoffs but had upset the Kings and Blues to reach the final four, where they had outworked the Islanders two years before. But the Isles were so very ready for this rematch. "The one thing Al was so good at, every series, was making sure we never forgot our losses," Trottier said. "We weren't dwelling on them, but we never forgot them either."

John Tonelli scored twice to break a 2–2 tie in Game 1, sending the Isles to a 5–2 win. In Game 2 Goring and Bossy scored twice to rally from a 3–1 deficit in a 7–3 romp. At the Garden, it was more of the same—5–1 in Game 3, 5–2 in Game 4. Bossy was a force with five goals, showing the Rangers could not contain him the way they had in 1979.

The Islanders may have lucked out in 1981, as the teams that finished second through sixth were all bounced before the semis. The Isles would face the No. 9 Minnesota North Stars in the Cup Finals, and there was no way the Stars could compete. Minnesota had a decent roster but had nowhere near the depth of the Isles, and that depth showed itself in the Finals. Bossy scored four more goals in the series, giving him 17 for the playoffs, two shy of the NHL record. But the second Stanley Cup run was defined by a breadth of strong performances.

In Game 1 at the Coliseum, Kallur and Wayne Merrick each scored twice, and Kallur and Trottier each scored shorthanded goals during a first-period major power play for Minnesota on the way to a 6–3 win.

Game 2 was the same 6–3 final score, with Potvin breaking a 3–3 tie in the third and Merrick providing three assists. "It was truly a team effort," said Goring.

He should know. A 7–5 Game 3 win in Minnesota put the Islanders on the verge of one of the most dominating Cup runs of the post-expansion era, and Goring, the deadline acquisition of a year earlier, had a hat trick.

The North Stars staved off elimination in Game 4, but Game 5 back on the Island was almost a foregone conclusion. Goring scored twice in the opening 10:03 of the game, sandwiched around a Merrick goal. The pluggers did just as much damage as the big guns, leaving the Stars helpless. A 5–1 win cemented the second Cup, with Goring the Conn Smythe Trophy winner as playoff MVP.

"Everyone had a certain job and did it," Goring said after the win. "We had the muckers as well as the scorers, and they all knew who they were. Bossy didn't go out and try to knock guys down, because that wasn't his role. And Bob Nystrom didn't go out to try and score a lot of goals. He was a mucker and Bossy was a scorer, but there was no jealousy, just a common goal. We all wanted to win like hell."

"I've never seen a team as up for a game as this team was," Gillies said. "This is a great team, and the proof is the Stanley Cup."

Asked if he scooped up the puck at the final horn, Goring gave some of his usual wisdom in that winning locker room. "No, I didn't, because I don't collect things," he said. "Well, Stanley Cups, maybe."

He was certainly right about that, and about how the core stars were just getting going. Bossy's 35 points in the 18 playoff games was then a league record; Trottier had at least one point in every playoff game, also a record.

"Guys like Bossy and Trottier are still very young," Goring said. "Everybody thinks they're 28 or 29, but they're kids. So are a lot of others on this team. And there's more coming up. We've got a lot of Stanley Cups ahead of us."

13 1982: No Letting Up the Third Time Around

When you ask the core players from the dynasty era which Cup-winning season was their best, you may not get very far. "Which year was my favorite? It's like asking which of my kids is my favorite," Trottier said.

The first one will always be special. The last one, when the Islanders fought off the hard-charging Oilers and the NHL wags who said there'd be a changing of the guard, is special too. But to get as close to perfection as possible—what Al Arbour and Bill Torrey strived for—the 1981–82 season of the third Stanley Cup might be the winner. "Al had it laid down pretty simple for us morons," Clark Gillies joked. "We knew what we had to do, how we needed to play. He wasn't easy on us, but we understood pretty clearly how we could win, and we did it."

Torrey had tinkered some, as always. On the eve of the season, he dealt away two more glue guys from the first two Cup teams; Garry Howatt, one of the original Isles, went to Hartford for a low draft pick.

The other trade just before the season was perhaps Torrey's masterstroke in terms of non–trade deadline deals. He sent Bob Lorimer and prospect Dave Cameron to Colorado for the Rockies' first-round pick—not in the June 1982 draft but in the 1983 draft, which would be loaded with talent.

He could afford to lose Lorimer off the defense because Tomas Jonsson, the Isles' second-round pick in 1979, had joined the team from Sweden—continuing the pipeline that began with Stefan Persson's arrival four years earlier.

The only hitch at the start of 1981–82 was Denis Potvin beginning the season injured. He'd torn his groin in the closing minutes of the Cup-clinching Game 5 win over the North Stars five months earlier and aggravated the injury at the 1981 Canada Cup—the international tournament featured six Islanders on Team Canada, two more on Team Sweden (Bob Nystrom, who was born in Sweden, was invited to play for them but declined), and Ken Morrow on Team USA.

So Potvin, who had missed the start of the 1979–80 season, now sat out the first 15 games of 1981–82. The Isles went 10–2–3 without him, but the captain, as he had two years earlier, slogged through a tougher-than-normal season in which he played only 60 games. "I could understand the occasional bad game or things like that, but what I could never understand was the body giving out," Potvin said later that season. "In my case, it's been injuries, something I never had to be concerned about my first seven years in the league."

Even as Potvin wrestled with that, the Islanders simply flew through 1981–82. They were 25–13–6 in January when they reeled off 15 consecutive wins—not squeakers, either. Billy Smith and Roland Melanson were cruising; Mike Bossy set a team record with 147 points and another 60-plus-goal season; Bryan Trottier hit 50 goals for the first time; and John Tonelli posted his best season of his four on the Island with 93 points.

There was no deadline deal to shake things up—the shakeup, such as it was, came right around Christmas, when Brent Sutter joined his brother on the Island. "I was having a good year [in Lethbridge] and Mr. Torrey called me up and said he'd rather I didn't go to play for Canada at the World Juniors," Brent Sutter said. "He told me, 'Go home, have Christmas with your folks, because it's the last one you're going to get with them for a while.'"

Sutter had 21 goals in 43 games, another young player seamlessly fitting into the champions' run. The Islanders finished the season with 118 points, again best in the league.

The 1982 playoffs featured a new structure: divisional semifinals and finals to open the postseason, followed by a conference final and then the Cup. The change didn't seem to faze the Islanders, who faced the Penguins in the opening-round best-of-five series—a Pittsburgh team that finished 43 points behind them.

And the first two games were laughers: an 8–1 Game 1 at the Coliseum followed by a 7–2 Game 2. These were warm-ups, basically, for the real challenges to come. "We get to Pittsburgh for Game 3, it's the Saturday before Easter Sunday," Jiggs McDonald said. "And guys are walking over from the hotel with their luggage—we're going to sweep and be home for Easter Sunday dinner. I noticed a lot of Penguins players driving into the parking lot as we walked over, and I think they noticed us too, with all our luggage."

The Penguins eked out a 2–1 overtime win in Game 3. Game 4 wasn't close, a 5–2 Isles loss in which Arbour put Melanson in net. The Penguins had pulled even and had nothing to lose going back to the Coliseum for the deciding Game 5. And they played like it. Three straight goals in the first period gave Pittsburgh a 3–1 lead that they held into the final six minutes of the third. After all the success—two straight Stanley Cups, scoring records, numerous trophies—it was all about to come to a screeching halt.

Arbour pulled a new one out of his bag of motivational tricks during an Islanders power play late in the third. He pulled Smith and put in Melanson, taking advantage of the rule that allows a new goalie a two-minute warm-up. "I've never done anything like that before," Arbour said, "but I had been thinking about it. It let everybody settle down and stop rushing things. And it worked."

That allowed his top power-play unit to rest. It came back out and produced—Mike McEwen swept in a rebound to make it 3–2 with 5:27 to play. With 2:21 to go, Tonelli pounced on a dump-in and snapped it past Michel Dion to tie the game and send it to overtime.

The Islanders had gotten themselves a chance to pull out the series, but nothing was assured. Penguins forward Mike Bullard led a two-on-one in OT and Smith got enough of his slapper to turn it a few inches by the side of the net. At 6:19 Tonelli was there again. He couldn't convert a partial breakaway but fought for the puck in the corner, fed Nystrom in front, and followed up the play to jam in the winner. "We were that close," Potvin said. "If Smitty doesn't make that save, we're not talking about the history that we made."

And it was Tonelli—yet another of the core group who wasn't considered a star—who had pulled it out of the fire. "I've had that label [a checker] since I first joined the Islanders four years ago," he said. "Although that's a definite part of my game, I always felt I could contribute more to the team, but I wasn't able to until this season."

The Patrick Division final was another meeting with the Rangers, who were now coached by 1980 U.S. Olympic coach Herb Brooks. They were a small, scrappy team and they pulled out Game 1 at the Coliseum 5–4 on a late goal. But the Islanders, chastened by the scare from the previous round, solidified. A 7–2 win in Game 2 was followed by Trottier's overtime winner in the Garden in Game 3 and Duane Sutter's tiebreaking goal late in the third period of a 5–3 Game 4 win.

The Isles wrapped it up at the Garden in Game 6, another 5–3 win. As the Isles emerged for the first Wales Conference final, they certainly realized that the only other two teams to break 100 points in the regular season were gone—the Canadiens were bounced in the opening round and so were the Oilers, who lost to the 63-point Kings in the first round.

So instead of a date with the Habs and a potential Cup Finals against Edmonton, the Islanders had the Nordiques in the conference final. A fourth-place team that had won a pair of deciding games on the road—Game 5 in OT over the Canadiens and Game 7 in Boston over the Bruins.

Quebec was one of the highest-scoring teams in the regular season and the Nordiques had scored 19 goals in their three games against the Islanders. The focus was to choke off their high-powered offense. And it was successful. The Islanders put Quebec down in the opening games at the Coliseum by scores of 4–1 and 5–2. The pivotal Game 3 in Le Colisée went to overtime, where the Islanders took advantage of a key mistake—Quebec goalie Dan Bouchard dropped an easy toss by McEwen from the point, and after swipes by Tonelli and Nystrom, Wayne Merrick shoveled the puck into the net.

The 4–2 final score in Game 4 brought the Islanders to the doorstep of a third-straight Cup. It wasn't high-flying, end-to-end play but just the methodical work of a team that knew how to close out a series, their 11th consecutive series victory.

"Sure, that may look like dull hockey," Smith said, "but all I care about is that it won us four straight games. I'm sure those guys would have done the same thing if they could have."

They were on the brink of another Cup—with another inexperienced opponent to come. The Campbell Conference final featured two sub-.500 teams, with the Canucks taking out the Blackhawks in five games. Vancouver had just 77 points in the regular season but had lost just two games heading into the final.

The Canucks also had Roger Neilson behind their bench. He was the coach of the 1978 Leafs, whose physical, hard-checking style had knocked off the top-seeded Islanders, who thought they were ready to win that year. In 1982 Neilson's shrewd tactics didn't stand much of a chance against the seasoned Isles.

The first two games at the Coliseum were hardly cakewalks. Vancouver fought back from 4–2 down to take a 5–4 lead with 6:54 to go. But the Islanders had their goal scorer ready to push back. Bossy scored his second of the game with 4:46 left to tie it, then he completed his hat trick with two seconds left in the first overtime when he stepped in front of an errant pass and snapped one over Richard Brodeur's shoulder.

Game 2 followed in a similar vein. The upstart Canucks grabbed a 3–2 lead after two periods and the Islanders stormed back with two goals in 47 seconds early in the third. At 4–4 it was Trottier this time who broke the tie on the way to a 6–4 win.

In Vancouver the Islanders finally got back to playing the way Arbour wanted. A 3–0 Game 3 shutout was punctuated by Bossy's ridiculous goal in the second, a wrist shot over Brodeur as Bossy was falling to the ice (he later said it was the best goal he ever scored). Smith had 23 saves, and the Islanders were on the cusp. Game 4 was the crowning achievement, as Bossy scored two second-period power-play goals to snap a 1–1 tie and send the Islanders to the title once more, with Bossy the easy choice as Conn Smythe Trophy winner. He had seven goals in the four Finals games.

"We did what we had to do to win," Arbour said. "That goes for this game, this series, and the whole playoffs. We expected them to try and get the jump on us tonight, for instance, and we contained them all the same. I just want to hand it to these guys for making a coach's job so satisfying."

Trottier set a single-season record with 23 assists and Bossy tied Jean Beliveau for most goals in a Finals.

There were plenty of observers who felt they were making it look easy, but the key was not forgetting the close calls—and also being able to succeed when everyone was looking to knock them off. "This has to be the most satisfying of the three years," Torrey said, "because every time you win it, the next one becomes even tougher."

That was certainly true then. A year later the Islanders would pass their toughest test and come away rightly feeling they were up there with the best teams in NHL history.

14 1983: Making History and Taking the Darlings Down a Peg

The Islanders opened the 1982–83 season in usual (for them) fashion: an 11–2–0 start to the season, plenty of the usual suspects scoring goals, and Billy Smith and Roland Melanson sharing the net equitably.

All was well and calm through the season with little fanfare—mostly because the hockey world was attuned to the scene in Alberta, where the Oilers were no longer the green kids the Isles had dispatched in the 1981 quarterfinals. Wayne Gretzky, Jari Kurri, Mark Messier, and Paul Coffey were putting up eye-popping numbers—Gretzky was coming off a 92-goal, 212-point season in

1981–82 and followed it up with a 71-goal, 196-point season in 1982–83.

It's safe to say the Islanders noticed. "They think they're so hot," Bob Bourne said of the Oilers. "They're damn cocky. The thing that really bugs me is, they don't respect us. They're not the Stanley Cup champions. We are."

Before the reigning champs and the presumptive title-takers could meet in 1983, the Islanders had to get through a tougher-than-usual regular season in which they finished with 96 points, a distant second to the Patrick Division–winning Flyers.

The Islanders dispatched the Caps in four games in the division semis and fully expected to see Philly in the next round. But it was the Rangers once more—a team not-so-affectionately dubbed the Smurfs by Flyers coach Bob McCammon—who swept past Philly to engage with their suburban New York rivals for the third time in four postseasons.

It had started to become a trying year for the Islanders' top forwards. Al Arbour put John Tonelli up with Bryan Trottier and Mike Bossy, with Gillies lining up on the left side with Brent and Duane Sutter. Bourne was still a big contributor, and Goring, the old goat at 33, had another capable season.

Against the Rangers, the scars were starting to show. Gillies missed the first two rounds with a knee injury; Trottier, always game to play hurt in the playoffs, also suffered a knee injury in Game 1 of the Rangers series and missed the next three games. But befitting a team that always had both its stars and its supporting cast ready to go in the playoffs, in that Rangers series the spotlight shone on the Sutter boys and Bourne, playing as a regular line for the first time.

"We're a western Canada type of line," Bourne said after a 5–0 whitewash in Game 2 at the Coliseum. Duane Sutter had a hat trick and Bourne had three assists. "Nothing fancy. If a guy's open, you give it to him. Sometimes a good player will wait for somebody to come at him before making a pass, but we pop it to the open guy right away. We don't do a lot of thinking out there."

The Rangers won both games at the Garden to even the series, but it didn't feel like an Islanders Cup run without a little adversity. Bourne and both Sutters scored in a 7–2 Game 5 rout, and the Islanders, as they had in their two previous series wins over the Rangers, closed it out at the Garden, a 5–2 win in a building many of them had grown to enjoy. "All of us love playing in the Garden," Duane Sutter said. "The fans are so…ugly."

The Islanders moved on to the Wales Conference final and a date with the Bruins, the team that had replaced the Isles as regular-season champs. But after splitting the first two games in Boston, the Islanders put the hammer down at home, with 7–3 and 8–3 wins to grab a decisive series lead. They closed it out in six games with another thumping as Bossy scored four times in an 8–4 Game 6 win.

And so it came down to the Islanders and the Oilers at last. Edmonton had lost just one game on its way to the Finals and the Oilers were feeling good about themselves. "We want to beat them more than anything," Gillies said. "You know why? Because they think they're the greatest thing since sliced bread."

The trash talk only intensified once the series got underway. And that meant the toughest talker on either side, Smith, was in his element. Smith had taken a back seat to Melanson at times during the regular season, and Melanson came in to win Games 3 and 4 of the first round against Washington. Smith was 32, and 11 years into his career, but he loved the big stage and he loved to play the villain. "Boston, Edmonton, the Garden—anyplace he knew he'd get booed, that's where he wanted to be," Goring said.

In Edmonton Smitty spoke with his play in Game 1. The Oilers threw everything at him and Smith turned aside all 35 shots to make Duane Sutter's first-period goal stand up. The Oilers were shut out for the first time all season—and Smith got in one of his trademark licks, a slash on Glenn Anderson that turned up the noise between Games 1 and 2.

Oilers coach Glen Sather called Smith "a maniac." Torrey fired back: "Sather was a yapping player, and now he's a yapping coach and a yapping general manager. Nothing's changed."

Game 2 came and the Oilers finally got on the board, but the Islanders held a 3–1 lead after one and 5–2 after two. And Battlin' Billy got in his licks again, this time whacking Gretzky behind the net. Smith got a suspect five-minute major penalty, then Smith went sprawling himself as Dave Lumley chopped him down near the end of the game.

Smith was in the Oilers' heads, and the mess was perfect for the Islanders, who just went about their business while Edmonton fumed. A 1–1 Game 3 entering the third became a 5–1 rout for the Islanders, with Bourne, Ken Morrow, and the Sutters all scoring in the final period.

Game 4 was a 3–2 game midway through the third when Anderson tried to exact a little revenge with a whack on Smith—who crumpled to the ice as Anderson had in Game 1. Anderson got a five-minute major penalty, the Oilers comeback stalled, and Ken Morrow sent his second empty-net goal of the series down to seal it.

Four straight Cups. And a thorough humiliation of the Oilers in the process. "This is a special group," Arbour said. "There's no team of greater character in any sport than this team right now."

"We're the best that ever skated," Denis Potvin said, "and if anyone doesn't believe it, they're kidding themselves."

It would be another spring parade down Hempstead Turnpike, another ring. And it never, ever got old. "It's a great feeling that will become greater with the years," Tonelli said after the fourth Cup. "I will be sitting on my couch, and other teams will be playing for the Stanley Cup, and I will smile. Then I will remember this night. And if I'm watching with someone, I'll just say, 'I played for the New York Islanders.'"

15 The Drive for Five

The Islanders gathered again in September 1983 for a run at a fifth Stanley Cup. The essential cast was still the same; Bill Torrey's trade with the Rockies on the eve of the 1981–82 season had produced the third overall pick in June 1983, which the Isles used on Pat LaFontaine.

Even at the start of the 1983–84 season, the anticipation of LaFontaine and Pat Flatley joining the team after the 1984 Olympics was on the horizon.

"We've always had our fuel injectors here," Denis Potvin told the *New York Times* on the eve of the season. "You know, guys who can get the machine going, like Trots, Clarkie, Bossy, and me. And we've had our share of guys with lesser talent who might be mediocre elsewhere but stand out here.

"What we've shown in the four Cups, I think, is a great deal of discipline, all of us. None of us feels any more important than the next guy. And we've shown that if we do the job, if we discipline ourselves, then the machine will work. The whole is often greater than the parts."

It was another strong season, with the Isles winning the Patrick Division with 104 points, three ahead of the improved Capitals. After a disappointing 1982–83 regular season, this was more like the championship mold Bill Torrey and Al Arbour had built.

Mike Bossy and Bryan Trottier were at their peaks still, with 118 and 111 points, respectively. Potvin had his best regular-season numbers since the 1970s: 85 points. Younger players such as Brent Sutter (34 goals) and Greg Gilbert (31–35–66) made big contributions. And LaFontaine and Flatley came on for the stretch run, given prominent roles that may have rankled some of the longtime veterans but energized the team as it headed toward the playoffs. After the two kids arrived, the Isles lost just three times in their final 15 games and barreled into the division semifinals against their old friends from Manhattan.

The Islanders had bounced the Rangers the last three years on the way to glory. Why should this best-of-five be any different? But it was. The series was even headed back to the Garden, and the Isles' wheels fell off in Game 3—a 7–2 loss that saw Billy Smith pulled when it was 5–0 midway through the second. These Rangers had finished just 11 points in back of the Isles in the regular season, and suddenly the dynasty seemed more in jeopardy than at any time since the 1982 division semis, when the Penguins rallied to put the Isles on the ropes.

It was 1–0 Rangers heading to the third period of Game 4. John Tonelli, the Islander who had saved the dynasty in Game 5 against the Penguins two years earlier, tied it up less than a minute in. Then it was Flatley, the 20-year-old kid who didn't have the weight of history on him, who turned the game around for good.

Flatley threw a hard shoulder at big Rangers defenseman Barry Beck, forcing a turnover. Beck was hurt by the clean hit and couldn't get back in position to deny Brent Sutter a clear look at a rebound, and Sutter backhanded one in with 8:56 to go for a lead that the Isles didn't give up in a 4–1 win.

Game 5 was still a nail-biter. Tomas Jonsson's goal with 12:04 to play gave the Isles a 2–1 lead, but the Rangers were controlling the game and managed to tie it with 39 seconds left on Don Maloney's batted-down rebound. If there were video replay like there is now, that review would have taken hours—Maloney's stick was right at shoulder height, which was the mark of a high stick back then (now it's the crossbar for goals).

But it stood, and they went to a deciding overtime. There was Ken Morrow, whose seeing-eye shot from along the right wall got through Glen Hanlon's pads to end it at 8:56 of OT. Sighs of relief rained down from the Coliseum faithful and in the locker room. "If we lost, it would have been impossible around here next year," Bob Bourne said.

The Islanders marched on, taking down the Caps in five games, then the Canadiens in six for their 19th consecutive playoff series win. No. 20 was what they wanted, and it was the Oilers again. Except this time Edmonton's kids were ready in a way they hadn't been a year earlier, when the old goats from the Island taught them a lesson. "We walked by their locker room in the corridor [in 1983] and saw after they won they were too beat up to really enjoy it and savor the victory at that moment," Wayne Gretzky said. "We were able to walk out of there pretty much scot-free. We had so much respect for the Islanders players and the Islanders teams that we learned immediately you have to take it to another level in order to win a Stanley Cup. And that's what we did. We learned from it and often credit the Islanders players and Islanders teams for teaching us exactly what it's all about and how hard it is to win."

And the Islanders weren't just bumped and bruised by the 1984 Finals; they were hurt. Bourne suffered a knee injury against Montreal and was out for the Finals. Nystrom was also hurt against the Canadiens and missed the first three games against the Oilers. Dave Langevin was injured twice in the postseason and was out as Game 1 at the Coliseum loomed. Wayne Merrick and Gord Lane, solid depth players the previous four postseasons, were extras this time around.

Still with all that, the difference in the series was probably that Game 1: a 1–0 Oilers win, which was such an unlikely result with all that firepower on both sides. The game was decided by an Edmonton goal from Kevin McClelland, one of the Oilers' depth guys.

The Isles stormed back to even the series with a 6–1 Game 2 win, but then a new wrinkle: The NHL changed the Finals format to give three straight games to the lower-seeded team, so Edmonton was headed home for three now. The Isles wouldn't even get a chance to get back to Fort Neverlose.

The turning point in the series was the final minute of the second period in Game 3. A 2–2 game, one that could have gone either way in those final 20 minutes, turned into a rout. Glenn Anderson scored with 48 seconds left in the second and Paul Coffey scored 17 seconds after that, two bad breakdowns by the Islanders that left them reeling. Game 3 ended with a final score of 7–2. And Game 4 ended by the same 7–2 score. Trottier and Bossy looked spent. Potvin was battling a virus by Game 5. The end came unceremoniously, with LaFontaine scoring twice in the third period to cut into a 4–0 Oilers lead, but it wasn't enough. The dynasty had ended and a new one was beginning.

"We were physically tired," Arbour said.

But still proud. "I know, down deep, that everyone gave what they had," Bossy said. "But I know I didn't get any good scoring chances in the last two games. Now it's not easy to look around and see the sadness on all the faces. I'm sure if we put our minds to it, we'll come back strong and have good times together again."

16 Easter Epic

By the time Game 7 of the 1987 Patrick Division semifinals came, the Islanders weren't just nicked up. They weren't just bruised. They were battered. There was some irony to the laundry list of ailments that hit the dynasty core of Islanders in that series against the Caps. Bossy, whose back had limited him to 63 regular-season games, suffered a knee injury in Game 2 that knocked him out of the series.

Potvin, who lost 17 games in February and March to a knee injury, missed the final three games of the Caps series with a back problem.

Trottier played—and played a huge role in the Easter Epic—but had a separated shoulder. When you watch clips from the game, he looks like he's about to audition for a monster movie, with one shoulder pad completely jacked up higher than the other due to the wrap on his shoulder.

Duane Sutter and Tomas Jonsson both had full face shields due to injuries. Brent Sutter hadn't played a game since March, and in a preview of his post-playing days, he was actually behind the bench with Terry Simpson and assistant Bob Nystrom for the deciding game in Landover, Maryland. "That was the first time I got to see the game from that side of it," Sutter said. "It was a fun little window into the behind-the-scenes part. I didn't know how crazy that game would get, obviously."

They'd been here before, the core guys—very recently, in fact: The deciding Game 5 of the division semifinals in 1985 was right on this same ice surface in suburban D.C., when the Islanders rallied from a 2–0 series deficit to force a winner-take-all Game 5 and eked out a 2–1 win, thanks in large part to Smith's 39 saves.

The run of five straight Cup Finals appearances ended in the next round at the hands of the Flyers. And the Caps got some measure of revenge with a three-game, first-round sweep in 1986, heralding the massive changes that the Isles underwent prior to the start of the 1986–87 season: Al Arbour retired and Terry Simpson came in. Gillies and Bourne were lost to the waiver draft. Sutter, LaFontaine, Flatley, and Hrudey—the younger core players—were starting to become the focus, even as the aging champions were still around and still contributing.

And there was the added benefit of the NHL making all rounds best-of-seven. The Caps jumped out to a 3–1 series lead in 1987—the Isles scored just seven goals in those four games. Potvin and Bossy were out, Sutter was already out, Trottier was hampered, Smith was on the bench. It didn't seem ripe for a comeback. "I remember one of the beat writers coming up to me on the off day between Games 4 and 5 saying, 'So what will you do for the summer?'" Hrudey said. "I was shocked, genuinely so. It just kind of hit home there that we weren't given much of a chance."

Hrudey posted 40 saves in a 4–2 win in Game 5 on the Caps' home ice. LaFontaine scored twice in a 4:56 span to rally the Islanders to a 5–4 win in Game 6 at the Coliseum. So there the Isles were, missing some of the big names of days gone by but trying to make history once more. Little did they know what they were in for.

Hrudey kept the game close until the midway point of the game, allowing only Mike Gartner's jam-shot rebound goal with under a minute to go in the first period. Flatley was somehow still in the game in the second after getting obliterated by Scott Stevens in the neutral zone—"I was basically crawling to the bench," Flatley said—and he tied it on a bit of a change-up wrister that snuck through Bob Mason's pads at 11:35 of the second.

The Caps took a 2–1 lead with 75 seconds left in the second on career minor leaguer Grant Martin's first and only NHL goal. The Islanders were being outshot 25–10 and didn't seem to have the gas needed to keep this fight up.

But inside of six minutes to go, Trottier came through. He was wearing the *C* that night with Potvin out and it would be the last stretch he'd get to do that. Torrey would name Sutter captain before next season when Potvin announced he'd be retiring after the 1987–88 campaign and handed over the captaincy.

So, with a C on one shoulder and a Frankenstein wrap on the other, Trots cruised up the ice on his off-hand side, took a feed from Alan Kerr and threw a backhand between Mason's legs to tie it.

"There's no Easter Epic without Trots," LaFontaine said. "The game went so long it's easy to forget that."

And perhaps the hockey gods were smiling on the Isles. Mason's skate blade had broken earlier without the Caps goalie being aware. When he went to close the pads on Trottier's shot, he had no support on one leg and the puck trickled through.

On to overtime, times four. The pace was pretty high and the Islanders, buoyed by Trottier's late goal, had the better of the play. Bob Bassen was denied all alone in front of Mason in the first OT. Randy Wood swept a rebound between Mason's legs and off the post in the second overtime while Mason had lost his helmet—perhaps one that would have been controversial had it gone in.

"If I'm giving my honest assessment, the Capitals outplayed us in regulation and maybe the first overtime," Hrudey said. "Then we started to dominate, Bob Mason was lights out."

Hrudey was incredible too. By the end of the second overtime he'd made 64 saves, including 17 in that fifth period. "That just shows you what will can do," he said.

The mood in the dressing room between periods was hardly somber. "Guys were getting giddier as the night went on," Sutter said. LaFontaine had a breakaway denied by Mason in the third OT and Duane Sutter whacked a rebound that Mason somehow kept out—everything but his catching glove was inside the net. Mikko Makela had two great chances with 30 seconds left in the third OT, then the Caps' Lou Franceschetti raced down and couldn't beat Hrudey before the horn.

On the bench in the fourth OT, LaFontaine couldn't believe what was happening. "I looked around the stands and saw people sleeping," he said. "[Equipment manager] Jimmy Pickard squeezed a water bottle down the back of my neck and says, 'Hey, you're gonna pop one in.' Then the organist starts playing the *Twilight Zone* theme.

"It was that crazy, 2 A.M. energy."

LaFontaine was nearing the end of a shift when Gord Dineen raced onto a puck and carried it around the Caps net. LaFontaine went to the right point to cover for Dineen, whose shot as he came around caromed off Kevin Hatcher's skate and skittered out to LaFontaine.

He swivels. He slaps the puck, sitting on end. All goes quiet in Landover as the puck clangs off the left post and behind Mason, who slumps down. The longest NHL playoff game in 36 years ended at 1:58 A.M. and the Islanders won it.

"I just stood there for about two seconds. I was in disbelief," said Hrudey, who finished with 73 saves, an NHL record that stood until the 2020 playoffs. "Half the guys went to Pat and half came to me."

And all the Islanders made it home to Long Island by sunrise. "I got home, went to bed for a bit, got up, went to Easter Mass, went back to bed, got to the rink and we were on a bus to Philly," LaFontaine said. "Two days later we started the series against the Flyers."

The Islanders nearly duplicated their first-round feat against the Flyers, falling behind 3–1 in the series before forcing a Game 7. It didn't end the same way, of course, and the Islanders didn't see the second round for another six years.

But the Easter Epic winner was a milestone of sorts for LaFontaine, who'd been a very good Islander up to that point. He started a run of six straight 40-goal seasons the next year, becoming the superstar that took the reins from the Islanders old guard, spurred on by ending the longest game of all of their careers.

"What propelled us really was the Islander way," LaFontaine said. "We were down 3–1 in the series, down in Game 7 and it's, 'Who wants to be the hero?' That was a moment that helped push me. It gives you confidence to go through a series like that. It gave us a belief we're going to continue to rebuild this."

17 The 2020 Playoffs

Everything about the end of the 2019–20 season was bizarre. The COVID–19 pandemic came to North America in February 2020. The Islanders continued their season for as long as they could, altering small procedures in a way that seems quaint now—holding media sessions outside the locker room, for instance, even though no one wore masks in a crowd of reporters in the hallway.

The regular season shut down on March 12, hours before a scheduled game in Calgary. Players went back to the Island, then home, for months, assembling back at Northwell Health Ice Center under new protocols on July 13 for a two-week training camp before heading to the Eastern Conference playoff bubble site in Toronto for a postseason without fans.

It was all new and jarring. The teams that could handle the new reality best would be able to go deep in the playoffs. "When you have a group, it's really important the group understands it's not normal, so you have to accept whatever's thrown at you," Barry Trotz said. "And you have to be somewhat resilient—what you're used to is not there. If you're looking for normal, you're probably going to fail. If you're a guy that's motivated by the crowd, good luck to you. You better find another way. That's where the players have to adapt, become better. As coaches we have to find methods and focuses that give our team a chance. There's going to be so much unpredictability."

This was where the Islanders benefited most from having Lou Lamoriello and Trotz running the show. Lamoriello's old-school rules—suits for everyone on the road, no long hair and no facial hair (he relaxes the last one for the playoffs)—helped the Islanders feel like they were preparing for something after four months of players trying to stay fit and focused when almost no one could.

And Trotz used that two-week camp not to evaluate who belonged where but to remind his team of what made it successful early in 2019–20, when a 15–0–2 run set a new franchise record for unbeaten streaks. Injuries to Adam Pelech, Cal Clutterbuck, Casey Cizikas, and Johnny Boychuk turned the Isles into a mediocre team for much of the last three months of that season, and they went into the 12-team Eastern Conference playoff as the No. 7 seed.

Once in Toronto teams had a few days to get settled, with the teams split into two hotels and restricted to their floor. Anders Lee and the other veterans tried to figure out ways to keep the group together and entertained with so much confined downtime between games and practices.

"We saw right away there was basically one thing they gave us: a Ping-Pong table," Lee said. "It was in a common room, and there was barely any space for guys other than the two that were playing. And it was great, don't get me wrong; the hotel there was doing its best.

"So we moved it to the area between the elevators on our floor. Guys would be coming back from lunch or practice, and it was there. It felt like guys were always playing. It became a little bit like a frat house or a dorm, guys' doors propped open, wanting to just spend time together."

That Ping-Pong table brought the Islanders instantly closer to one of their new teammates. Jean-Gabriel Pageau was a deadline acquisition from the Senators, a 27-year-old center for whom Lamoriello paid a big price: first- and second-round picks, plus a six-year contract worth $5 million a year an hour after the deal was done on February 24.

Pageau scored goals in each of his first two games after the deal, but the Islanders went 0–4–3 with him in the lineup. He went home to Ottawa during the pause, had time to breathe a bit, and came back refreshed. He also tore through the Ping-Pong tournament in the bubble hotel while scoring the first goal of the playoffs in the preliminary round against the Panthers.

"You knew by the way he played all his years in Ottawa that he fit in with what we do on the ice," Lee said. "In the bubble it was great to get to know him away from the ice too, and he fit there just as well. One of the boys."

Pageau came out on fire. So did Anthony Beauvillier and Semyon Varlamov, who'd replaced the incredibly popular Robin Lehner in goal and had an up-and-down first season with the Isles.

They whipped the Panthers in four games, then the Capitals in five, a series punctuated by Mathew Barzal's speed rush for the Game 3 overtime winner. Technically it was the first time since 1993 that the Islanders had won two playoff series, but they were still in the "second round" facing the Flyers.

It was a wild series on the ice and off—the teams joined their fellow quarterfinalists in calling for a two-day pause of games after police shot Jacob Blake, an unarmed Black man, in Kenosha, Wisconsin. The series was tied 1–1; the Islanders calmly got back to work, winning the next two games before losing Games 5 and 6 in overtime and double OT.

In Game 7 the Islanders returned to their foundation: stifling defense, aggressive forechecking, and contributions from the whole roster. Scott Mayfield and Andy Greene, two light-scoring defensemen, had first-period goals on the way to a 4–0 win with Thomas Greiss, who'd barely played to that point, posting a 16-save shutout.

That meant a trip to the conference final, the first since the miracle run in 1993. It also meant leaving the Toronto bubble—and that Ping-Pong table—and heading to Edmonton, where the conference finals and Stanley Cup Finals would be held.

The Lightning was waiting. The Isles flew across Canada on September 6 and played Game 1 on September 7, a predictably ugly 8–2 loss. But the killer was Game 2, a tie game into the final seconds of regulation when Tampa Bay's Nikita Kucherov snapped home the winner with 8.7 seconds to play.

The Islanders had their moments in the series, including Jordan Eberle's double-OT goal off a feed from Lee to keep the Isles alive in Game 5, but Anthony Cirelli beat Varlamov in OT in Game 6 to end the series. An improbable run fell two games short of the Finals.

"It was so unique it felt like a different life at times—our only responsibility was getting ready for the next game," Lee said. "It was so hard to be away from our families, but we achieved a level of focus that might not be matched again."

18 Beating the Penguins in 1993

Even nearly 30 years on, it's hard to believe the Islanders pulled it off. They got past the Capitals in the Patrick Division semifinals and were headed into the lion's den—a date with the two-time defending Stanley Cup champion Penguins, the team with Mario Lemieux, Jaromir Jagr, Ron Francis, Larry Murphy, Kevin Stevens, and Joe Mullen, and Scotty Bowman behind the bench.

The Islanders didn't have Pierre Turgeon. They had Al Arbour, of course, but aside from that, it was a completely unproven bunch of Islanders pretty far removed from the glory days.

"I still have no fucking idea how we won that," Glenn Healy said.

Well, here's how it all went down:

The Islanders caught a break in Game 1 in Pittsburgh when Lemieux left the game barely three minutes in after a collision with Brad Dalgarno. Lemieux had suffered through Hodgkin's lymphoma during the 1992–93 season, making a triumphant return from cancer treatment after missing two months to still win the regular-season scoring title despite playing only 60 games.

Lemieux was believed to have had a recurrence of the back spasms that had plagued him for a few years. Even without him for the bulk of Game 1, the Islanders were still treading water and looking for breaks.

Healy was just getting started with the acrobatics he'd need to pull off the upset. He helped kill a Penguins five-on-three late in the first period with the game tied when Tom Fitzgerald tipped a pass out of the zone just as Ray Ferraro was exiting the penalty box. Ferraro, who had eight goals in the six-game win over the Caps, continued his crazy scoring pace with a breakaway shorty to give the Isles a 2–1 lead.

"This is how insane that was," Ferraro said. "I have never, in my entire career, scored a shorthanded goal. The only time a coach would ever let me on the ice during a penalty kill was in the last 10 seconds. So here I am out of the box, and I'm going straight to the bench so one of our good PK forwards can come on; instead Fitzy tips a puck to me and I'm off. Unreal."

Benoit Hogue added another shorthanded goal in the third, and the Islanders had pulled off Game 1. "We certainly weren't overconfident or anything like that," Fitzgerald said. "But we had Al telling us every day, 'Can you win one shift? One period against these guys?' And then we [won] the first game, and maybe we [were] starting to believe a little more."

Without Lemieux the Penguins clamped down for a 3–0 Game 2 win, then a 3–1 win in the Coliseum in Game 3 with Super Mario back in uniform. The result started to feel a bit more inevitable after the Turgeon-less Islanders could only muster one goal in those two games. But the wackiness factor returned in Game 4, and it turned the series on its head.

It was a 1–1 game late in the second, and the Islanders were again shorthanded. Fitzgerald and Hogue misfired on a two-on-one and the Penguins gathered the puck for one last rush. But Fitzgerald picked a pass out of midair and blasted one by Tom Barrasso for an Islanders lead entering the third.

On the same penalty kill, Fitzgerald and Hogue again went down two-on-one. This time instead of trying to thread a pass, Fitzgerald kept it and snapped one by Barrasso. Two shorthanded goals on the same penalty. "And I shouldn't have even been out there—I definitely high-sticked someone and they took Claude [Loiselle] off instead of me," Fitzgerald said. "There's all these little things you think of after the fact; if they'd gone a slightly different way, you probably have a different outcome. But most of them went our way."

Game 4 was far from over at 3–1 early in the third. The Penguins tied it with two goals in 21 seconds, then Derek King untied it 38 seconds after that. Pittsburgh tied it, the Isles took a 5–4 lead, the Penguins tied it again at 10:50. And finally King put the Isles ahead for good with 7:49 to go. Six goals, all on Barrasso, just enough to keep the Penguins at bay and a tied series.

Lemieux was back to his old self in Game 5 in Pittsburgh, scoring his first two goals of the series in a 6–3 Penguins rout. Again Arbour implored his team to forget about who was on the other side and remember how his team could win.

The Islanders also had a crazy 20-year-old kid on defense who wasn't afraid of anyone. Darius Kasparaitis had thrown some big hits in the series, but his mission in Game 6 was to make sure Lemieux got checked every time the two were on the ice together. In the second period, Lemieux shoved Kasparaitis off a puck. Kasparaitis got up and shoved Lemieux down, making the much bigger Penguins star turtle with an extra shove. Later in the same shift Kasparaitis went in again, taking Lemieux's stick up high but somehow getting called for roughing.

The Penguins tied the game on the ensuing power play, but Kasparaitis was making Lemieux play with his head on a swivel. "The thing [we] loved about Darius is he played the same way every shift," Fitzgerald said. "Against a fourth-liner or Jagr or Mario, he was the same. Just a pit bull."

Brian Mullen scored early in the third to put the Islanders back in front, and they held on for a 7–5 win, sending the series back to Pittsburgh for Game 7.

Turgeon returned to the lineup with his separated shoulder in a harness, but he wasn't the same player. Then a huge collision between Stevens and Rich Pilon resulted in a scary injury for the Penguins forward in the first. He was knocked out by the hit and fell face-first, shattering several facial bones. It set an eerie tone for the game.

The Islanders held a 3–1 lead into the final four minutes of regulation before the Penguins rallied to tie with a double deflection off a Murphy point shot that hit off Rick Tocchet's skate and went in.

"Heading into OT there wasn't any panic or feeling like we'd blown it," Ferraro said. "Al was the same as he always was. 'Can you tie a shift? Can you tie a shift against Lemieux, against Jagr?' That's all he asked. If you could do that, you could get a break."

It came 5:16 in. Ulf Samuelsson entered the Islanders zone and his centering feed hit off a skate and went the other way. The Islanders had a three-on-one—Ferraro, Vladimir Malakhov, and David Volek. Malakhov picked off a scrambling Penguin, and Ferraro stayed wide and hit Volek perfectly for a one-timer. Then silence in Pittsburgh. Except for the Islanders screaming themselves silly.

"Someone, some line, stepped up every game that series," Fitzgerald said. "It was the ultimate team moment."

19 John Tavares

As hard as fans may try these days, you can't erase the John Tavares era from Islanders history. Someday, maybe someday soon, fans will give Tavares a warm welcome. OK, maybe not soon, but the appreciation for what Tavares gave to the Isles and their fans over nine seasons will return. "I hope so," Anders Lee said. "He wanted to win here as bad as anyone. As time passes, people will understand that."

From the moment Garth Snow called Tavares's name onstage at the Bell Centre in Montreal in 2009 to the time a little past noon on July 1, 2018, when Tavares announced he'd signed with the Leafs, he was all in on the Islanders. No one who ever played with him or encountered him ever doubted how serious and committed he was to making the Islanders a good team.

And when you look back to see what Charles Wang's austerity budget left Tavares to work with his first few seasons on the Island, you can see his impact even clearer. Matt Moulson, whose younger brother had played with Tavares when they were kids in Toronto, came in as a low-budget free agent and went immediately on Tavares's left side.

For the next three years Moulson, who was 25 when he lined up alongside the 19-year-old Tavares, scored 30 goals or more, the first Islander to do that since Ziggy Palffy 15 years earlier.

P.A. Parenteau was another Islander reclamation project when he signed on prior to the 2010–11 season. Parenteau amassed 120 points as the right wing with Tavares and Moulson in the next two seasons and signed a four-year, $16 million deal with the Avalanche before the 2012–13 season. "You couldn't help but be a better player with Johnny," Parenteau said. "He worked hard and he was extremely talented. You needed to do the work or you couldn't keep up."

Moulson was traded away early in the 2013–14 season prior to signing a five-year, $25 million deal with the Sabres. Kyle Okposo, who ultimately played more minutes with Tavares than anyone, signed with the Sabres in 2016 for seven years and $42 million, thanks in no small part to his time as Tavares's right wing.

Josh Bailey's numbers went up when he was the top-line right wing in 2016–17 and 2017–18. Lee was the Isles' first 40-goal scorer in his second season with Tavares in 2017–18, the first Isles player to reach that mark in nearly a dozen years.

Tavares himself was a two-time Hart Memorial Trophy finalist and averaged more than a point a game in three of his nine seasons and barely less than a point a game in two others. He was a bogus Jamie Benn assist away from a share of the NHL scoring title in 2014–15, which would have been the first Art Ross Trophy for an Islander since Bryan Trottier in 1978–79. He did it while always facing the opposition's best defensemen, best checking centers. And he never complained, except about how he felt he'd failed if the team didn't play well.

"Back then, there was just no off switch for him," said Colin McDonald, who roomed with Tavares for two seasons (2012 to 2014) on the Island, when both guys were single. "As focused as he was at the rink, there wasn't much difference at home—we'd watch hockey, he [was] foam-rolling, whatever it took to be ready, be better. It was an eye-opener for me. Here [was] a guy who [had] enough talent to do whatever he want[ed] in his spare time, and he spent most of it trying to be even better."

His goal to win the 2016 first-round series against the Panthers will always be iconic. That it was Tavares who jumped off the bench and stuffed in the tying goal in Game 6 with 53.2 seconds to go made sense—he was a force that series, with that goal his fourth in the six games.

The individual effort on his double-overtime winner—the shot, the follow, and the backhand wraparound—one of the more difficult shots in hockey—will never be forgotten. "We had a real group effort that series, with some guys people didn't really know much about who made big contributions," Jack Capuano said. "But Johnny was our leader, and he did it in the biggest moments. That goal was skill and hard work combined. That's John Tavares."

It won't happen yet. It may not happen soon. But there will come a time when the best Islander of the 21st century gets his due.

20 The Old Barn

Everyone has a Coliseum story. For a place that was seemingly falling apart from the time the first Stanley Cup banner was raised—a place with too few seats, too few suites, endless bathroom lines, leaks, and that was once declared unfit for office workers to be in—everyone who rooted for, worked for, and played for the Islanders from 1972 to 2021 (with that Brooklyn detour from 2015 to 2018) has a warm feeling about the Old Barn.

"It's a dump, but it's our dump," fans and players would say about the Nassau Veterans Memorial Coliseum. The progression of owners who tried in vain to make money off the place might say those words with a little more resignation and a little less pride, but Islanders fans of all ages have great memories of the little arena with low ceilings, terrific sight lines, great space for tailgating, and a whole lot of noise when it was full—even at a capacity that never went above 16,297. "You can't count the number of times our fans gave us the energy we needed," Bob Nystrom said. "When we'd get out there during the Stanley Cup years, we felt invincible."

Fort Neverlose was the nickname for the Coliseum during those 19 consecutive playoff series wins. The Islanders were 11–1 at home in the Finals, losing only Game 1 of the 1984 Finals—a series that plenty of the core dynasty Isles and their fans believe could still have ended differently if the NHL hadn't switched that postseason to a 2–3–2 format for the Finals, meaning the Isles didn't get a chance to fend off elimination back home.

But even during the odd playoff appearances over the last 25 years, no one will forget what the building was capable of. "Before my first playoff game in 2015, we were staying at the Marriott [across the plaza from the Coliseum], and it was a day game,"

Johnny Boychuk said. "At like 8:00 AM I heard people outside my window. I thought they were washing the windows at the hotel or something, but it was fans setting up to tailgate. It was amazing to see that."

The Capitals were the Isles' opponents that first round in 2015, and Barry Trotz was Washington's coach. He said—and legendary hockey play-by-play announcer Mike Emrick has said it too—that the loudest building he's ever been in was the Coliseum when John Tavares scored 15 seconds into that afternoon Game 3 to win it. "You couldn't hear yourself think in there," Trotz said.

It was the same in 2013, when the Islanders made their surprising playoff appearance. Same even in 2007, when the Isles squeaked into the playoffs on the last day of the season. "I was in the stands in '07 since I was skating with the extra guys," Frans Nielsen said. "The energy was incredible. It didn't matter that we were the last team to get in and the Sabres were the best team in the conference—the fans were so excited to have the games that mattered.

"And all I wanted the next few years was to get back there. So when we did in '13, it was everything I thought it would be."

Local Long Island government brought the Coliseum into existence, but it was Nassau county executive Ralph Caso who oversaw the construction and helped bring the Islanders into the world and into the new building. The World Hockey Association's New York Raiders eyed the new arena as their home, but Caso and county leaders didn't think the WHA was viable.

The NHL agreed, awarding a franchise to Long Island essentially to block the WHA team from trying to move in. "I'm delighted by the action," Caso said. "It solidifies my belief in the position I've taken all along—that the Coliseum would settle for nothing but the best. We're going first class all the way. I believe the NHL is the prominent hockey league, and I opted for it all along."

The Coliseum opened on February 11, 1972, with Roy Boe's other team, the ABA's Nets, defeating the Pittsburgh Condors 129–121. Just fewer than 8,000 attended.

When the Islanders made their Coliseum debut eight months later, the place was just about full. And it stayed full even through that dismal 1972–73 expansion season, when the Isles mustered only 12 wins in 78 games. "We knew we weren't very good," Ed Westfall said, "but we didn't want to disappoint the fans."

The Flames' Morris Stefaniw scored the first-ever goal in the Coliseum in that opener on October 8, 1972. Westfall scored the first Islanders goal. Cal Clutterbuck had the "last" goal in the Coliseum, an empty-netter to seal Game 6 against the Capitals in 2015—that was until the Islanders returned on December 1, 2018, when Anders Lee scored the "first" goal in the renovated Coli.

There won't be another "first" goal there by an Islander. The building that saw three Cups won, four championship banners raised, and countless fans go through the place will live on for a while. In Islanders fans' memories, it'll always be the Barn. Our Barn.

21 The New Barn

And now, Islanders fans, your reward for five decades of feeling less-than to all your fellow hockey fans who have enjoyed upgraded or new hockey arenas to watch their teams play. The UBS Arena at Belmont Park will soon open for business. And it's got a lot of elements you asked for. But everything good comes to those to wait.

"One of the reasons I walked around the Coliseum all the time instead of sitting in the box was the chance to talk to hundreds and hundreds of fans," Isles co-owner Jon Ledecky said last year. "All of whom were excited about Belmont but all wanted input. They wanted the intimacy of Nassau Coliseum. They wanted a bowl that was close to the ice, so we're going to have more lower-bowl seats than any arena in the league. We're going to take that feeling and move it over to UBS, but we're going to leave behind the 30-minute wait for a bathroom, we're going to leave behind the 20-minute wait for a cold hot dog."

It's more than the details, of course, though the details are pretty sweet. Parking for 12,000 cars so the tailgaters can set up. An expanded Long Island Rail Road stop so those who don't want to drive don't have to.

Inside there are eight bars, some with standing areas to watch the action. And there's a wide array of food choices—that was Barclays Center's best draw, really—that will leave the nostalgia of the Coliseum nachos way in the past.

For the higher-end seats, there are suites at ice level with access to watch the Islanders walk out from the locker room to the rink. But the suite experience is not the dominant one. "We got rid of a lot of the suites because it was more critical to build a great bowl to enjoy the show," said Tim Leiweke, CEO of Oak View Group, which built and is managing UBS Arena. "We're not the show. Our job is to complement the show."

In short, it's the best arena you'll ever have been in to watch your team at home. That in itself is an amazing thing given the starts and stops and dead ends so many Islanders owners encountered trying to get a new building off the ground.

This one, though blessed by New York State, was driven by a unique partnership between three different entities with strong footholds in the New York sports scene: Ledecky and principal owner Scott Malkin; Oak View Group, the arena construction and management firm led by Leiweke and backed by Madison Square

Garden; and Sterling Equities, the real-estate arm run by former Mets owner Fred Wilpon.

So yes, in a way the Rangers helped the Islanders get a new home. Feels like the right thing to do given it was the Rangers who had the Isles in major debt from the start in 1972.

The current Islanders are certainly excited to have this new home, but so are the long-ago Islanders who got to play in the Coliseum when it wasn't outdated. "I'm beyond thrilled it's come to this conclusion," Ken Morrow said. "It's been, I don't know, well over 10 years that this team has been without a permanent home. I'm very thankful they're still on Long Island. I can't imagine that they wouldn't be there. Thankfully it never came to that. There's really bright days ahead."

22 Pat and Pat Arrive

It had worked so well for the Islanders at the 1980 Olympics, with Ken Morrow making the incredibly seamless transition from gold medal–winning Olympian to Stanley Cup–winning New York Islander. Why not try it again in 1984? There was no Miracle on Ice in the '84 Games in Sarajevo. Pat LaFontaine's U.S. squad finished seventh and Pat Flatley's Canadian team finished fourth, with the high-powered Soviet Union team taking its spot back on the gold medal podium.

Bill Torrey was eager to get his top picks from each of the past two drafts into the fold, however. LaFontaine, the third overall pick in 1983, was the product of one of Torrey's shrewdest trades, when he sent Dave Cameron and Bob Lorimer to the Colorado Rockies on October 1, 1981 (by 1983–84 they were the New Jersey

Devils) for the perennially awful Rockies' first-round pick in the 1983 draft.

Flatley was the last pick of the 1982 first round, one of the first-ever first-rounders taken out of the U.S. college hockey ranks. Flatley, a Toronto native, spent two seasons at Wisconsin before spending the bulk of the 1983–84 season with the Canadian national team in preparation for the Olympics.

They arrived for practice on February 27, 1984. "That first practice was a little shaky," Flatley said. "I told Al, 'I'm really not this bad.' He said, 'I hope not, because you won't be here very long if you are.'"

Coming to a team about to try for its fifth-straight Stanley Cup might make anyone nervous; coming to take two regular forwards' jobs with 16 games to go might make you a little nauseous. Anders Kallur, the fourth-line dynamo for all four Cup years, reportedly cracked on meeting one of the Pats for the first time: "He's Flatley. I'm history."

LaFontaine started out centering Bob Bourne and Bob Nystrom; Flatley was on the wing with John Tonelli and Brent Sutter. Torrey and Al Arbour were giddy at having a much deeper group behind Bryan Trottier and Mike Bossy at the top and Butch Goring centering the fourth line.

And it didn't take long to see why. On his first shift in Winnipeg two nights after that brutal practice, Flatley bowled over the Jets' Lucien DeBlois, took a feed from Tonelli, and scored his first goal on his first shot during his first shift. "Thought I was gonna score 50," Flatley said, laughing. "Obviously, I did not." He still had four points in his first two games.

LaFontaine broke out in his second game in Toronto. He already had his first goal and an assist late in the second period when big Leafs defenseman Jim Korn tried to rough up the new kid. Nystrom got involved as well, and all three went to the penalty box.

"We're sitting there, it's my first NHL penalty, and Bobby goes, 'When we get out, just put your head down and go straight to the bench,'" LaFontaine said. "So I do that, and I turn around to see Bobby just pummeling Korn. It was about 20 punches to one.

"Here I am, my second game with a team like we had, someone takes a couple liberties with me, and Bobby Nystrom, the guy who scored the 1980 Cup-winning goal, is standing up for me. My dad was there that night, and he said to me after, 'Now you see why they win all the time.'"

LaFontaine finished that game with a hat trick and five points. He'd put up 13 goals and 19 points in 15 games before the playoffs began, then another 9 points in the playoffs. Flatley finished the short regular-season stint with two goals and nine points, but he was a key contributor in the playoffs, second on the team with nine goals during the run to the Finals that fell short.

"They've given us a breath of fresh air," Arbour said that March. "A little youthful enthusiasm is pretty useful to have around at this time of year."

23 The Trade

We've come to think of the NHL trade deadline now as a frenzy, and rightly so: There are at least a dozen deals at or right before the deadline in late February as teams jockey for position to make the playoffs or try to give themselves that extra push to a Stanley Cup. And the first one of those can be traced back to March 10, 1980. Not the first deadline deal, of course, just the first one that had a profound impact on what came next.

First we have to back up a bit. The Islanders entered March 1980 as a team not in disarray but far from the commanding group that had finished first overall the year before. Mike Bossy was on his way to another 50-goal season and Bryan Trottier was on his way to a third-straight 100-point year.

But the Isles missed their captain, Denis Potvin, who finally returned after a three-month absence due to a thumb injury he sustained at the Coliseum on March 1. "I don't think anyone in this room recognized what it was like for Denis," Bob Bourne said then. "He didn't talk to any of us. Most of the time he never came to practice. We'd go days at a time without seeing him. It hurt him and it hurt us."

When he returned on March 1, 1980, Potvin had a very unfamiliar face as his defense partner that night against the Red Wings: a 24-year-old rookie named Ken Morrow, making his NHL debut just days after winning gold with the Miracle on Ice team in Lake Placid. "It was a lot of change at one time," Potvin said. "But I just wanted to give our team some confidence when I got back. I hoped that would settle us down."

They lost that night to Detroit and went 2–2–1 in the next five games. Bill Torrey, meanwhile, knew he needed some more punch down the middle, with Trottier, Anders Kallur, and Wayne Merrick unable to generate enough consistency. Torrey tried in vain to pry Darryl Sittler out of Toronto. So on the eve of the deadline, he swung a deal with the Los Angeles Kings. Torrey surrendered Dave Lewis, a mainstay on defense for five years, plus Billy Harris, the well-liked winger who had been the first Islanders draft pick in 1972, for Butch Goring.

Goring had basically been on the trade block for nearly a year, even though he'd signed a six-year extension with L.A. just a year earlier. And when he was notified of the trade by Kings coach Bob Berry after a 6–3 loss in Montreal, Goring was reluctant. "Heck no,

I was angry," Goring said. "We were in shock. My life was in L.A., I'd been there 11 years. I didn't want to leave."

And the Islanders, a team that had seen a few guys go—Jean Potvin, Denis's brother, had been dealt to Cleveland for Wayne Merrick during the 1977–78 season and signed back on with the Isles to be a spare defenseman prior to 1979–80, for example—had not experienced losing two core, longtime teammates such as Harris and Lewis. "Those were longtime friends," Bob Bourne said. "It was a little tough for some of us to take, even if we knew about the business side of things."

"I walked into the Coliseum for practice that day, and before anybody said a word, I sensed that something big had happened," Bossy said. "Before I could ask, I knew. There were Lewie [Dave Lewis] and Harry [Billy Harris] in the dressing room, both red-eyed from crying, both shocked beyond belief. These were two of the best-liked guys on the team."

But Torrey was firm in his belief that his team needed something that Goring could bring. "When things aren't going right and you know what the problems are, you've got to correct them," Torrey said the next day. "I did what we need to get over the top. There are people who think this season is a dead end. I don't think so. I still think the best part of the season is ahead of us."

The immediate aftermath certainly proved Torrey's instincts correct. The Islanders didn't lose a game the rest of the regular season, going 8–0–4 down the stretch to rescue the fifth overall seed in the playoffs.

And after the initial shock wore off for everyone, the Islanders and Goring realized they might be good together. "I was able to say, 'OK, where am I now?'" Goring said. "They had Billy Smith and Jean Potvin, who I played with in Springfield. I wanted to win a Cup, and I didn't think it was going to happen in L.A. And I knew how good these guys were.

"The best thing for me and probably for Al and the team was I wasn't a kid. I was 30. I knew why they brought me there. Al came from the old Toronto Maple Leafs school—checking, defense. That was my game. He didn't say much to me, honestly. I just played."

"When Smitty told me, 'Trots, you're gonna love this guy,' I had a good feeling about it,' Trottier said. "Hanging with Butchie and Smitty, it was great. Butchie is a little guy who should have been about 6'10" with how he carried himself. Cocky, no-nonsense—he was a shot in the arm for us."

Early after he arrived, Goring spoke up to his teammates for the first time after a soft period of play. "I just remember him standing there telling us, 'You guys don't know how good you are,'" Denis Potvin said. "He was a huge presence."

24 Watch *30 for 30: Big Shot* and Cringe at the John Spano Debacle

There's too much to the John Spano saga to put into words here. What you must do to understand the full extent of the bizarre Spano-Islanders saga that spanned pretty much the entire 1996–97 season is sit down and watch Kevin Connolly's 2013 ESPN *30 for 30* episode on the whole mess, called *Big Shot*.

Big Shot gets to the heart of the matter: The Islanders of the mid-1990s were a mess, with Bill Torrey pushed out before the 1992–93 season and Al Arbour retiring after the 1993–94 season. John Pickett tried to find local owners for the team he himself rescued from near bankruptcy in 1978, gave four Long Island investors control of the team, and watched them make bad decision after bad decision, culminating in the Fisherman logo rebrand of 1995.

Pickett's search for someone to take the team off his hands led him to an unassuming 32-year-old "millionaire" based in Dallas named John Spano who had unsuccessfully tried to buy the Stars a year earlier. Spano came to save the day and made huge promises about turning the team's fortunes around.

Connolly was uniquely situated to tell the story. An actor and producer who grew up in Medford, he was a die-hard Islanders fan from an early age. He intercuts scenes from the Isles' glory days on into the miserable 1990s with interviews with some of the key people from that '90s era, including Mike Milbury, NHL commissioner Gary Bettman, and Spano himself.

It's a story that, if it showed up on Connolly's door as a fictional script to be turned into a movie, would be rejected for being so ridiculous: A young guy holds himself out as a multimillionaire, gets almost no vetting from an established sports league, has fans chanting his name at the Coliseum, and is slowly revealed to be a fraud after the local paper digs into his past and finds a serial fabulist whose net worth is closer to five figures than nine.

"In his head John Spano was the owner of the team," Connolly said when the documentary was released. "He wasn't playing a role."

That Spano was able to secure an $80 million loan—half of the purchase price—and also take control of the team from Pickett while his specious money sources were being checked on is incredible. That he was also able to accomplish some business is even more so. He convinced Milbury, who was then GM and coach, to relinquish the coaching job—a sensible decision by anyone's measure.

And Spano managed in his web of lies to secure a solid deal with Cablevision that still pays the Islanders $30 million a year. Spano didn't make that deal for any other reason than to try and secure enough actual money to cover the cost of buying the club (he probably would have secured a loan against the future cable income), but still, it's been a boon to future owners.

It's all laid out in detail in Connolly's documentary. Even those who lived through that crazy year still can't believe it all happened. "We went to the guy's house in Dallas, with family portraits on the walls, all of it," Bryan McCabe said. "And then when it all comes crumbling down, you hear he's just renting the place—it was nuts!"

"It's true that he could never quite look you in the eye," Howie Rose said of Spano. "I remember talking to him in Tampa during that year, and I asked him if he'd made any headway with Nassau County on a new arena. He shook his head and said, 'If I have to build it myself, I'll build it myself.' And that guy couldn't build a fort with LEGOs."

25 The Fisherman

John Pickett's decision to cede control of the Islanders to a group of four Long Island investors in December 1991 seemed wise at the time. Pickett was an absentee owner, living in Florida and unwilling to spend as much time as he once did on the club. He'd been publicly accused of failing to come through on contract promises made to Pat LaFontaine, the Isles' star player, who had been traded a couple months earlier. The time seemed right for Pickett to step back from the day-to-day operations as he sought a buyer for the team and let a few guys from the Island who still lived there shepherd the club while he hoped they or someone else would take the whole team off his hands for $75 to $100 million.

Looking back now, all you can see are the Fisherman jerseys. Sure, there were other missteps by the Gang of Four—investors

Stephen Walsh, Paul Greenwood, Ralph Palleschi, and Robert Rosenthal—including pushing Bill Torrey aside and elevating Don Maloney, then a 33-year-old recently retired player, to the GM role; seeing Al Arbour retire; approving Maloney's trade of Pierre Turgeon and Vladimir Malakhov to the Canadiens for Kirk Muller; and hiring Mike Milbury as coach.

But nothing—nothing—can stand the test of time like the rebranding of the Islanders the four men spearheaded. Nick Hirshon's amazingly detailed book, *We Want Fish Sticks: The Bizarre and Infamous Rebranding of the New York Islanders*, describes the exhausting process that the Gang of Four initiated in the search for a new logo for a franchise that was barely 20 years old. "We also are attuned to the winds of change," Walsh said at the June 22, 1995, press conference announcing the logo change. "And quite frankly, we believe the time for a new uniform has come."

Unfortunately what came was a laughingstock: The desired image of a rugged bayman of Long Island instead was remarkably similar to the one on the side of a Gorton's Fish Sticks box, along with a change to softer tones than the clear blue and orange of the team's previous two decades.

Fans hated it; sportswriters derided it. The players on the 1995–96 team? "Safe to say it was disliked among the guys as much as it was [by] the fans," said Bryan McCabe, who was a 20-year-old rookie on that squad. "I would have been happy to wear any jersey as long as it was an NHL one. But that one was tough."

"We talked about it in the room a lot—why didn't they ask us? We were the ones that had to wear 'em," Scott Lachance said. "In warm-ups you'd look over and the guys on the other teams were just laughing. It wasn't fun."

Pat Flatley was the captain of that 1995–96 squad, the last of his 12 seasons with the Islanders. After all the ups and downs of his time on the Island, he doesn't look back too fondly on those sweaters. "I have lots of friends on the Island who love to fish, and they don't like it either," he said. "I just never knew the reason for changing it."

Coupled with Milbury's first year as coach and the ongoing Muller fiasco, the Fisherman jerseys just exemplified another mistake in an organization that was too quickly becoming known for them. With Torrey gone and Arbour retired, changes were already happening; the total rebrand attempt to completely sever the team from its successful past struck too many fans as gauche—a desire to force the team into a new direction before it had any sense of where it was headed.

The jerseys lasted two years and disappeared into the ether. Milbury stuck around for another decade, mostly as GM. Walsh, Greenwood, Palleschi, and Rosenthal faded into the woodwork, with Walsh and Greenwood convicted of securities fraud in 2009 for bilking investors out of some $800 million.

Pickett resolved anew to find an owner. The next one he hit upon, at the start of the 1996–97 season—John Spano—made the Fisherman jersey fiasco seem quaint by comparison.

The funny part now is how younger Islanders fans view the logo—with a kitschy pride. When the NHL teams unveiled new third jerseys before the 2020–21 season with the theme of Reverse Retro, a noticeable number of Islanders fans pleaded online for the Fisherman logo to make a comeback. It didn't win out, but you can pick up any number of Fisherman-logoed items at the Isles team store. Somehow the worst thing to happen to the Isles in the mid-1990s is now a fashion statement.

26 Roy Boe's Money Woes

The best thing Roy Boe did as Islanders owner, aside from being the lead investor among a crowd of nearly 30 limited partners to start the franchise, was hire Bill Torrey. The second-best thing he did was let Torrey run the team without interference. There was no third-best—everything else from the birth of the Islanders to the day in 1978 when Boe sold his controlling interest to John Pickett, one of those limited partners, was a mess.

Some of it could be pinned on Boe, a big dreamer who didn't let the massive debt he took on to start the Islanders deter him. He'd already spent $1 million on the Nets a year earlier when he and his cadre of partners won the rights to the New York franchise awarded by the NHL in late November 1971. The expansion fee was $6 million. The territorial rights fee owed to the Rangers was $4 million. In all, Boe and his partners had $2.3 million cash on hand. It was already a recipe for disaster.

As Torrey was patiently building a winner, Boe's money problems were pretty walled off from the team. Players' contracts contained a lot of deferred money, but no one was making huge enough sums for it to matter; Torrey and Jim Devellano, his top scout, also deferred money through the mid-1970s and were owed plenty.

All the while Boe focused on spending big on the Nets as the interest on the expansion fee for the NHL and the rights fee to the Rangers piled up. Boe bought Julius Erving, the Long Island native and budding ABA star, for $1.3 million in 1973, trying to use star power to get into the NBA.

The Islanders played to packed crowds at the Coliseum almost as soon as they started, even through the awful 1972–73 expansion season and the not-much-better 1973–74 season. But Boe barely made a dent in his hockey debt. "There were times on road trips where [Torrey] would carry a briefcase full of cash with him to pay our hotel bills—this was because the Islanders' credit had become so bad nobody would take a credit card from us," Devellano wrote in *The Road to Hockeytown.* "Boe had a heart of gold really, but that cost him in the long run."

Devellano also detailed a time when Boe asked Torrey to trade a draft pick to the Atlanta Flames as a peace offering to the family that owned both the Flames and the ABA's Hawks, whom Boe had outbid for Erving.

The real problems came in the 1976–77 season, just as the Islanders were becoming a force under Torrey and Al Arbour. Boe finally got the Nets into the NBA for a $3 million fee and $800,000 of $4 million in territorial rights to the Knicks. To get there, Boe sold Erving to the 76ers for $3 million but was still short.

He decided to slide $3.5 million off the Islanders' books to pay off the Nets' debts. When that was discovered by Thomas Thornton, one of the myriad limited partners of the Isles, he sued Boe for $10 million in the spring of 1978, bringing the mountain of debt the Isles were under to light. All told, it amounted to nearly $22 million, barely six years since the club started playing.

"Roy's a very optimistic person by nature," Torrey told the *New York Times.* "Even in the worst of times, he always kept saying, 'It's going to turn around. Everything will be great,' even though we knew we were on the *Titanic.*"

Everyone knew what had to come next: a sale. How it happened, though, is as big a part of the story of the Islanders as the four Stanley Cups that came soon after.

27 Pickett (and Torrey) to the Rescue

With Roy Boe pushed out due to the Islanders' overwhelming debts in 1978, things could have fallen apart quickly for the team. When Bill Torrey and the remaining limited partners—all 30 of them—examined the Isles' books closely, they found a mess: 13 pending lawsuits, $22 million in debts, and a similar amount owed creditors on the Nets' side of the ledger.

One lawsuit stemmed from Boe trying to sell the television rights to Islanders games without realizing (or perhaps without acknowledging) that Cablevision, a then-fledgling company founded by Charles Dolan, already owned said rights. The interest on the debt owed to the NHL for the expansion fee and to the Rangers for the territorial rights amounted to nearly the full $10 million Boe initially owed in 1972. The team ran an operating deficit of $1 million a year and had $10,000 cash on hand. "If this had been a widget manufacturer, I'd have never put a dime into it," investor John Pickett said.

What would have made the most sense was to find a deep-pocketed buyer, possibly somewhere else besides the Island, and simply sell the team off. But Torrey, there since the beginning, fought hard to find a solution. And Torrey courted Pickett out of all the limited partners. Pickett, an investor from tiny Ozark, Arkansas, married a woman from Long Island and had put $100,000 into Boe's venture six years earlier. Now he was with Torrey, poring over accounting statements and letting the GM convince him to take things over.

"I didn't know Bill that well," Pickett told the *New York Times* in 1982. "We got to know each other late at night sitting poring over numbers and talking to lawyers and accountants. As things went along, I saw how much involved this guy was in it and how dedicated he was to something, and I started, I guess, feeling sorry for him, and at a certain point it turned into a challenge, as these things do.... We had to make a decision whether to let it go and walk away or try to save it, and I said, 'The hell with it. Let's go, Bill!' And that's the way it was."

Torrey had his backer, this time one with enough money to sort out the many financial woes. Pickett bought out several other limited partners who balked at selling a large stake in the Isles to Dolan; Pickett also recruited another limited partner, Nelson Doubleday, to put in a larger amount that helped stave off more losses. Ultimately Pickett wanted to put the Islanders on the right track and fade into the background. "If I had my way, you'd never know who owned the Islanders," he told the *Times*.

Pickett sorted out the debts just as the Islanders began their march to glory in 1979–80. By 1981 he was putting in "gallery boxes," the suites at the top of the Coliseum, to generate more high-end ticket revenue. Pickett and Dolan, whose Cablevision company owned the Islanders TV rights, agreed to a 30-year contract to broadcast the team's games.

And Torrey could count on getting whatever he needed for his emerging dynasty squad. "John Pickett was more businessman than hockey fan," Jiggs McDonald said. "Mrs. Pickett was the hockey fan. Bill would make the appeal to Marilyn—more for payroll or a key trade. That was his way of getting things done."

However it worked, it certainly did work for nearly a decade. Torrey didn't just build the dynasty; his efforts on the business side—and Pickett's shrewd moves—helped save the dynasty before it even began.

28 Bob Bourne

Just about all of the emerging standouts when the Islanders were growing into a formidable team were drafted by Bill Torrey. But Bob Bourne had a choice in the summer of 1974, and he *chose* the Isles.

Bourne had been drafted by the Kansas City Scouts in the 1974 draft, 38th overall—11 picks behind Bryan Trottier and 29 picks after Clark Gillies, his old friend from the Western Canada Hockey League and minor league baseball (more on that later). But Kansas City wasn't interested in keeping Bourne around, and he was fortunate enough to be asked where he wanted to go. "I told them the Islanders," Bourne said. "I was familiar with seven or eight guys on the team; I knew Clark, I grew up with Dave Lewis in Saskatchewan. They asked and I told them."

Bill Torrey gave up the rights to two of his 1972 expansion-draft picks, defenseman Bart Crashley and forward Larry Hornung, both of whom had bolted to the WHA rather than play for the first-year Isles. It was a steal almost immediately. Bourne isn't in the Hockey Hall of Fame, and his No. 14 isn't in the UBS Arena rafters. But he's part of the dynasty core, and it was apparent quickly that he had what it took to fit into the Torrey/Al Arbour mold. "I was so intimidated when I went down there. I was green as grass, just came off the farm in Saskatchewan," he said. "I was overwhelmed but had a really good first half of the year, then things slowed down."

Bourne scored 16 goals in his rookie year and displayed some of the speed and tenacity that would be his hallmark in a dozen Islanders seasons. He also carried a bit of a chip on his shoulder from his first preseason game at the Coliseum in early October

1974. "We came out of Peterborough back to Long Island from camp; my first exhibition game was against the Rangers," he said. "I would say 95 percent of the fans wore Ranger jerseys—I was a little bit taken aback by that. The thing I was shocked about—we'd go to a deli, restaurant-type place before practice; the guys who owned it, ran it, worked there were all Ranger fans. Certainly that was a huge thing for us—it pissed all of us off. You get a bunch of western Canada guys out there feeling pissed off, it was a huge incentive to become better and beat the Rangers all the time."

Bourne spent the bulk of the 1975–76 season in the minors, playing in Fort Worth of the Central League—playing, ironically enough, with Crashley, the guy he'd been traded for a year earlier. But that was a small detour. By 1976–77 Bourne was back as an Islanders regular and had back-to-back 30-goal seasons the following two years. And he proved himself to be one of the better playoff performers on the roster during the Cup runs, scoring 31 goals in the 1980–83 postseasons.

"We just hated to lose so much," he said. "You talk to any one of the guys from those teams and you think, *What if we didn't have a Dave Langevin? A Gordie Lane? A Garry Howatt?* Take one guy away, and we might not have won any Cups."

And it started with a simple request: "Trade me to the Islanders." In 1974 that may not have seemed so smart. But Bourne, like the rest of the group that was coming together in the 1970s, just needed a chance to prove himself.

29 Lucky and Good: The Story of Ken Morrow

You can call it luck, but there's more to Ken Morrow's hockey career than that. If anyone knows how fortunate he was, it's Morrow himself. His personality matches his playing style during his decade in the NHL—straightforward, no flash, and incredibly humble. "There have been times where I've thought, *Why me? Why did all this good fortune happen for me?*" Morrow said. "I'm just thankful for everything that happened."

To talk about hockey in the winter of 1980 didn't mean the Islanders; it meant the U.S. Olympic team. Morrow was one of the 20 American hockey players in Lake Placid for the Miracle on Ice, a gold-medal run like no other. "We were in the middle of our season and we were as transfixed by it as everyone else," Denis Potvin said.

Morrow had come from Bowling Green, where he played for U.S. Hockey Hall of Fame coach Ron Mason. Herb Brooks, the Olympic coach, was also a Hall of Famer of course. And then, as soon as the Americans had dispatched Finland for the gold medal, Morrow got a chance to play for yet another Hall of Fame coach and general manager. The Islanders had drafted Morrow in the fourth round of the 1976 draft; now, nearly four years later, Morrow was being welcomed into a new and somewhat unexpected situation. "When Bill [Torrey] called and said I'd be going straight to Long Island, it was a huge relief for me," Morrow said. "I didn't know if I was going to Indianapolis [the Isles' IHL farm club]; I had no idea. I just wanted to fit in."

Here was Morrow's week at the end of February 1980:
- He and the Americans pulled off the Miracle on Ice, beating the Soviet Union on February 22.
- On February 24 the U.S. squad beat Finland to win the gold.

- On February 27, a Wednesday, Morrow headed to Long Island.
- On February 28 Morrow took the ice for his first practice with the Islanders.
- And on March 1, eight days removed from the biggest win in American hockey history, Morrow stepped onto the Coliseum ice in his No. 6 sweater for his NHL debut.

Oh, and he was paired with Potvin, playing his first game since November 30 due to a thumb injury. "It was probably good that I didn't have much time to think about anything," Morrow said. "It was really just a continuation of what I'd done with the Olympic team, except you're trying to earn a living now."

Torrey's instinct on Morrow was the correct one. His simple, steady game was the right fit, allowing Torrey to feel confident nine days later when he traded mainstay defenseman Dave Lewis and Billy Harris, the franchise's first draft pick, to the Kings for Butch Goring. It's a legendary deal, perhaps the most important of the many Torrey made. But it would not have happened without Morrow sliding right into the lineup after winning gold. "Kenny was so easy to play with," Potvin said. "Pass the puck over or get it up the wall. There was no confusion to his game."

And lest you think Morrow was just there to witness history Forrest Gump–style, he had one of the most important goals of the 1980 Cup run. It also happened to be his first NHL goal. The Islanders went into their first-round best-of-five against the Kings feeling good, having closed the regular season on an 8–0–4 streak to grab the fifth seed. They torched L.A. 8–1 in Game 1. But the reverse came in Game 2 at the Coliseum, a 6–3 Kings win that was never close. And out in Los Angeles for Game 3, the Isles were down 3–1 entering the third, certainly wondering if the playoff failures of the previous two seasons were haunting them so early in this postseason. They got it tied and went to overtime. In OT

Morrow sent a slap shot that was "going about 10 feet wide," he said. "It hit off a defenseman's leg and went behind Mario Lessard [for the score]. It turned out to be a pretty important one for the team." The Isles exhaled after that, blowing out the Kings in Game 4 on their way to the ultimate triumph.

Morrow finished his NHL career with 17 regular-season goals in 550 games and 11 goals in 127 playoff games—three of them OT winners. On the NHL's all-time playoff OT goals list, there are only 20 names ahead of his, and he's tied with Mike Bossy. And of the 50 players with at least three, there are only two other defensemen, the Hawks' Brent Seabrook and Carolina and San Jose's Niclas Wallin.

His greatest moments came in the 1983 playoffs, especially that year's Cup Finals against the Oilers. Morrow had three goals in that four-game sweep, the last into an empty net to seal Game 4 and the fourth Cup. "He outscored Gretzky, for heaven's sake," Potvin said.

Morrow's last OT winner was perhaps just as memorable as his first. Morrow threw a shot from the side wall through Glen Hanlon's legs in overtime of the deciding Game 5 of the 1984 Patrick Division semifinal against the Rangers, a hard-fought series that could have gone either way on the drive for five straight Cups. "For a guy who didn't score too many, those are great memories to have," he said. "It's nice to look back and know you did your part."

Knee problems forced Morrow to retire after the 1988–89 season. He coached in the minors for two seasons, then rejoined the Isles as an assistant to Arbour for the 1991–92 season. Torrey named Morrow his director of pro scouting in July 1992, a month before Torrey was forced out as GM. Morrow stayed and hasn't left, holding that same position for 28 years and through half a dozen owners and almost as many general managers. He went from the Miracle on Ice to four straight Cups to three decades in management for a team whose mantra hasn't exactly been "stability" since he joined the front office.

"It's rare in this business," he said. "But I always tell people: If you cut my arm, I'd bleed blue and orange. It's been an amazing run, and I'm so fortunate that they even drafted me all those years ago."

30 Dog and Pup: The Sutter Brothers Take Long Island

It didn't take long after Duane Sutter arrived in November 1979 for his nickname to be cemented. "Always talking, always yapping," Bryan Trottier said. "The kid was just hilarious." Dog wasn't Sutter's nickname only because of the constant barking—either in his own locker room or at opponents on the ice—it was also for his tenacity, a willingness to do whatever it took.

Bill Torrey had selected Duane Sutter 17th overall in the June 1979 draft—just barely. Torrey called Duane on the eve of the draft and said if he were available at the Isles' pick, they would take him. "I said, 'Thanks, but no thanks,'" Duane Sutter said. "I told him straight out that I didn't want to play in a big city like New York with all those skyscrapers. But when my older brother, Brian, heard about it, he called me and screamed, 'The Islanders are one of the best organizations!'"

So he relented. And perhaps it's no coincidence that Sutter's arrival happened just a few months before the dynasty began in the middle of a season in which the Islanders seemed to be carrying the burden of recent failed playoff trips.

He had 15 goals in 56 games that season, then another three in the playoffs—including the second Isles goal in Game 6 of the

1980 Finals. He was one of the prime examples of Torrey and Al Arbour knowing the right time to inject some youth or new blood into the lineup. So much so they would do it again two years later with Duane's kid brother Brent.

Brent Sutter was the fifth of the seven Sutter boys, another star in the making for Lethbridge of the Western League, the closest team to the family farm in Viking, Alberta. Brian and Darryl Sutter were already in the NHL when Duane arrived; the year after Torrey selected Duane 17th and just a month after the Islanders hoisted their first Cup, Torrey went to the same well and selected Brent 17th overall in the 1980 draft. "We considered the genes," Torrey said. "We took them [at age 18], so we knew they were a year or two away. But they were available because the teams at the bottom needed help right away."

The Islanders could afford to wait. Brent Sutter joined the Islanders for three games in late February 1981 and had two goals and two assists. He looked like he belonged. But Torrey was patient, as always. Even when Brent Sutter led the team in scoring during the 1981–82 preseason and looked like he was ready for a regular role. "They wanted to be loyal to the guys that had just won them a couple Stanley Cups," Brent said. "You're eager, but you understand."

He returned for good just after Christmas and, like Duane, posted phenomenal rookie numbers in barely more than half a season: 21 goals and 22 assists in 43 games. His comfort was increased by being able to live with Duane and his wife, Cindy, who were already three years into their stay on the Island. Dog now had Pup alongside him.

"It was such a huge help for me," Brent said. "You're there in a new situation, the middle of the year with a team like that; it could have been uncomfortable. But Bill and Al understood—even though guys have families to support with their jobs, you can't let anyone get complacent. I've been on the management and coaching end of it, and I've seen it myself all these years later. If someone can come in to improve the group, it keeps everyone on their toes."

The Sutters got to win two Cups together, and they played huge roles in the last one. With Bryan Trottier and Clark Gillies missing time in the 1983 playoff run, Duane and Brent lined up with Bob Bourne, and that trio led the charge past the Rangers in the Patrick Division finals and in the Cup Finals against the vaunted Oilers. Duane led all scorers in the sweep of Edmonton with seven points in the four games; Brent had five points.

It was a heady way to start what ended up being lengthy NHL careers. Duane played eight seasons with the Isles and three more with the Hawks before stepping into coaching and front-office roles with various NHL teams over the last 30 years.

Brent was named captain of the Islanders after Denis Potvin stepped aside in 1987 and wore the *C* until he was traded early in the 1991–92 season. He played 7 seasons with the Hawks after 11-plus on the Island, coached the Devils and Flames, and now is back in Alberta, where he's the owner and GM of Red Deer in the WHL.

They're Alberta farm boys, two of the six Sutter brothers who played in the NHL. Darryl won two Cups behind the Kings bench in 2012 and 2014, but only Duane and Brent won as players. "We never [wear] our rings around our brothers," Brent said. "It's too much like gloating." As Duane put it to the *New York Times* during the 1983 Cup run: "On special occasions, I might [wear a ring]. But I sure don't want to wear it when I'm out shoveling horse manure."

31 Go to Northwell Health Ice Center

You can still go to at least two of the other practice facilities the Islanders called home on the Island. Iceworks, where the team practiced for more than a decade, is over in Syosset; it's maybe the coldest building on Long Island, and you could usually catch a bunch of professional hockey players working out between the building and the Long Island Rail Road tracks behind it during training camp.

There's also Cantiague Park, a public rink that's a short drive from the Coliseum. This was the Isles' practice home in their 1980s heyday. "Nothing to write home about," Bob Nystrom said, "but that's not how the practice facilities were in those days."

To see a place you want to write home about, go where the Islanders currently call home during training camp and non–game days. Northwell Health Ice Center, tucked inside Eisenhower Park, is a practice facility with only a few equals around the league.

Even before UBS Arena went up, the Islanders leveled the playing field when Charles Wang bought what was then called Twin Rinks for a song—an $8 million purchase in 2015 for a two-year-old facility that cost nearly $52 million to build.

Wang was about to sign a lease to renovate Cantiague Park and make that the team's practice and office home, using money he'd deposited with Nassau County during his previously failed Lighthouse Project. But when Twin Rinks went into bankruptcy, Wang saw a better opportunity closer to where most of the Islanders lived in nearby Garden City, and with a much nicer footprint.

The place has undergone a couple face-lifts, mostly in the private areas under the Isles' control. But it's still a public skating rink on county property, so you can go in and take a spin or a hockey clinic during available times. Many of the Island's amateur hockey teams play games there, and the Isles hosted a prospects game before the pandemic that would draw several thousand fans.

The Islanders Pro Shop on-site at Northwell is a serious upgrade from past team stores as well. Want a replica Fisherman jersey with Ziggy Palffy's No. 16 on the back? Done. A vintage Isles sweater with Mike Bossy's No. 22? Also done. It's a great store befitting a state-of-the-art facility.

When Matt Martin was in his two-year exile in Toronto, he still hosted his summer hockey camp at Northwell. The Leafs' young star Mitch Marner came down one day to speak to the campers and marveled at how much Northwell reminded him of the Leafs' high-end practice facility in suburban Toronto.

For all of the arena follies the Isles have endured even in the last several years, having Northwell as their home base eases a lot of minds. With facility amenities such as underwater treadmills, a personal chef, an expansive kitchen, and a huge workout space for the players, the Islanders have been able to showcase the place their team spends most of its time well enough, even without the great new arena. Now they have both. Those are great selling points.

As a fan, you may not get to hang around and watch practice at Northwell, though season-ticket holders do get special access throughout the year. But even walking through the lobby and the pro shop is a fun experience; taking a spin on the ice where the team practices isn't bad either.

32 The 3–0 comeback of 1975

After slaying the local rivals in the 1975 playoffs for their first playoff series win in the franchise's first playoff appearance, the Islanders went right into their quarterfinal matchup with the Penguins and promptly tripped over their own skates. A pair of close losses sandwiched a 3–1 Game 2 defeat to put the Isles in a 3–0 hole. Up to then, exactly one team in NHL history had rallied from 3–0 down, and that had been 33 years earlier.

In hindsight, Al Arbour's famous practice speech between Games 3 and 4 sounds great; the fact that his young Islanders pulled off the incredible comeback gives his words so much more meaning. But to his players, most of whom had never been in a playoff game before that spring, the willingness to believe grew stronger thanks to Arbour.

"He called us over to the corner of the rink after practice. There was a lot of snow built up on the ice," Chico Resch said. "He piled up some snow, drew it into a line with his stick, and said, 'I understand if you don't think we can come back and win. I think we can. Whoever thinks we can do it, cross that line.'

"And of course we all crossed it. I don't know if we all believed we could do it, but we all went across."

Resch, who had been pulled for Smith for the deciding Game 3 against the Rangers, returned to the net for Game 4 against the Penguins at the Coliseum. And Chico, whose stature in the history of Islanders goalies trails Smith's by a long way, had his finest run in blue and orange, starting with a 3–1 win.

He stood on his head in Pittsburgh with 36 saves in a 4–2 Game 5 win, the first time the Islanders had ever won in Pittsburgh.

Game 6 was another strong goalie performance—31 saves in a 4–1 win that was a one-goal game until the final minute.

Then came Game 7, when Resch started kissing goalposts. "They must have hit two or three posts the first couple periods that game," he said. "I just got so excited I leaned over and kissed one."

It was 0–0 deep into the third period. And lest you think Arbour was more about messaging than tactics, he'd changed the Isles' forecheck strategy from trying to throw pucks on Penguins goalie Gary Inness to dumping them into the corner and winning battles—pretty modern stuff by 1975 standards.

On one of those corner dump-ins, defenseman Bert Marshall won a puck and handed it off to Ed Westfall, who came out of the corner unmolested and flipped a backhand by Inness with 5:18 to play. Fitting that the old captain, who'd piloted the Isles through their expansion-year mess, would end up getting the winner.

And with a little history accomplished, the Islanders got a reminder the next day that Long Island was taking notice. "We landed at LaGuardia and there were maybe 100 fans there to cheer for us," Resch said. "That was a big deal for us kids from Canada. You know, we won the Cup [Resch was only an Islander for the first one], and that's every player's dream. But beating Pittsburgh, that was just euphoria—a bunch of kids mostly who'd never been to the playoffs being able to do that. It was the second building block for us."

Even Westfall, the seasoned vet, looked back on 1975 as something special. "Even though I'd won two Cups as a player," Westfall said, "that time in '75 was the most exciting time in hockey for me."

33 The Isles' First Training Camp

Chico Resch remembers that first training camp in the fall of 1972 quite well. "We had our practice jerseys, they were blue and white, but there was something a little different about them," Resch said. "They didn't have numbers. The guys had to pin their numbers on with little safety pins! We knew we were an NHL team, but it just didn't quite seem like it."

The collection of players was wild that first year, when Torrey assembled his ragtag expansion gang in Peterborough, Ontario, where the Isles would hold training camp in their first few seasons. The expansion draft didn't yield good players the way it does now—they were all castoffs or veterans past their prime.

Resch was among those young guys, having been acquired from the Canadiens in June, the very first of Torrey's many, many shrewd deals. All of the Isles' first draft class was there too, including first overall pick Billy Harris, who had just signed a deal to make him the first $100,000 rookie in the league.

The team's third-round pick was on hand as well after an inauspicious beginning to his Islanders career. "I remember that summer [1972] I was working framing houses," Bob Nystrom said. "And we're at the bar after work, same as always. And I got a call at the bar from my dad, who told me I'd been drafted. 'By who?' I asked him. He said the New York Islanders. When I heard 'New York,' I just thought, *Geez, I better go buy a gun.* Because that's what we'd heard about New York back then in Canada."

Even before Nystrom got to see and fall in love with Long Island, he had to get through that training camp. Torrey invited 90-odd players. "You have never seen such an inept bunch in your life," Ed Westfall told *Sports Illustrated* in 1982. Torrey admitted to a reporter during camp: "The secret to this team is to get rid of everyone just as fast as I can."

Westfall gave the group an air of legitimacy. He was a two-time Cup champion with the Bruins, having won his second title just the year before. He was so unsure of this new venture that his family stayed behind in New Hampshire and the licensed pilot bought a plane to fly back and forth from the Island to see them during breaks in the schedule.

Torrey too clearly knew what he was doing. He sent Nystrom, Resch, and Garry Howatt, three of his promising young players, down to AHL New Haven to get away from the stench of that first season. "We'd follow their games, and we knew it was a struggle," Nystrom said. "We were just waiting for our chance."

Nystrom and Howatt were called up and played the final eight games of the regular season after Torrey had changed coaches and made yet another small, smart deal, acquiring a capable young defenseman named Jean Potvin from the Flyers for veteran Terry Crisp. (The Islanders' woeful season had just about assured them of the first pick in the 1973 draft and Potvin had a kid brother who was everyone's pick at No. 1.)

The future was on the horizon. It just took a brutal training camp and a brutal season to get there.

34 Mike Bossy's 50 in 50

By the 1980–81 season, everyone knew that Mike Bossy was the premier goal scorer in the game. His 53-goal rookie season (after telling Bill Torrey he'd get 50 as a rookie) in 1977–78, followed by his career-high 69 goals in 1978–79, had already settled matters.

Plus there was that first Stanley Cup in 1980, when Bossy shook off a hand injury earlier in the playoffs to score four times in the six-game Cup Finals win over the Flyers.

Even just three years into his NHL career, there wasn't much to prove. Maybe he could take a run at Phil Esposito's 76-goal record for a regular season, but there was one the Montreal-born Bossy wanted more than anything: to equal Canadiens legend Maurice "Rocket" Richard and score 50 goals in 50 games, which Richard had done in 1944–45.

It's unthinkable now. If you're an Islanders fan, it's been 29 years since you saw one of your own score 50 in an entire season; heck, there have only been two 40-goal scorers since the 21st century began.

But Bossy was determined—and vocal about it. As the first half of that 1980–81 season got going and he got going—Bossy had 19 goals in the first 16 games—he wasn't shy about his desire to match Richard. "Boss was different," Chico Resch said. "And boy, was he driven. The great ones, you can see it. We loved him for that individualistic personality he had.

"And then this [Wayne] Gretzky guy comes along and he starts getting all the attention. I remember [Bossy] saying to me, 'I've been doing this three years now and all I hear about is Gretzky!' You saw his pride there, and we wanted him to get what he wanted. And what he wanted was to score goals."

The numbers grew. His team ripped off a 13–0–2 streak into December. Another hat trick—Bossy's fifth of the season, in a 9–0 dismantling of the Hawks in Chicago—got him to 37 goals in 36 games just before Christmas of 1980. Then he had another burst in January: four goals at the Coliseum against the Penguins on January 13, another three against the Caps on January 17. Now Bossy stood at 48 goals in 47 games and attaining the 50-in-50 goal seemed like a two-foot putt.

But then silence. Nothing in a 5–0 shutout of the Flames, followed by the same nothing in another shutout of the Wings in Detroit. "What hurt the most," Bossy said later, after he had tied Rocket's record, "was that I had brought all this on myself by telling everybody I wanted to beat the Rocket's record. I had announced my goal, and now it looked as if I wasn't going to get it. I had three games to get two goals, and I was about to fail."

His last chance was a Saturday night visit from the Nordiques. Earlier that day, he bypassed his usual pregame nap to watch the Kings' Charlie Simmer, who entered his own 50th game with 46 goals, nearly steal Bossy's thunder by scoring a hat trick in a matinee in Boston. "Boy, that gave me a start," Bossy said later that night. "What a great try by Charlie."

He would tell Stan Fischler after the game that the day just dragged. "Today waiting for the babysitter to come was the longest 5 to 10 minutes I've spent in the last while," Bossy said.

And the game was a grind for him. As he recalled in 2017, "I dreaded that game because Michel Bergeron was the coach and he coached against me in junior," Bossy said. "Alain Cote used to check me all the time when we played Quebec, and I thought, *Oh boy, this is going to be murder.* And it was. I was tired physically, I was tired mentally, and I went the first two periods without a shot on goal."

It was into the final minutes of the third and Bossy was still coming up empty against a Quebec team that sported an 11–24–12 record and had journeyman backup Ron Grahame in net. And it was a tie game as an Islanders power play wound down late in the third.

Stefan Persson tried a centering feed for Bossy that banked off a Quebec skate and went to Bossy as he crossed in front of the net. A quick backhand and he finally had No. 49 with 4:10 to play. "I figured if I was going to get one, I might as well get two," he said after the game.

The last one was pure Boss: Trottier, his forever running mate, picked off a clearing attempt and just found his friend. The puck hopped on edge for a second and Bossy whipped it through Grahame's legs with 1:29 to play, sending the Coliseum crowd and the players in white into a frenzy.

Bossy's Running Man celebration was one of a kind. "I can still visualize that dance on the ice," Potvin said. "I'd never seen anything like it."

It was relief, joy, pride—everything that made Bossy special. In his postgame TV sit-down with Fischler, Bossy looks like he just finished off a four-overtime game.

He got a telegram from Richard after the game. "I know what he's going to say when I see him," Bossy said. "He'll claim he still holds the record because I scored my 50th in the last minute and he scored his with two minutes to go."

Years later he still recalled how drained he was. He went on to finish with 68 goals for the season, and in the playoffs—when it counted most—he scored another 17 as the Isles braced the league for their second Cup. "It was physically and mentally tiring," he said, "but it was all worth it."

35 Scott Malkin and Jon Ledecky

The first thing Islanders fans noticed about their new owners back in the 2016–17 season at Barclays Center: One of them was seemingly everywhere the fans were. Jon Ledecky doesn't have the financial stake in the team of his old high school and college buddy Scott Malkin, but it was clear from the start who would be the public face of the ownership tandem. Ledecky sat in the stands in Brooklyn, chatting with fans—and let's be honest, he rarely sat, since he could usually be seen roaming around.

He was at community events. If you were an Isles fan in another NHL city or one who occasionally traveled to see your team, he was there too—he might have been sitting a row or two behind you on the flight from LaGuardia.

"If the fans aren't happy, they aren't going to come," Ledecky said at a luncheon in the summer of 2016, just after he and Malkin took majority control of the team from Charles Wang. "Successful franchises have this connection with their fan base. They listen and they try to make improvements. They don't pay lip service."

The good side of all that input includes some of the details that will be part of the experience at UBS Arena, such as shorter bathroom wait times (they even touted those in television ads for season tickets) and phone-app ordering for food at your seat. Ledecky wasn't just shaking hands the last few years; he wanted to hear what Isles fans had to say about their game-going experience.

The downside to getting lots of input: When Ledecky went on a season-long "listening tour" during the 2016–17 season, sitting down quite publicly with former players such as Wayne Gretzky, to whom Ledecky offered a front-office job that he turned down. Also he sat down with agents and former team executives, which led to then-GM Garth Snow to wonder if he was free to do his job while his new bosses talked with everyone under the hockey sun about a role in the organization.

When Malkin and Ledecky did decide to move on from Snow, it was only because they'd found the right person available at the right time. Lou Lamoriello came in with strict assurances that he wouldn't be hearing about personnel decisions from ownership, and that is exactly what the Islanders needed in the spring of 2018.

It was too late a move to keep John Tavares, who may have been a bit turned off at seeing Pat Brisson, his agent, invited to half a dozen meetings with Malkin to keep apprised on the state of

the Belmont development and other high-level doings in the organization. Snow was pushed aside in that relationship, which was a
miscalculation on the owners' part that Tavares would want to feel
more special than any of his teammates or hockey operations staff.

But still Malkin and Ledecky hired Lamoriello, who hired
Barry Trotz (with the help of Malkin's deep pockets to give Trotz
the $4 million per season that the Caps refused to pay him). The
owners focused on UBS Arena while Lamoriello and Trotz focused
on restoring the franchise.

Everyone made out perfectly. The fans love Ledecky's accessi-
bility, and he and Malkin have done what no other Islanders owner
could: They've delivered a state-of-the-art arena to the Island.
They've also delivered the most accomplished GM and coach
combination in team history, and the success in the last three years
hasn't been matched in decades.

And we've left perhaps their most important contribution
for last: the welcoming back of every former Islander, whether he
played 1 game or 1,000. The Isles alumni weekends are populated
by some stars and some "Hey, I remember that guy!" types, all of
whom are treated like royalty by Ledecky and the business side of
the operation. "They've made us feel a part of it again," said Kelly
Hrudey, who left in a trade in 1989 and felt some bitterness toward
the organization that dissipated over time. Now, with monthly
alumni newsletters in his email inbox, it's gone for good and has
been replaced by Islanders pride. "I've never been able to make the
alumni weekends, but to get 50 to 60 guys, some of whom might
have been forgotten, it's incredible."

36 Lou Lamoriello Takes Charge

The end of the 2017–18 Islanders season was tense and disappointing. Islanders owners Scott Malkin and Jon Ledecky—after their first full season as majority owners—had chosen to stick with Garth Snow as general manager and make interim coach Doug Weight the permanent coach after a strong finish to 2016–17.

Part of that was to maintain some continuity. Part was to try and appease John Tavares, who had decided in the summer of 2017 to play out the final year of his contract, never a good sign. And part was the ownership group had spent a large part of the 2016–17 season talking to various retired players, former NHL executives, and agents to gauge what the Islanders needed to become a more consistent winner—that so-called "listening tour" didn't sit well around the league, given Snow was already on the job.

And then it all fell apart in 2017–18. The Isles had Mathew Barzal, on his way to a Calder Trophy, but they were a disaster defensively and allowed the most goals of any team in the league. The tension around Tavares's pending decision boiled over often, and the Isles finished that season 17 points out of the playoffs. The tension grew after an angered Ledecky delivered a terse statement on April 9 before a year-end press conference with Snow and Weight, then left the GM and coach to answer questions.

On April 30 Lou Lamoriello was relieved of his GM duties by the Leafs. And the ball was rolling toward one of the most respected men in the game coming to grab the Isles' reins. By May 22 it was a done deal: The Islanders hired Lamoriello as team president, removing that title from Snow. The 75-year-old Lamoriello had been running NHL teams for 30 years, and now he was coming into a volatile situation with the fates of a GM and coach in his hands and a star player's future to figure out.

Within two weeks Lamoriello had made his first key decisions: Snow, a longtime friend, and Weight were out. Lamoriello named himself GM and was to set about finding a coach who fit how he wanted to remake the team. "It is my opinion at this point that there is a culture change that's needed, and there are new voices needed in different areas, and because of that, the change is made,"

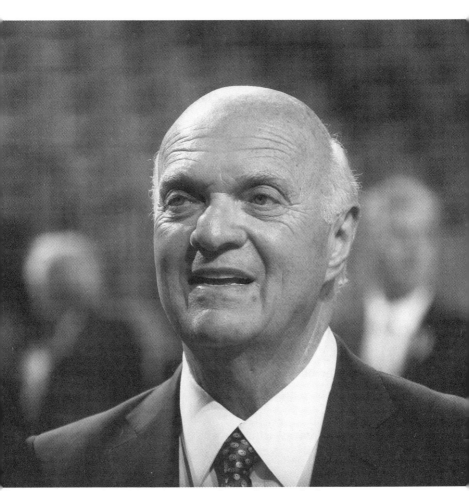

Lamoriello in a lighthearted moment during the 2018 draft.

he said. "*Culture* is a very overused word and underdeveloped. It's just doing the little things a certain way, a different way, a consistent way. So I really couldn't define that. It's only going to be time before we see exactly how it works out."

Other than Snow, who would be at the Isles draft table three weeks after his firing for one last public event with the team he'd run for 12 years, Lamoriello changed very little. He added some scouts and an assistant GM to work on salary-cap concerns, but he left Snow's front-office infrastructure intact. Much as his coach hire would do with largely the same cast of players, Lamoriello focused more on bringing some discipline to the organization. Even beyond his elimination of facial hair and other small rules he implemented, Lamoriello commanded a respect in a way that the more laid-back Snow did not.

"It won't be a challenge for him—the challenge is for everyone [on the Islanders] who is willing to adapt, adjust, and grow," Yankees GM Brian Cashman told the *Athletic* right after Lamoriello's hiring. The two have been friends for years. "Each environment is unique, and obviously I've never worked with Lou directly, so I know he's going to assess every aspect of what's going on there. But the Lou Lamoriello I know, people are going to have to adapt to Lou and what he wants. It's chain of command. Lou will set the tone and everybody else will follow. If they won't, well, they better raise their hand sooner than later to say this isn't the place for them.

"He's going to eliminate anything that's between where they are now and the ultimate goal of being a Stanley Cup contender. Anything that could erode that, take away from reaching that goal, he'll get rid of it."

Three years into his tenure, that's exactly what Lamoriello has done.

37 Barry Trotz Comes Aboard

Of all the decisions Lou Lamoriello has made while running the Islanders, his first hire will always be his best. He announced on June 5, 2018, that Garth Snow and Doug Weight were out as GM and coach. Lamoriello took the GM job and set about finding a coach. Two nights later, the Capitals finished off the Golden Knights in five games to win their first Stanley Cup. Washington's coach, Barry Trotz, resigned 11 days after that over a refusal to increase his salary; by the time that happened, lots of executives around the league figured Lamoriello was already talking to Trotz and opening ownership's checkbook.

On June 21, the day before the draft, Trotz signed on. Like it had been with Lamoriello, the Islanders hired a coach who garnered as much respect around the league as anyone. "From a professional standpoint, he's one of the most organized coaches I've seen in any sport," said Ken Hitchcock, a friend of Trotz's for more than 35 years and, like Trotz, one of the five winningest coaches in NHL history. "As organized and as disciplined in his long-term plan as anybody around."

During his first season with the Islanders in 2018–19, Trotz also hit a couple significant milestones: He won his 800th game behind an NHL bench in March, joining Hitchcock, Joel Quenneville, and Scotty Bowman as the only men to do so.

Before he hit 800, on New Year's Eve in Buffalo, Trotz won No. 783—passing Al Arbour on the all-time list. That he did it as the Islanders' coach made it even more special. "I didn't know Al at all, but I admired what he had done," Trotz said. "I said to my wife when I did reach that mark, 'It is pretty cool to be standing behind that bench—it's always Al's bench.' That's how I look at it.

It is pretty cool to match his mark, and finally pass it on the same bench he'd have stood on. It's always Al's bench, no one else's."

It makes sense. The Islanders from Arbour's two decades as coach describe him in glowing, almost parental terms—Arbour understood better than most coaches of his era that getting to know all the players meant almost as much as teaching them systems or playing styles.

There are plenty more coaches who do that today, but Trotz has no equal in player relations. He's firm but fair and honest.

Trotz meets the press in 2019.

"It's about personalities, about knowing what makes people tick, and I think you've got to play games sometimes, pull strings," Cal Clutterbuck said. "He's done it with everyone in this room in different ways. You don't always know why he's doing things, and you have to trust in the reason. When you do that, that's how you become a coach of his stature. He's very methodical and knows people very well."

Trotz also knows how to win: His 83 victories in his first two seasons with the Islanders are more than any coach in team history starting an Islanders tenure.

38 Go to Madison Square Garden and Laugh at *That* Chant

"A friend of mine from Florida went up to New York maybe 10 to 15 years ago around Christmastime to see the tree [at Rockefeller Center] and take in a Rangers game," Denis Potvin said. "It's not a minute into the game and a guy sitting right near him starts the whistling and yells, 'Potvin sucks!'

"So my friend plays dumb and asks him, 'Who's this Potvin guy?' And the Ranger fan says, 'Oh, I don't know, I think he's dead now.'"

The chant lives on in the Garden, game after game, whether the Islanders are the opponent or not. It's remarkable in a lot of ways—for its longevity, for its ridiculousness, for everything. And you have to get there to hear it.

Potvin can laugh about it now for any number of reasons. Time has healed most of the hate from Rangers fans toward the greatest Islanders captain, whose hit on Ulf Nilsson back on February 25, 1979, was the thing that started it all. Both Potvin and Nilsson know the truth: It wasn't a dirty hit. Nilsson's skate caught in a rut and he was injured before Potvin shoved him into the boards. It was a broken ankle for Nilsson, playing his first NHL season with fellow Swede Anders Hedberg. They were two of the Rangers' stars that season, and even though the Rangers managed to upset the Isles in the semifinals that year, they fell short against the Canadiens in the Stanley Cup Finals. "I think they blamed that hit, blamed me, for not being able to get past Montreal," Potvin said. "And then we went out the next year and reeled off four straight Cups."

So it's jealousy, really, that kept the "Potvin sucks" chant going through the 1980s. The Rangers stumbled and the Islanders were hitting their stride.

It's more than that too. The Rangers, even without a Cup since 1940, were the established hockey team in New York. Roy Boe went so far into debt starting the Islanders, fueled primarily by the $4 million territorial fee he had to pay the Rangers, that there was no way the new kids could feel superior. Except the Islanders grew quickly into the better franchise. They pulled off the first-round upset of the Rangers in 1975, the Isles' first trip to the playoffs, and won both games in their best-of-three series in the Garden.

The loss in 1979 was painful, but the Islanders dominated the rivalry for years afterward, going through the Rangers and the Garden on their way to the last three Cups—and every year, the Isles clinched the series on Garden ice.

In recent years, the Islanders fans at MSG have become almost as loud as the Rangers fans at the Coliseum—there's something to be said for having an arena right on top of the Long Island Rail Road's terminus in the city, the place where hundreds of thousands of Long Islanders start and end their workdays. So you'll have friendly company. And since it was renovated several years ago, the Garden is a great place to see a game—during the Isles' stay in Barclays Center, many Isles fans preferred going to see them play the Rangers at MSG because it's built for hockey.

And you can chuckle when you hear the whistling start, usually by the first television timeout of the opening period. When the Rangers crowd yells "Potvin sucks!" you can just smile, knowing how much those fans would rather have your team's history.

Even Nilsson knows it. He and Potvin met through a mutual friend in the 1990s, before Nilsson moved back to Sweden, where he still lives. "It was at a shooting club outside of New York," Nilsson said. "People were saying, 'How can you have Nilsson and Potvin at a place with guns?'

"But it was so long before, there were no hard feelings. I always told Denis, 'I'd rather have your Cups than worry about that chant.' He's one of the best defensemen to ever play the game. I think the Ranger fans were just mad we didn't do what his teams did."

Shawn Bates and the Shot Heard 'Round the Island

The 2002 playoff series against the Leafs stands out for so many reasons. It was the Islanders' triumphant return to relevancy after seven incredibly bad years. There was so much nastiness in those seven games that Islanders fans of a certain age might still hate the Leafs 20 years later even if John Tavares didn't go there.

The Leafs won Games 1 and 2 in Toronto before the Isles stormed back in Game 3 with a 6–1 win in the first home playoff game since 1994. Game 4 was a tight affair, with the Isles rallying from a goal down to take a 3–2 lead with 5:04 left in the third on a long blast by Roman Hamrlik. And the Coliseum showed it could still shake to its foundation, especially late in that Game 4 when one of the unlikelier heroes of Isles lore got his chance and made it count.

The Leafs pulled even with 3:26 left, setting up what looked to be overtime to decide it—either the Isles would be even or they'd be headed back to Toronto down 3–1, a huge swing.

But the swing came quickly, before the end of the third. Chris Osgood denied Alex Mogilny and Alexei Yashin retrieved the rebound and snapped a long pass off the boards. Shawn Bates raced to it in stride and stepped around Leafs defenseman and former Islander Bryan McCabe, who swept his stick out and took down Bates.

Referee Brad Watson called for a penalty shot. Bates almost called for the Pepto Bismol. "I thought I was gonna puke," Bates said after the game.

As Bates collected himself, Isles captain Michael Peca skated over to offer some advice on how to approach Leafs goalie Curtis Joseph. "He told me not to deke because he's pretty good at that and the ice was pretty bad," Bates said. "He said, 'Make sure you take your best shot.' I decided to go for my shot."

Bates sped in and snapped a wrister over Joseph's blocker, sending the Coliseum crowd into delirium. Dave Scatchard tackled Bates near center ice as the Isles took and held on to a 4–3 lead.

The wait between the penalty-shot call and Bates stepping up to take it was torture for everyone. On the video you can see Garth Snow, the Isles' backup goalie at the time, itching to say something to Bates; Mark Parrish, Bates's housemate, was just praying. "No offense to Batesy, I wasn't feeling very confident," Parrish said. "And then he scores and the place—I can feel the hair on the back of my neck standing up now just talking about it! Lavy [coach Peter Laviolette] was right behind me, and there was no way I could hear a word he was saying."

In a series marked by drama, viciousness, and so, so much trash talk from both sides, the Bates goal stands out. Leafs coach Pat Quinn and his players were livid about the penalty-shot call, saying Bates didn't have a clear path to the net. Isles GM Mike

Milbury had already publicly complained about Toronto's dirty tactics between Games 2 and 3, and the Leafs now countered that the officials were moving too much in the other direction. "If Mike Milbury's quotes can influence the game that badly, the whole game's in trouble," Gary Roberts said.

Roberts and Darcy Tucker figured prominently in Game 5's ugliness, but before that, Bates got to make the Coliseum roar once more.

40 Eddie Westfall, the First Captain

Jiggs McDonald got to see the Islanders win three Stanley Cups in his first three seasons behind the microphone. The guy next to him in the booth for those years had plenty of knowledge of the Islanders—and not a shred of envy that the team finally climbed the mountain without him.

Eddie Westfall is probably better known to a generation of Islanders die-hards as the smooth-voiced color analyst who paired with McDonald for a decade of television broadcasts. But he was the first Islanders captain and perhaps the most important veteran Bill Torrey brought in during the 1972–73 expansion year, the one with a real NHL pedigree and an interest in shepherding the young Islanders into becoming confident pros. "I think everyone that played with Eddie knew how important he was to those championship teams," McDonald said. "He contributed so much on and off the ice."

Westfall was coming off his second Stanley Cup with the Bruins in 1972 when expansion hit the NHL. The Islanders and Atlanta Flames were going to pick the bones of the established teams, and Westfall, thinking he was safe, headed overseas for a golfing trip to St. Andrews. "I remember saying to myself jokingly, 'I wonder which team I'll end up on,'" Westfall told *Sports Illustrated* back in 1982. "A few days later, when I was clearing customs, I could see my children waiting beyond the glass with sad, forlorn faces. Little did I know it was because Daddy was now a New York Islander."

Torrey named Westfall captain of that motley crew, and as the Islanders slowly crawled out of the muck from the first season to a marginally better second season under Al Arbour, Westfall made a point of embodying what the *C* on his sweater implied. "He was a fantastic captain," Denis Potvin said. "Myself, Bobby Ny, Clarkie, Bryan—Eddie would make sure we were always included. He'd say, 'You can have a beer, a Coke, an ice cream sundae, whatever it is. You have to come with us to lunch.' To make the young guys feel welcome like that, it was so important for all of us, and Eddie never left anyone out."

"I'm on the Island my first year, 1975, 19 years old, and Eddie's in my ear: 'You got a place to eat, kid? Come to my house,'" Bryan Trottier said.

That 1975–76 season Westfall was 35, but he could still play too—he scored 25 goals, matching his career high. He didn't retire until after the 1978–79 season, but his days as a regular were done after 1976–77, the same year he surrendered the captaincy to Gillies.

And like a lot of players over the years who came to the Island rather reluctantly, Westfall stayed once his playing days were done. He moved directly into the broadcast booth for the 1979–80 season and got to see the guys he had shared a locker room with—and also shared some early losing and then several years of playoff disappointment—finally win a Stanley Cup. Then a few more after that, of course. "He would never admit it, but there was a pride there," McDonald said. "People would joke with Eddie, 'Geez, if you'd retired a year earlier, we could have had five Cups.' But he would never let that sort of thing bother him. He's always had a happy-go-lucky outlook."

Westfall was no pushover in the booth, either—not that there was much to criticize in those first few seasons. Billy Smith stopped speaking to his old captain, and Westfall found it uncomfortable to go in the locker room in his new role. "It's awkward, but time will take care of that," Westfall told the *New York Times* in 1986.

Westfall retired from the booth after the 1997–98 season with 25 years of service to the Islanders and their fans. Most of us may only remember his commentary, but his time as captain to a bunch of green young Islanders shouldn't be forgotten.

41 Villains: Dale Hunter

Let's get a couple things straight nearly 30 years later: Dale Hunter was a great player. He also committed one of the more heinous acts on the ice that anyone, Islanders fan or no, has ever seen. "The guy had 1,000 points—he wasn't out there running guys [over] every second," Ray Ferraro said. "But he only knew one way to play, and that was with emotion. And what happened in '93...there's no excusing it. But if you knew Dale, you knew what he was about."

And if you're an Islanders fan, you know what happened in the Coliseum on April 28, 1993. Even if you were just a hockey fan watching the NHL's divisional semifinals, you probably remember back that far.

The Islanders entered that postseason feeling better about themselves than they had in quite a while. Don Maloney's first full season as GM—after Bill Torrey was not-so-gently pushed out of the job he held for two decades by the minority ownership's Gang of Four—had been a qualified success, mostly thanks to moves Torrey had made before relinquishing control.

The Pat LaFontaine trade from October 1991 could have been a disaster, with LaFontaine holding out and holding a grudge thanks to broken promises of ownership. Torrey wrangled Pierre Turgeon, Benoit Hogue, Dave McLlwain, and Uwe Krupp from the Sabres. He also received Steve Thomas and Adam Creighton for Brent Sutter in a trade that same October day 18 hours earlier.

Turgeon had 132 points in 1992–93, the best season for a non-dynasty Islander in franchise history. Thomas, on his wing, had 87 points, the best season of his career. Hogue, on a line with Ferraro and Pat Flatley, had his second-straight 75-point season.

Three kids on defense brought some vital new energy: Darius Kasparaitis and Scott Lachance had been the Isles' first-round picks in 1991 and 1992, plus a 10th-rounder named Vladimir Malakhov, who was the best of the three, having played four pro seasons for the Red Army team in the USSR before coming over.

And in goal, Glenn Healy, the veteran who'd had three middling seasons sharing the net with young Mark Fitzpatrick, improved his play enough to earn Al Arbour's trust and the net for the division semifinal against the Caps. It was the Isles' first playoff appearance in three seasons, and after all the turmoil of the prior few years, there was relief that the team was back in the hunt.

It was a dogfight of a series. Hunter led the Caps in scoring; Ferraro began what was an unconscious run that postseason with eight goals against Washington, including back-to-back OT winners in Games 3 and 4 at the Coliseum to give the Isles a 3–1 series lead.

In Game 6 the Islanders were simply holding off the Caps with a two-goal edge in the third when Travis Green scored on a two-on-one at 9:58. They were just about there. Hunter, near the end of a shift 90 seconds later, tried a pass out of his zone that Turgeon picked off. He went in alone, beat Don Beaupre, and pumped his arm in celebration.

And there was Hunter, delivering the dumbest hit you've ever seen—while Turgeon, his teammates, and 16,000-plus Islanders fans were celebrating the team's first playoff series win since 1987, over these same Caps. Turgeon went flying into the boards. Hogue, coming in for a hug, didn't know what to do. "When you're right there, you can't believe your eyes," Ferraro said. "Benny was a tough SOB too."

Rich Pilon came flying in from down the ice and nearly drop-kicked Hunter into the glass. The officials hustled Hunter off the ice, and Turgeon needed assistance to get to the Isles' room. "I've kicked my fair share of Gatorade coolers over," Healy said. "He did something incredibly stupid, and to me, it was over with."

Not to all of his Islanders teammates. The game ended 5–3, the series ended 4–2, and the Isles managed to shake hands with the remaining Caps and get to their locker room in what was supposed to be a moment of glory. "We had a couple guys in Richie and Mick [Vukota] who weren't about to let that thing slide," Healy said. "It's about 40 yards between the dressing rooms, and if it wasn't for a few of Nassau County's finest, things would have gotten ugly."

"It's amazing how the charge of the win completely turned," Ferraro said. "We were elated, then angry, then concerned. We had Pittsburgh, the best team in the league, coming up, and we're wondering if we'll have Turge."

As we all know now, they would not. The Isles found out the next day that Hunter had separated Turgeon's shoulder—the same day they likely all heard Hunter's lame excuse that he was "finishing [his] check" and didn't know Turgeon had scored. Apparently those 1,020 career points didn't sink in enough to remind Hunter what players do when they score. "The worst excuse in the history of excuses," Ferraro said.

A week later new NHL commissioner Gary Bettman handed down a 21-game suspension to Hunter, one of the longest in league history. "He got off too light," Thomas said.

"If being boiled in oil is the high range and 21 games is the low range," Maloney said then, "he's within the range."

The Islanders had to forget, with the two-time defending champion Penguins looming. But no one else on the Island ever has. "I truly believe Dale is one of the good souls in our game," Healy said of Hunter, who coached the Caps for one season in 2011–12 and recently coached Canada's entry at the World Junior tournament. "We had to turn our attention to Pittsburgh—and I still have no fucking idea how we won that."

42 Villains: Darcy Tucker

It doesn't matter that, according to the NHL Rule Book circa 2001–02, Darcy Tucker's low hit on Michael Peca in Game 5 of the Isles-Leafs first-round epic was not a dirty hit. It will never matter. You can tell the age of any Islanders fan by who their most hated opponent of all time is: Older fans will always say Dale Hunter, and who's to argue with them? Slightly younger fans will always say Tucker. Even now the former Leafs agitator still gets the occasional hate tweet, and he always knows where it's from. "Oh, definitely Long Island," he said. "They have long memories down there."

This book has many chapters about 2001–02 and that playoff series, and rightly so—even two decades on, among some players and coaches who went on to win Stanley Cups, that first-round battle is still their favorite.

Which means Tucker's low hit on Peca, which tore the Islanders captain's anterior cruciate ligament, will live on in infamy, even if Tucker didn't get so much as a minor penalty for it. "My temperature's rising just talking about it now!" Mark Parrish said. "Pecs meant so much to us that year, and we needed him.... You look at that play, and you know it was dirty. The league did too; they changed the rule the next season."

It was a doubly tough pill to swallow because of a much, much dirtier hit earlier in Game 5 of a series that was tied. Gary Roberts crushed Kenny Jonsson with a hit from behind, a dirty shot that resulted in an obvious concussion. Roberts got a major penalty but wasn't ejected and wasn't suspended—it would have been a 7- to 10-gamer in today's NHL, but even though this wasn't the wild days of the 1990s or earlier, it was still eons ago compared to now.

Tucker had been doing what he did best in his career that series: getting under the skin of various Islanders. The Leafs controlled the first two games, Mike Milbury delivered his expletive-laden video session to reporters, and the Islanders rallied for the next two games at the Coliseum, with barbs being thrown from all sides as the series shifted back to Toronto.

It was a lopsided Leafs win, one that was pretty well out of reach when Peca threw a puck out of his zone and Tucker cruised in, bent deeply at the waist, and took out Peca legs-first. It happened along the boards in the opposite zone from the Islanders bench, so few players knew what happened initially; they clearly knew what happened once Peca had to be helped to his skates and went off slowly, as Jonsson had a period earlier. "It was obviously tough to watch that go down," Steve Webb said. "But that's who Darcy was: a really skilled player who walked the line."

When the teams came back to the Island for Game 6, the fans were prepared. They booed the heck out of Tucker from the time warm-ups began. "You don't love seeing signs with your name on 'em, that's for sure," Tucker said. Webb delivered a huge hit to

Tucker near the end of the second period, then Shawn Bates and Tucker fought (wrestled, more like) a couple of minutes before the end of that 5–3 Islanders win.

Where Tucker sought to engage Peca until their fateful Game 5 encounter, Webb sought to do the same with Tucker…and about everyone else in Leafs blue. "That was called opportunistic, right?" Webb said. "Just so happened when he was on the ice I ended up getting a shift. It's a grinding series, it gets tiresome to handle the punishment every shift. You wanted to make sure you contributed."

That the Leafs prevailed in seven games likely adds to the hate for Tucker, who ended up playing with Peca in Toronto for a season five years later. "Our kids went to the same preschool," Tucker said. "It was over for us then. I definitely tried to always leave what happened on the ice once I was off it."

Islanders fans, though—long memories. "I'm glad," Tucker said. "If you don't want rivalries or that sort of passion, then you don't want guys like me or Steve Webb or Eric Cairns in the game. It was an amazing series, maybe the best one I was ever a part of. They may not remember me in the best way, but I'm glad they remember."

43 Kirk Muller, Public Enemy No. 1

Kirk Muller's career is pretty impressive: the second overall pick in 1984; Stanley Cup champion in 1993; 1,349 NHL games and 16 seasons as an NHL coach, 10 of those with the same Canadiens he helped to a Cup.

And it's safe to say he's the most hated player by the Islanders fan base, at least among those who wore blue and orange. Fans of a newer vintage might not even know Muller was an Islander. Fans of an older vintage might never let you forget his 27 games over two seasons, 1994–95 and 1995–96, and that his time here quite certainly cost Don Maloney the GM job.

Let's begin at the beginning. Maloney was in his third season as GM, having taken over for Bill Torrey—big shoes, to say the least. After the exhilarating run of 1992–93, the Islanders managed to get back to the playoffs in 1993–94 but suffered a humiliating sweep at the hands of the Rangers, scoring just three goals in four games. Al Arbour stepped down, this time for good. Lorne Henning, Arbour's old assistant, took over as head coach.

After the three-month lockout reduced the 1994–95 season to 48 games, the Isles were just brutal in the shortened season, mired at 10–20–4 in the first week of April. Maloney felt the team needed a shakeup, so he dealt Pierre Turgeon, their best player during his three-plus seasons on the Island, along with top-pair defenseman Vladimir Malakhov to the Canadiens for Muller and Mathieu Schneider.

The problem was that Muller—then the Canadiens' captain—had no interest in leaving Montreal. GM Serge Savard had reportedly told Muller he wasn't going to be traded, but the Canadiens couldn't resist adding Turgeon when the chance came along. Muller refused to report to the Island, and Maloney acquiesced. "The New York Islanders organization is more than willing to give him the time he needs to get his affairs in order," Maloney said. "He was terribly upset about the deal.… He needs some time to get himself straightened out." Apparently there was never a good time for that. Muller reported five days later, played the final 12 games of the season, and departed, allegedly with a promise from Maloney that the Islanders would try to trade him before the 1995–96 season began.

Mike Milbury arrived as head coach before the 1995–96 season, and the Isles had a very no-nonsense guy behind the bench. Muller moped through the first 15 games of that season as the Isles started 2–11–2, and Maloney and Milbury decided to send Muller home on November 12, just as the Islanders departed on a four-game California road trip. "We have decided to ask Kirk to go home," Maloney said. "He will not play for the New York Islanders again."

Three weeks after that, the Islanders fired Maloney, and on December 12 Milbury was named GM and coach. The reign of Mad Mike had begun, and his first order of business was revoking Muller's suspension with pay. He asked Muller to return to the team on December 16; Muller declined and was suspended without pay on December 20.

Finally, on January 24, 1996, Milbury swung a complicated three-team deal that sent Muller to the Leafs and brought in Bryan Berard, the first overall pick in 1995, who'd basically refused to report to the hapless Senators after being selected. "'Relief' is an understatement," Milbury said.

In retrospect, all the blame can't be laid at Muller's feet. He went from the Canadiens, one of the premier NHL franchises, to an Islanders team that was in ownership turmoil and then, during his brief tenure, decided to don the Fisherman jerseys. "I'll tell you, it's a direct reflection of [how] the organization was perceived at that time," Mick Vukota told Nick Hirshon in *We Want Fish Sticks*, a book about the 1995–96 logo and jersey change.

The Islanders were on their way to being a joke around the league. Muller wanted no part of it. He went on to play another eight NHL seasons, and now he's one of the most experienced assistant coaches in the game, so his reputation hasn't suffered. Don't tell that to Islanders fans, though. Muller will remain their most hated Islander for a long, long while.

44 Go to Bridgeport and Watch the Kids Play

The ferry from Port Jefferson takes about 75 minutes and drops you a few hundred yards from Webster Bank Arena. If you're not that far out on the Island, the drive to Bridgeport isn't short—unless you're already in Connecticut. But it's worth the trip. The Sound Tigers are ringing in their 20th season in 2021–22, and while their history has been as up and down as the Isles' has over that same span, to sit in a cozy building and watch the future of the franchise is always worth the trip.

Amazingly it all started with Roy Boe. The original Islanders owner never could quite get his financial footing and sold his interest in that team to John Pickett in 1978, before the Isles took off. Boe returned to hockey in the 1990s as owner of the Worcester IceCats in the AHL before starting the Sound Tigers in 2001–02. Within a few years he was again forced to sell, with the team piling up unpaid bills. Islanders owner Charles Wang bought the team in Bridgeport in 2004, and it's been an Islanders-owned affiliate ever since.

And yet under Boe, the Sound Tigers had their greatest success. They haven't come close to achieving what they did with future Isles coach Steve Stirling behind the bench in 2001–02, when they made it to the Calder Cup finals behind 20-year-old goalie Rick DiPietro. "It was one of the closest groups of guys I've ever been around," DiPietro said. When Mike Milbury took DiPietro first overall at the 2000 draft, it took some convincing to get the goalie to turn pro right away—and he ended up playing in Chicago of the IHL since he was under 20, the age minimum for the AHL.

That ended up working out well, with the Sound Tigers coming in and Wang signing an affiliate agreement with the new team just across Long Island Sound. The franchise's first affiliate was in New Haven in 1972–73, but that was the closest the farm team had ever been before Bridgeport came along.

And even though the prospect cupboard wasn't exactly full in 2001, the Sound Tigers had some decent talent. Their leading scorer was a big winger named Trent Hunter, who Milbury had scooped up from the Ducks for a fourth-round pick the year before. The top line of Hunter, center Jason Krog, and wing Juraj Kolnik led the way. Recent first-round Islanders picks Raffi Torres and Branislav Mezei contributed as 20-year-olds. Heavyweights Ray Schultz and Eric Godard kept the fists flying. "It was just like a college atmosphere," DiPietro said. "That league was no joke, but we were a good team and we were having fun."

The Sound Tigers lost to the Chicago Wolves, the Thrashers' first-year AHL affiliate, in the finals in five games. Bridgeport not only hasn't been back to a Calder Cup final since, they've won exactly one playoff series in 19 years—and it came in the first round of the 2003 playoffs.

But if you're an Islanders fan now, you're rooting for players who have paid their dues and matured in Bridgeport. Brock Nelson is one of just two players in Sound Tigers history to score 25 goals in Bridgeport and 25 goals for the Isles in a single season (Hunter is the other). Anders Lee had 22 goals in 54 games with the Sound Tigers in 2013–14 before earning his regular spot in the NHL.

The Isles have had greater success developing defensemen in the last few years. Scott Mayfield played 223 AHL games before becoming an Islanders regular; Ryan Pulock (163 games), Adam Pelech (105), and former Islander Devon Toews (116) all played multiple seasons in Bridgeport before the Islanders deemed them ready. "When you grow up together like we did, it's a great time," Mayfield said. "A bunch of us lived together near Bridgeport; we formed a real bond."

And now, with Lou Lamoriello and Barry Trotz running the Islanders so well and being so dependent on veterans, the prospects are multiplying at the AHL level. It's great to catch them early and in an environment such as Webster Bank.

My only bit of advice: Maybe don't take in one of the school-day games, with a few thousand raucous elementary schoolers going nuts for an 11:00 AM puck drop.

45 Joanne Holewa, the Woman behind It All

Garth Snow had a phrase he must have said 500 times during his 12 years as GM: "Before you do anything, run it by Joanne first."

Joanne Holewa has been with the Islanders since 1979, when Bill Torrey brought her in. She's still there more than 40 years later, now with the title manager of hockey administration. She's worked closely with every Islanders general manager—seven men of vastly different temperaments and levels of success. And not one of them could have done the job as well without her.

"When you come into a job like this, it helps to have people around you who know the organization and the league inside and out," Snow said. "I knew Joanne when I was a player, and I knew she was incredibly helpful then. When I got the GM job, I realized she's not just helpful—she's a godsend."

Holewa's job description covers a lot of ground. There are contracts to draw up, adherence to the CBA (which has changed a few times over her 40 years), booking charter flights and hotels, and immigration and visa requirements for players on the Island and in Bridgeport. She does it all without a bit of fanfare—she's refused interview requests for decades, only allowing the Islanders team website to write a piece on her day-to-day responsibilities back in 2010.

Torrey said then: "She's remarkable. At times, the business can be high pressure, and at deadlines you really have to know what you're doing. I really don't know if anyone in this league today has a better knowledge of how a hockey team has to function and all the aspects that go with it."

And between changing league rules and changing U.S. laws, Holewa manages to keep up with the times and keep players and their families moving and happy. When the Islanders traded for Jean-Gabriel Pageau at the 2019–20 deadline, there was some question about whether Pageau could get the necessary travel documents to make it down from Ottawa in time to face the Rangers the next night. The pandemic was just starting to have an effect on travel around the world, and there were also tightened restrictions on foreigners obtaining work visas in a timely fashion.

Pageau was on the ice for the Isles' morning skate barely 18 hours later. "You know Joanne?" Barry Trotz said when asked how Pageau made it so quickly. "She handled it."

Coming into the pro sports environment when Holewa did— Jiggs McDonald said she had worked for the Penguins, which is where Torrey knew her from when he hired her—was incredibly rare for a woman in the 1970s. That she not only stayed on the job under Torrey but continued on through the chaotic ownership stints, Mike Milbury's reign, Snow, and then for Lou Lamoriello is a testament to how good Holewa is at her job and how much she cares about the organization.

So much so that she once opened her home to an 18-year-old draft pick who needed a place to stay before training camp. "They were so good to me," Josh Bailey said of Joanne and her husband, Walter. "Snowy wanted me to come down in the summer after they drafted me to train, and I just ended up at Joanne's. To develop a good relationship with someone in the organization was great for me, and it stays to this day—whenever [my wife] Meg needs anything, Joanne just says, 'Have her call me.'"

"She is a bit of a mom to the whole team," Snow said. "That doesn't mean people look at her differently, just that she has the respect of every player and person who comes through the organization because she cares. It's not an easy business to develop that sort of reputation."

And she's kept all the crazy stories of the Islanders to herself, also no mean feat. What a book that would be. Said Torrey in 2010: "I have never bought a hockey book, but I have always told Joanne that if she ever writes an autobiography, that is the first hockey book I am going to buy."

46 The Poke Check

Wade Dubielewicz might have only been known for having played the most games in net in Bridgeport Sound Tigers history—164, in case you were wondering. But just say the word "Dubie" to an Islanders fan, and you'll get two words in reply: "Poke check."

Dubielewicz authored one of the greatest weeks in Islanders history outside of 1980 to 1984. Even if you include the dynasty, it's still one of the unlikeliest Islanders tales ever told: the time a goalie with 13 career NHL appearances got the Isles to the playoffs.

Rick DiPietro suffered a concussion on March 13, 2007, when he collided with the Canadiens' Steve Begin; on March 25 against the Rangers, DiPietro suffered another concussion and was sidelined indefinitely. So the Islanders summoned Dubielewicz, who'd spent the bulk of the previous four seasons in the AHL backing up Mike Dunham. Except Dunham, who would retire at season's end, wasn't playing well enough. Dubielewicz relieved Dunham in each of the next two games, then made 42 saves in a 5–2 loss to the Senators on March 31. The Isles had lost four straight and sat 11th in the Eastern Conference, needing to leapfrog three teams to grab the last playoff spot.

First-year GM Garth Snow had pushed his chips to the middle of the table a month earlier when he sent his 2007 first-round pick and two prospects to the Oilers for pending free agent Ryan Smyth. The Isles had been absent from the postseason for a year, and Snow was hoping to make a minor splash; the goalie problems threatened to derail that hope.

The Islanders hosted the Rangers with four games to go and what coach Ted Nolan called "a million-to-one shot" to make the playoffs. Dubielewicz and the Isles went to a shootout, and only Miroslav Satan had scored for either team when Jaromir Jagr stepped up to try and keep the shootout going.

Dubielewicz, all 5'10"(ish) of him, shot out his stick to knock the puck away from Jagr. Game over; the Isles won to stay in the hunt. "I'm not going to lie; I was pretty happy," Dubielewicz said. "He's one of the best players in the world. Anytime you can come out on the better end of that one, you've got to be pretty excited."

"We're not eliminated yet," Brendan Witt said. "We have to take it literally one game at a time. I hate to say that stupid cliché, but it's true. We have to focus now on Toronto coming in here."

Two nights later the Leafs, who were a point behind the Canadiens in ninth, came calling to the Coliseum. Again Dubie got the call. No need for shootout heroics this time: Jason Blake scored his 40th goal of the year to break a 2–2 tie in the third, part of a 5–2 win. And the Islanders got some unlikely help—the Rangers beat the Canadiens at the Garden 3–1 to leave the Isles' hopes intact.

Two nights later the Islanders went into Philadelphia needing a win and even more help, as the Leafs and Canadiens were facing each other in those teams' season finales. The Islanders needed a Leafs regulation win to stay alive, plus a win of their own over the Flyers, who were closing up their worst season in franchise history.

The Isles got out to a 3–0 lead and held on for a 4–2 win, with Dubie making 28 saves. While that was going on, the Leafs rallied to win a wild one in Toronto 6–5 to get to 91 points and eliminate Montreal. The Isles, sitting with 90 points, simply needed two points any way possible to get the last berth. "I've got to go to church on Sunday," said former Islander Bryan McCabe, who scored the winner for the Leafs.

That Easter Sunday brought the Islanders into the Meadowlands to face the Devils, who had long ago locked up their playoff berth, which meant Martin Brodeur was on the bench. The Islanders grabbed a 2–0 lead on Richard Park's second goal of the game with 12:09 to go. Inside of five minutes to play, it looked like the Islanders would get there without much fuss.

But this was the Islanders—they were made for fuss in the 1990s and 2000s. John Madden tipped a shot past Dubielewicz with 4:13 to play to make it 2–1. The Devils pulled their goalie and poured it on in the closing seconds; the Islanders were a few ticks away. But Dubie tripped over his own skates trying to get to his right and Madden flipped a backhand over him with 0.7 seconds left. The Isles were incredulous, but it was tied. "That was probably the toughest thing I've ever had to deal with," Dubielewicz said. "I just couldn't believe it. I really couldn't believe that we were that close. I was pretty confident that we were going to win the game at that point. They just kept plugging away and they were able to get it."

After the short break, the overtime went scoreless. Back to the shootout. Satan went first and scored, answered by Zach Parise. Viktor Kozlov made it 2–1 Isles on the next attempt, then Brian

Gionta steamed in for the Devils—and Dubie used the poke check once again.

Smyth couldn't convert with a chance to clinch it, so it came down to Dubielewicz vs. Sergei Brylin. Brylin tried to pump-fake and go backhand—he never saw the poke check coming. "I play fairly aggressive," Dubielewicz told *Newsday* a few days later. "A guy that's two or three inches taller can play three or four inches deeper in the net. At the same time, it makes sense that I'm a little bit quicker than a big guy. And I've always been told by coaches that I do an excellent job of reading the play. The brain between my ears is probably my best asset. I've really got to think the game and be ahead of the play somewhat."

As with a lot of great stories about this team in the 1990s and 2000s, it pretty much ended there. Dubie got the call in Game 1 of the first-round series against the top-seeded Sabres, and it was a 4–1 loss; DiPietro was cleared and played the rest of the five-game series defeat.

Dubielewicz earned his spot as DiPietro's backup the next season, making 20 appearances for the Isles and posting a more-than-respectable .919 save percentage. But he wasn't offered a chance to return, bounced around a bit, and retired after the 2010–11 season.

For one week, though, he was unbeatable. And for that, he's an Islanders legend.

47 The 2012–13 Revival

The slog of the previous five seasons led into a 2012–13 that didn't hold much promise for the Islanders. The three-month lockout certainly wasn't good for the game of hockey, but perhaps, in a strange way, it wasn't all bad for the Isles. "We really used that time to evaluate a lot of guys, in the AHL in particular," Jack Capuano said. "You know it's going to be a season where you have to have guys ready to go. We were looking for guys who could do that."

And for a young team, everyone kept busy. Many players who wound up with regular roles on the Isles for that 48-game season played the first half of the year in Bridgeport; John Tavares went with Mark Streit to Switzerland, Josh Bailey to Germany, Andrew MacDonald to the Czech Republic. When the time came to pull together for a one-week training camp in January, the Islanders had plenty of holes to fill. They went through the waiver wire and picked up what looked like scraps—former fourth overall pick Thomas Hickey out of the Kings organization, 34-year-old center Keith Aucoin from the Leafs.

The only really competitive game during that weeklong camp was a scrimmage between those who came to Islanders camp and the Sound Tigers—a few of whom, Nino Niederreiter most notably, were feeling hot about being excluded from the big camp. "For me, I'm 28 years old, I finally feel like I have a chance to make it in the NHL, and we go out and lose to the AHL team where I'd been playing all year!" Colin McDonald said. "I was like, 'I'm so close to making it and now this happens?'"

With a bunch of new faces, the Islanders stumbled out of the gate on that shortened season, kicking it off 4–7–1 with a five-game losing streak. But Lubomir Visnovsky, whom Garth Snow had acquired at the draft the previous June, arrived on the Island after balking at the trade and then delaying his arrival due to a surgery for his son at home in Slovakia. The 36-year-old defenseman came in with the right attitude and the ability to make his team better.

The same was true for another reluctant Islander: Evgeni Nabokov. His return to the NHL in the 2010–11 season was supposed to be with the Red Wings; the Islanders claimed him on waivers, he didn't want to come, and he finally arrived for the 2011–12 season. By 2012–13 Nabby was the No. 1 goalie, and his unorthodox style of leadership rubbed off on Tavares and the rest of the young core. "I think these guys knew they could have a good team, but they didn't have a chance to be part of one," Nabokov said. "You have to have some faith in yourself, and when you lose a lot, maybe you need some people reminding you how good you are."

The Isles started, slowly, to put it together. There was a rally from two goals down to win a 4–3 shootout against the Rangers in the Garden on Valentine's Day followed by a 5–1 thrashing of the first-place Devils two nights later. There was the bizarre sight of Nabokov skating in front of the Isles bench during a television timeout in Montreal a week later, giving his dejected teammates an in-game pep talk after they fell behind the Canadiens 2–0. They rallied again, with Hickey winning that game in overtime.

And then, with 17 games to go and the Isles sitting at 13–15–3, it all clicked. Tavares turned a good season into a great one, with 11 goals over the last 17 games. Nabokov played 15 of the 17 games. The gap-fillers such as McDonald, Keith Aucoin, and Brad Boyes produced. Kids such as Travis Hamonic and Casey Cizikas played regular spots. And they picked up points, going 11–2–4 to grab the last Eastern Conference playoff berth. Which meant their first playoff series in five years would be against the Penguins, the dominant team in the East. The Isles were supposed to be a speed bump, but it didn't quite work out that way.

John Tavares was one of the players who made the 2012–13 season fun to watch.

In the first game, it did. The Islanders seemed in awe of the moment, taking a 5–0 thumping. "It was the first time there for a lot of us," Bailey said.

In Game 2 the Isles were trailing 3–1 when Kyle Okposo, who'd had just a four-goal regular season, delivered a shot heard 'round the Island. It wasn't a goal, though. Okposo took overdramatic offense at Matt Niskanen's open-ice hit on Matt Moulson and challenged Niskanen to a fight. It was one-sided to say the least—Niskanen left the ice bloodied, and the Islanders remembered they too could put up a fight.

McDonald and Matt Martin scored to tie it in the second, then Okposo scored the winner in the third. All three goals were ugly ones on Marc-Andre Fleury, and not only had the Isles evened the series, they'd dented Pittsburgh's confidence in its All-Star goalie.

Game 3 was an afternoon tilt at the Coliseum, the first playoff game there since 2007. The Islanders stayed at the Marriott across the plaza the night before. "It felt like there were fans tailgating at 6:00 AM," Bailey said. "You walk over a few hours before a noon start and the lot's just packed."

The noise and chanting started the minute fans got into the building. "You just said 'Game 3' to me and I got chills thinking about how loud it was," McDonald said. "We're going through our routines in the locker room before the game, everybody's doing their thing, and you just have this background roar going on. It was incredible."

The Islanders scored twice in the first 5:41, fell behind 4–2, tied it up in the third, and lost in overtime. This was a roller-coaster ride, and it didn't let up in Game 4, another seesaw contest in which the Isles rallied from 4–3 down in the third to win 6–4, with Tavares scoring the eventual winner.

Game 5, with the Penguins turning to veteran Tomas Vokoun, was another clunker—a sign that this ragtag Isles band wasn't quite ready to put the hammer down. But back in the Coliseum for

Game 6, it was mayhem again—a game that was nip and tuck all the way until Brooks Orpik's 50-footer eluded Nabokov in OT.

The Penguins were supposed to win that series, with Sidney Crosby and Evgeni Malkin and a Stanley Cup just four years earlier. The Islanders were still supposed to be a couple years away—if they ever got to legitimacy at all. But they were able to put together a fun, fast, furious season that gave the fan base a jolt after five straight bummers.

"Johnny was unreal that year, and we had that core of young guys getting better," McDonald said. "For a lot of us, guys like Hickey and Aucoin and me, we got to show we belonged."

48 Sit Up (and Sing Along) with the Blue and Orange Army

It's not just any fans' group that can handpick their section before the team's arena is even finished. The Blue and Orange Army is not just any fans' group. The Army has been loudly cheering, chanting, and singing in support of the Islanders for more than a decade now, formed back when the Islanders were struggling to get their rebuild going.

Now the Section 329 fixtures at the Coliseum are on their third arena, and they've made each one home—so much so that co-owner Jon Ledecky promised the Army well before UBS Arena was completed that there'd be a section 329 just for the group. "They're the best owners by far," Tom LoFaso, the Blue and Orange Army cofounder, said of Ledecky and principal owner Scott Malkin. "They're willing to talk and engage with the fans. Mr. Ledecky came and sat with us a few times."

LoFaso and some of his fellow Islanders fan friends from Levittown organized the group in the 2008–09 season, when any gathering of more than a dozen fans in any Coliseum section constituted a movement of sorts—the Islanders were last in the league that year in attendance, averaging 13,773 fans, though the actual numbers were probably quite a bit lower.

Up in Section 329, LoFaso and his friends, all big European soccer fans, devised a group that would be like a Premier League supporters' section. "We made games where we were getting blown out fun," he said. "It's kind of crazy to see where we are now."

That goes for both the Islanders, who've come a long way since that ugly season, and the Army, which can count on 10 times its original 10- to 15-person group at games these days. "We've had the last three to four rows full of people at the Coli," LoFaso said. "Some sit further down because they don't want to stand the whole game, but they sing with us."

Ah yes, the songs. The most recognizable one over the last few seasons is for Josh Bailey, the longest-serving Islander. It goes to the tune of the 1961 pop hit "Hey! Baby" by Bruce Channel:

Hey, Josh Bailey
Oh Ah
I wanna know, will you score a goal?

There's some irony to it, because Bailey has never been a prolific goal scorer, with 162 goals in his 919 Islanders games. There's been a debate that's raged among Islanders fans almost since Bailey arrived in that brutal 2008–09 season about whether he's truly an elite player, and the Blue and Orange Army has declared which side it's on. "It's pretty special to say the least," Bailey said. "My kids look forward to it a lot."

"My friend John Ballantyne came up with that one; he's been singing it since the Isles drafted him," LoFaso said. "I think a lot of people thought we were making fun of the guy at first. Now the whole building sings it."

Among the other Islanders songs emanating from Section 329 is one called "When I'm on Long Island," sung to the tune of Depeche Mode's 1981 hit "Just Can't Get Enough":

When I'm on Long Island
I know just what to do
I just can't get enough
I just can't get enough
I was born an Islander
I bleed orange and blue
I just can't get enough
I just can't get enough
We stand and cheer the entire year
And I just can't seem to get enough of you

These may seem silly to the average fan, but these are right in line for any fan sitting in the supporters' section in the UK for a soccer match. And the energy the Army brings is infectious. UBS Arena will be packed, but if you can find your way to Section 329, sing along with the group. The Blue and Orange Army welcomes all newcomers. "As long as you're an Islander fan," LoFaso said.

49 Peter Laviolette's All-Too-Brief Coaching Tenure

Peter Laviolette badly wanted to be the Bruins' coach. He'd led Providence, their AHL club, to a Calder Cup in 1999 and was a finalist for the big club's job the next year, but it went to Mike Keenan. Laviolette was an assistant to Keenan in 2000–01, then a finalist again, but the job went to Robbie Ftorek. "It was getting late in the process and jobs were filling up, so I was frustrated I didn't get that job," he said. "I remember going for a run, I came back, and my wife said Mike Milbury had called."

Islanders general manager Milbury had interviewed some veteran NHL coaches—Ftorek, Kevin Constantine, Ted Nolan, and Bryan Murray among them. With second-year owner Charles Wang ready to spend, Milbury flirted with some heavy hitters behind the bench. But he went with a 36-year-old with no NHL experience instead, hiring Laviolette ahead of his team-transforming moves (a month after hiring Laviolette, Milbury traded for Alexei Yashin, Michael Peca, and Adrian Aucoin, with veteran goalie Chris Osgood coming in right before the season in the Waiver Draft).

"I remember going into the Island with the Bruins [in 2000–01], and there were maybe a few thousand people in the Coliseum," Laviolette said. "Then we had maybe 15 to 16 sellouts my first year. Mike made all those moves and that generated some buzz, and we started off with four straight wins on the road."

Laviolette may not have known he'd have a veteran team given the sad state of the Islanders over the few seasons prior, but he didn't coach any differently from day one of training camp in Lake Placid. "He meant business right from the start," Mark Parrish said.

"He expected you to work hard and let you know if you didn't. I loved it."

Those Islanders were ready to work hard. The 9–0–1–1 run to open the season is still the best start to any Islanders season in franchise history. Laviolette and his assistant coaches—longtime Canadiens assistant coach Jacques Laperriere, who coached with Laviolette in Boston; former Ranger and Capital Kelly Miller; and Greg Cronin, a holdover from Butch Goring's Islanders staff—had a terrific feel for this mostly new team and kept a steady hand on the reins as the Isles finished with 96 points, a 44-point improvement from 2000–01.

The epic playoff battle with the Leafs is legend. "It was so brutal," Laviolette said. "You still see the intensity of playoff hockey now, but maybe not with the nasty edge of that series. We had Eric Cairns, we had Steve Webb just tracking guys all over the ice. They were a tough team, and they took some liberties, but we fought them every step of the way."

After falling in that seven-game series, Islanders fans surely thought the team that had fumbled its way through the majority of the 1990s was finally long gone. And that they had an heir to Al Arbour's coaching throne just getting started in his NHL career.

But the next season was simply a grind. Word started leaking out from that veteran dressing room that Laviolette was too demanding, too relentless. "The last couple years were good," Jason Blake said on the eve of the 2003–04 season, when Steve Stirling had replaced Laviolette, "but we were always on edge." Yashin took a step back from his strong first Islanders season. Peca and Kenny Jonsson weren't the same players after their injuries in the Leafs series.

The overall mood of the team never quite jelled the way it had the year before, and the ever-antsy Milbury didn't try to fix things. Laviolette was fired a month after the Islanders fell to the top-seeded Senators in five games as the No. 8 seed in the East. "I'm not talking about strictly the results," Milbury said in announcing the firing. "I'm talking about a methodology in coaching and communication with players. If you don't have it, it's pretty tough to succeed. And it looked to me as if it had been lost." He added: "He'll surface again, and I hope shortly. I think he's learned some things from the experience. I know I have."

Within a year Laviolette was hired by the Hurricanes midway through a disappointing 2003–04. His intense ways galvanized a Carolina team that had been to the Cup Finals in 2002 but had a long history of playoff disappointment. Coming out of the 2004–05 lockout, Laviolette had his team up and running. Sound familiar? They finished second in the East and pulled out Game 7 wins in the conference final over the Sabres and the Cup Finals over the Oilers. Three years after Milbury chose his team's comfort over quality coaching, Laviolette was a champion.

Milbury has perhaps been proven right over the years, as Laviolette's intensity and demanding nature have worn thin. He's on his fifth NHL job, with the Capitals. But the results are there: top 20 all-time for wins, games coached, playoff wins, and playoff games coached. He's taken three teams to the Stanley Cup Finals. And it took the Islanders 15 years to find another coach who could marshal his players, albeit with a very different tone.

"I owe a lot to Mike," Laviolette said. "He gave me my chance, and we had a great team that first year. There's no ill will toward him; there never was toward Charles. My family and I had a great time on the Island. We got to be there for a rebirth of sorts, and the fans were great."

50 Tavares Leaves and the Isles Band Together

The puzzle pieces were fitting in a way that Islanders ownership and Isles fans wanted after the 2017–18 season. Lou Lamoriello was pushed aside as Leafs GM and Scott Malkin and Jon Ledecky pounced, making Lamoriello Islanders president. He fired Garth Snow and Doug Weight, naming himself GM. Two weeks later Lamoriello brought Barry Trotz on board. Things were moving in the right direction after two listless seasons.

But it was too late to make the last piece fit. Lamoriello met with John Tavares even before he took the president's job on May 22 and spent pretty much every day after that in contact with Tavares or his agent to try and keep the Islanders captain in blue and orange. Tavares had asked Snow and ownership not to trade him while he played out the final season of his contract, a request that was granted; Malkin and Pat Brisson, Tavares's agent, met often during the 2017–18 season as the Isles principal owner kept Tavares's camp apprised of plans for UBS Arena and any other organizational issues.

It wasn't enough. The contact window arrived, and even though Lamoriello flew from the draft in Dallas straight to Los Angeles on the same flight as Brisson and stationed himself out there as Tavares and his camp hosted teams at the CAA offices, the Isles' hold on Tavares was slipping away.

The Leafs, his hometown team, made a compelling pitch. He ultimately accepted their seven-year offer for $11 million per, about $1.5 million less per season than the Islanders had offered. Once Tavares's camp tweeted out a picture of him as a kid with Leafs bedsheets, Islanders fans were livid. Videos of Isles fans burning

No. 91 jerseys littered social media. "Don't blame them," one Islander told the *Athletic* the next day. It was a devastating blow.

And yet it was also an opportunity—one that Trotz, ever the master motivator, seized upon. "Everyone had us written off, and that was a pretty big motivating factor," Josh Bailey said. "Lou and Barry set the tone for us in a positive way. They put in a winning mindset, brought a lot of accountability. And we had the guys willing to buy in and put the team first."

That's not to say Tavares would have done anything differently had he stayed. But Trotz in particular was able to emphasize "we over me," as he likes to say, and used Tavares's departure as a reminder that one player doesn't make a successful NHL team.

And it was just another day of being an Islander in the 2000s. Lamoriello and Trotz didn't have that baggage, but most of the team returning for 2018–19 did—and that fueled what came next as well. "I've been here long enough that even when we started to be good in 2014–15 or so, we were never anyone's pick in a preseason poll or anything like that," Anders Lee said. "People love to give us a knock. And we see it—we're not oblivious. So when Johnny left, there absolutely was a chip on all our shoulders."

The team without Tavares went out and posted its best season in 35 years and hosted Game 1 of a playoff series for the first time in 31 years. "Johnny gave everything to this organization," Lee said. "It's nothing personal with him; we're all still friends with him. But this was never about one guy. We had something to prove."

51 Kelly Hrudey and the Trade He Never Wanted

Kelly Hrudey falls into the same category in Islanders history as Pat LaFontaine—an heir apparent to the dynasty crew who served the Islanders very well but never got to see any kind of sustained success.

Hrudey's shining moment with the Isles was the Easter Epic. That 73-save performance capping an Islanders rally from 3–1 down in the playoff series to the Caps was his biggest achievement in the Islanders net. It propelled Hrudey from a young goalie who was sharing time and being outshined by an aging Billy Smith to becoming the No. 1 on the Island.

"It was our little team at the time, not the dynasty guys but the new wave trying to make their own name," Bryan Trottier said. "Kelly was at the center of it, him and Pat. If that team had stayed together, it would have been the next great Islander team, no doubt."

But even before LaFontaine soured on the Islanders and the broken contract promises from John Pickett, Hrudey was out the door. He was the first of the second wave of promising Isles to be traded by Bill Torrey, dealt on February 22, 1989, to the Kings for Mark Fitzpatrick, Wayne McBean, and future considerations. A 28-year-old goalie hitting his prime dealt to Wayne Gretzky's new playground for a couple of kids, the Kings' first- and second-round picks in the 1987 draft.

The Islanders were in the midst of a slide in that 1988–89 season, their first without Denis Potvin, who'd retired after the previous year. Mike Bossy had missed all of 1987–88 and announced his retirement in October at the start of the 1988–89 season. Smith was in his final year. So it made sense for Torrey to go even younger and capitalize on getting the best price he could for Hrudey, who had been a Vezina Trophy finalist a year earlier but, like his team, wasn't at his best through the bulk of 1988–89.

Except it never made sense to Hrudey. "That's the only time we were really floundering and I was wondering where things were headed," Hrudey said. "I felt completely betrayed by the organization. I was of the mindset that I hoped they lost every game for 40 years. I knew there was a lot going on, but I didn't care. I was so mad at the organization, I hoped they were imploding. I don't feel that way anymore. At the time, I was completely shocked by the trade."

The genesis of the trade seemed to come from the 1989 All-Star Game, which was held a few weeks earlier in Edmonton. Gretzky made a triumphant return to his old stomping grounds, winning MVP of the game. In the players' hotel a day earlier, Gretzky sidled up to Torrey and asked a question: "What would it take to get Kelly Hrudey from you guys?"

Torrey had a quick reply: "Janet."

That joking reference to Gretzky's actress wife aside, the Great One seemed quite serious about getting his new team to acquire a solid No. 1 goalie. The trade was made a few weeks later, and Hrudey—after being drafted following the Isles' first Cup and making the team in the 1984–85 season—was off to play for a true contender.

It took a few seasons, but Hrudey backstopped the Kings to the 1993 Cup Finals, where the Canadiens beat them in five games— three of which were overtime wins by Montreal. It also took some time to get over the Islanders trade and reconnect with Al Arbour, who had returned to the Islanders bench during that 1988–89 season after Terry Simpson was fired. "I did run into Al after I retired. I was a broadcaster; it was All-Star weekend, at the dinner

Hrudey takes care of business in goal during a 1988 game.

the night before the festivities," Hrudey said. "I sat beside Al, and I remember he said, 'Do you still hate me?' I may have teared up because I loved Al so much. I said, 'I never hated you.' At the time, he felt he had to be really stern with us, and I think he didn't want to be—it wasn't in his nature, I don't think…. It was kind of cool Al and I had that interaction for me to let [him] know what I truly thought of him."

Hrudey and Torrey never quite made up in the same way. The GM's job is tougher than the coach's in that regard; it has to be a business for a general manager to make it work. "I still respected him," Hrudey said. "I just didn't like what happened to me."

52 Charles Wang Hires Garth Snow

Charles Wang was the first to admit he knew almost nothing about hockey when he bought the Islanders in the spring of 2000. "I asked Mike [Milbury], 'What do you guys do at halftime?'" Wang said in 2016. "I'd gone to two hockey games in my life, never made it past the second period. I didn't have any idea. I remember that so vividly."

His approach to owning the team was just as unusual. When he kicked Milbury upstairs in 2006, he listened to those who told him to hire an experienced general manager. He went with Neil Smith, the onetime Islanders draft pick and scout who had led the Rangers to their only Stanley Cup in the last 80 years.

But Wang insisted on leadership by committee, and Smith couldn't abide that. Wang fired Smith—who hadn't even signed his contract—after 40 days and immediately hired the guy everyone told him not to hire when he went through the process initially:

his backup goalie. "I went with another general manager, but I picked Garth first," Wang told *Newsday* a decade later in his last interview as majority owner. "And at the last minute, I chickened out. Because everybody was hounding me—this guy, that guy, he has this experience. But I thought, *They're all part of the same club. They just rotate around the league, it seems.* I wanted another way of thinking.

"He saw the game as a player. And I love the man. That's the guy. But at the last minute, I thought, *If I bring him in, a backup goalie as my general manager, I'm going to get laughed out of town. I can't do it.*"

There were plenty of chuckles still. Snow had carved out a serviceable 12-year career as mostly a backup goalie for five teams, finishing his career with four seasons on the Island. When he knew he was retiring after the 2005–06 season, he thought he might try his hand at college athletics. Snow earned bachelor's and master's degrees in his five years at the University of Maine. "I thought maybe I'd be a coach or an athletic director," he told the *Athletic* in 2018. "I was going to play as long as I could and maybe turn in that direction."

When he threw his hat into the ring for the Islanders GM job, he was well prepared. It wasn't just his personality meshing with Wang's that got him to the top of the list. "I thought going from playing to managing, I knew the league better than any scout or manager at the time," he said in 2018. "I went from being on the ice, on the bench, at ice level, where you get a better appreciation for the talent, the character of teammates and guys you play against. There's a lot you see down there that you can't see in a press box. That's true even today. I was fortunate in that regard."

After the backlash subsided, Snow had to get to work—with perhaps the smallest front office in the league. Wang had already owned the team for six years. He was deep into planning for his Lighthouse Project to develop the area around the Coliseum; once that failed, Wang pulled back on the financial reins even more, forcing Snow to be creative with the roster even as he tried a complete rebuild starting in 2009. "Don't forget the constraints he was working under," Wang said in 2016. "It's not like we were a big team."

Wang stuck by Snow until the end of his ownership tenure, which covered just four playoff appearances in 11 seasons. They were as friendly as any owner-GM combo around and could be found playing pickup basketball outside of the Iceworks practice rink in Syosset during the summer—an incredible sight, the 6'4" Snow and the 5'7" Wang squaring off against Islanders coaches or employees. "I always made sure to be on Garth's team," Wang said. "I'm no dummy."

53 The 2009 Draft: It Was Always Tavares

Garth Snow knew from April 14, 2009, that the Islanders would be picking first overall in the most consequential draft for the franchise in nearly a decade. He also knew, barring any unforeseen events between that night and June 26 in Montreal when he would be announcing that first pick, that the Islanders were taking John Tavares. "You always want to keep your options open," Snow said. "There's people who will say right away, 'We're taking this guy,' because they want the player to be excited about his new team. We felt we were going to take John, but there was still a process to go through."

That process meant Snow had Tavares, Victor Hedman, and Matt Duchene to Long Island for spring visits. They were the clear top three draft picks that year: Duchene, a skilled center; Hedman, a hulking but smooth-skating defenseman; and Tavares, the prodigy who got to the OHL at 15 and scored 72 goals in that league as a 16-year-old.

There were dinners on the Island with the three prospects. But for Tavares, there was more. Because Snow knew he was likely taking the star center, Tavares spent a weekend at Snow's house. They played golf and watched some playoff hockey. "Just sitting down and talking with him, seeing how he watched a game and what he thought, it was a real window into what kind of young man he was," Snow said. "My kids were little, and he jumped right in with them. It was partly to see how he handled himself and partly to help him see what we were about."

Snow had been GM for three years by then and had inherited nearly all of his scouting staff from Mike Milbury. There were a few on that staff who were pushing Snow in a different direction than Tavares, which is part of the reason Snow didn't tip his hat about the pick to anyone except a few confidants on his staff—he used the run-up to that draft to weed out some staffers he felt weren't making the right call on the top pick.

And there were some curious leaks. *Newsday*, the only outlet that covered the Isles regularly then, had a couple of stories in the weeks and days before the draft that the Isles were going to select Duchene; the nerves that rippled through the draft party crowd of fans at the Coliseum that night were palpable, especially given what had happened nine years earlier with the first overall pick: Milbury dealt Roberto Luongo the night before and drafted Rick DiPietro, who was in 2009 still struggling to play through injury.

But Snow had his mind made up long before. He, owner Charles Wang, and his top scouts strode to the podium in the Bell Centre with only one thought in mind: *We're making the right call.*

"You can look back now that John didn't stay with the Islanders and Hedman's won a Cup [and think] that maybe it wasn't the right choice, but this is a long way out," Snow said. "For nine years John gave the Islanders everything he had and made our team better."

On the podium, Snow whispered in Tavares's ear to ease the tension, bringing out a big laugh from the top pick. "I told him the happiest guys on the Island were the pros at my golf club," Snow said. "All the money he'd be spending on lessons after how awful he played."

54 John Tonelli and the Fire That Never Went Out

The most recent jerseys to go to the Coliseum rafters—ones you'll see at UBS Arena, naturally—went up fewer than two years ago. John Tonelli's No. 27 being "retired" (Anders Lee still wears it, but he'll be the last Islander to do so) on February 21, 2020, was more than three decades in the making. JT was a firebrand of a forward when he played, one of the lesser-known but still crucial members of the dynasty core. And he was the first to leave—a day that stayed with Tonelli so long it took years before he was able to come back and be celebrated.

Tonelli was one of the more intense Islanders of the Cup era. He told the *New York Times* in 1982 that he'd had migraines every game day since he was a preteen. "The doctors told me it was from being nervous and being intense," he said.

When he joined the Islanders before the 1978–79 season, that intensity was easy to spot right away. He was labeled as a worker, a lunch-pail sort of guy, but in addition to his ability to dig pucks out and never give up on a play, he figured in some pretty big goals. It was Tonelli, of course, who set up Bob Nystrom for the

Cup-clinching goal in 1980. The biggest goals he scored as an Islander were likely the tying and winning goals in Game 5 against the upstart Penguins in the first round in 1982 after Pittsburgh nearly pulled off a rally from 2–0 down in the best-of-five. He tied that game with fewer than three minutes to go in regulation and won it in OT with a typical Tonelli effort.

And Tonelli could handle himself in a starring role, never more so than in 1984–85, when he posted a 100-point season playing mostly on a line with Brent Sutter and Mike Bossy. "I hate being characterized as just a digger," he said in 1982. "It makes me so mad. I'm other things; I can score goals and make plays too."

By the 1985–86 season, he was looking to be paid like a top player—he was the first Islander under Bill Torrey's reign to hold out from camp, coming back after three weeks to sign a deal worth a reported $350,000 a year, up from $225,000. Even though some around the team (Torrey included) felt Tonelli's play suffered after the holdout, he still had 68 points in 74 games as the trade deadline approached.

On March 11, 1986, the group that had just two years earlier gotten to a fifth-straight Cup Finals was gobsmacked by the news: Tonelli was traded to the Flames for Steve Konroyd and Rich Kromm. As it happened, Calgary was on the Island for a game that night, so the players sat in stunned silence as the teams' equipment managers wheeled the players' gear between locker rooms at the Coliseum.

"That's as close as 16 guys could be," Denis Potvin told the *Athletic* in 2018. "There [were] a lot of changes, which I didn't like, of course, and JT was one of the first casualties. Things happened that were just completely not understandable—this incredibly bad plan to send all these champions away. Terrible plan."

Tonelli played that night in a red No. 27 jersey. "I never should have played," he said recently. It was a bitter pill to swallow but a sign of things to come for the Islanders—and a decent restart for Tonelli. It was his Flames that reached the 1986 Cup Finals, losing to the Canadiens in five games. The Islanders continued to dismantle the old core, with Al Arbour retiring after the 1985–86 season and Torrey leaving Clark Gillies and Bob Bourne exposed in the 1986 waiver draft to be snapped up by the Sabres and Kings, respectively.

Tonelli played six more seasons in the NHL, including three with the Kings and Wayne Gretzky. After starting his pro career with the Houston Aeros in the World Hockey Association, Tonelli ended up being the only player in hockey history who scored goals assisted by Gordie Howe and Gretzky.

It was decades before he was coaxed back to the Coliseum. Potvin, Bossy, Bryan Trottier, Nystrom, Gillies—all had their jerseys retired over a 10-year span in the 1990s and early 2000s. But Tonelli, for whom a Facebook page was created in the 2010s to plead with the Isles to honor him, remained at arm's length until current owners Scott Malkin and Jon Ledecky did their best to bring him back to the fold.

It culminated with the ceremony to honor him a few weeks before the pandemic shut things down. "Never in my wildest dreams did I think this would happen," Tonelli said that day. "Ever since I got the call [from Lou Lamoriello], I've been in a different mood. It's just been constant excitement and a great feeling."

55 Draft Floor Wizardry: The 2015 Draft

In the 2014–15 season, the Islanders looked like what Garth Snow and Jack Capuano had envisioned: a team that played fast, rolled lines well, and had a good mix of young, homegrown talent and veterans that they rode to a 101-point season, the franchise's best showing since 1983–84.

As they went into the off-season, one thing was missing: their first-round pick in the 2015 draft, to be held in June at the Florida Panthers' arena in Sunrise. Snow's trade in October 2013, when he sent Matt Moulson and two draft picks to the Sabres for Thomas Vanek, was a bust through that dismal 2013–14 season, and here it was still haunting the Isles.

Snow had the option to surrender either his 2014 or 2015 first-rounder and held off until 2015, when it was the 21st overall pick. At least that part of the trade was the right call, because the Isles picked fifth in 2014.

But here was Snow, who had been trying to rebuild the Islanders for years through the draft, stuck without anything to do on the draft floor that Friday night as teams jockeyed around him in one of the most talent-laden first rounds of the 21st century. He had a plan. The Oilers had yet again won the lottery and did it at just the right time; their prize for getting the Ping-Pong ball alignment in their favor was Connor McDavid, a generational talent. The Sabres got bumped to No. 2, and their consolation prize was Jack Eichel, the best American player in a few years.

Snow had his eye further down the first round, on a talented, confident kid from suburban Vancouver who had struggled with a knee injury in his draft year. If there was a way to pick Mathew

Barzal in the middle of the first round, Snow was ready to pounce with a deal so lopsided it's amazing it even happened.

Edmonton was looking for a defenseman heading into that draft. "When Dougie Hamilton went from Boston to Calgary the night before, that's when my phone started ringing," Snow said. The Oilers held the 16th pick in addition to the top choice and were willing to part with it for a defenseman who could help them sooner than later. Snow dangled Griffin Reinhart, the fourth pick from 2012 who had yet to develop into a consistent pro player. Reinhart had been a star in Edmonton in juniors, and the Oilers were interested.

"We weren't doing it unless Barzal was there [at 16]," Snow said. "Our scouts were really high on him; we had him rated top 10 on our board. So as the middle of the draft unfolded, we were just hoping." The pivotal stretch comprised picks 13 through 15, all held by the Bruins. They had a first-year general manager, Don Sweeney, who the month prior had taken over for Peter Chiarelli—ironically then the Oilers GM who was waiting to see what his old team would do before completing a deal with Snow.

The Bruins took their time with all three picks, but none of them were Barzal. Snow pounced, getting back into the first round and getting Chiarelli to surrender the 33rd overall pick as well.

The Islanders took Barzal, then packaged the 33rd and 72nd picks to trade with the Lightning for the 28th pick and selected Anthony Beauvillier. Without a first-rounder entering the night, Snow had finagled two—and, in hindsight, provided the Isles with a pair of top-six forwards as their young foundation for years to come. "Obviously you look back now and see what those two have become, and you're happy you made the right call," he said. "Even at that first camp when you saw Barzal on the ice, just the skill, you felt pretty good about it."

So did his scouting staff. In the team suite at the draft after that first round ended, a scout grabbed this writer's shoulders and screamed, "Can you believe that? Someone's getting fucking fired for sure!"

56 2/11/11: Fight Night at the Coli

Happy memories aren't so plentiful from 2007 to 2012, when the Isles missed the playoffs for five straight seasons, the second-longest streak in team history. They were bad enough in 2008–09 to draft John Tavares first overall, but even with Tavares in the fold, his first three seasons were a struggle. So perhaps it's somewhat understandable that most Islanders fans' favorite night from that downtime came from exacting a bit of revenge—on the scoreboard, sure, but mostly with their fists.

February 11, 2011, was Fight Night at the Coliseum. Everyone who played in that one remembers it well. "Everyone grew an inch, everyone was 10 pounds heavier after that," Bruno Gervais told the *Athletic* in 2019. "We'd taken a few punches, not the literal kind, that year. I think we told everyone that night that we weren't going to be pushed around."

"We kept some fans on board with that one," Zenon Konopka said.

First, the background: As the 2010–11 season dragged into February, the Islanders were already out of the playoff picture; a 1–17–3 slide through November and December saw to that. Jack Capuano replaced Scott Gordon and the Islanders showed some life over the last half of the season, but they were still mired in the bottom of the Atlantic Division playing out the string.

Then came a February 2 trip to Pittsburgh. Max Talbot, the Penguins winger, delivered a borderline hit to Blake Comeau that sent the Islander forward to the locker room with what was later diagnosed as a concussion. It was the sort of hit that even a few years later would have drawn a penalty and possibly even a suspension, but it got neither.

At the end of the night, Rick DiPietro, who was at the tail end of his Islanders career and his years-long battle with knee problems, got into it. He bumped Penguins agitator Matt Cooke in the waning minutes, initiating a scrum; Penguins goalie Brent Johnson motioned down the ice to see if DiPietro wanted to fight, and Rick was willing. "Here's Ricky. The knock on him is maybe he's a little soft, and he squares off. We were impressed," Konopka said. "And he chose the wrong door."

Johnson decked DiPietro with one punch, breaking several bones in DiPietro's face to prematurely end another frustrating season for him. As Johnson skated to the bench, the cameras caught Marc-Andre Fleury, the Penguins' top goalie, laughing on the bench. As if the indignity weren't enough, there was that at the end of a 3–0 loss. "That didn't sit well with us," said Matt Martin, who was a rookie that year.

Nine days later the two teams met again at the Coliseum. In the interim, the Islanders had made sure they were prepared—Micheal Haley was called up from Bridgeport and Trevor Gillies was back in the lineup. "During warm-ups, I'm not sure Gillies even touched a puck," then–Penguins forward Joe Vitale said.

On the scoreboard, the game was extremely satisfying for the Islanders. By the time Haley scored his first NHL goal—a pretty breakaway move to beat Johnson—at 3:46 of the second, it was 6–0 Islanders. The downside to such a rout was that the nonsense was about to begin in earnest. Haley and Gillies had played their parts, each with a first-period fight—Haley fought Pens veteran

Craig Adams and Gillies squared off with former Islander enforcer Eric Godard.

But soon after Haley's goal, the Islanders started to go after the Penguins they held responsible. Martin grabbed Talbot near center ice and sucker-punched him, drawing a huge crowd. Martin, Josh Bailey, and Travis Hamonic were all ejected; Deryk Engelland, Mike Rupp, and Pascal Dupuis got the gate for the Penguins. And the wildness was just getting started.

Fleury had replaced Johnson for a spell in the second, but Johnson came back in just before the Islanders made it 8–2 heading to the third. Early in that third period, Gillies delivered a high hit that clearly concussed Eric Tangradi, but Gillies threw a few punches as Tangradi fell to the ice. That drew a crowd and bodies were everywhere. In the pile, Haley found Talbot. "It was like, 'Hello! Just the guy I was looking for,'" Haley said.

All four officials were pulling players away, and one of the referees simply sent Haley to the penalty box alone. As Haley skated there, he glanced down the ice to see Johnson gesturing to him. "I'm thinking, *Maybe I can get a couple shots in on this guy,*" Johnson said. "And if they wanted to kick me out, fine—no one cared where the puck was that night anyway."

Haley got a couple pops in on Johnson as the crowd roared, and Godard raced from the Penguins bench to interrupt. More players got tossed, including Gillies, who was seen on the game footage yelling at what everyone thought was a clearly injured Tangradi. Turns out Gillies was jawing with longtime Penguins trainer Chris Stewart. "It looked bad for Gillies, but their trainer was the one who got it going," Konopka said. "This little Chihuahua is yapping at a pit bull! And right after Gillies was in a scrum."

There were several more players tossed by the time the final horn mercifully sounded. A 9–3 Islanders win with 346 penalty minutes and barely more than a dozen players combined on the teams' benches. One of them was Talbot, who got ragdolled around all night and never got thrown out. He did, however, get a birthday present (Talbot turned 27 that day) from his longtime friend Gervais. "We always got each other a nice bottle of Scotch, something like that," Gervais said. "I felt bad that the guys kept going after him."

"I was pissed!" Talbot said. "I told him, 'You got me a gift? You should have got me a fucking wheelchair.' That was a strange night. I can't blame them. They were upset about the last game and they were having a bad season. I might have done the same thing."

The aftermath kept the story of that night alive. Penguins owner Mario Lemieux—who had heavyweights such as Godard, Engelland, and Rupp on that roster, not to mention the oft-suspended Cooke—wrote an open letter to the NHL decrying the Islanders' behavior after the league handed down suspensions two days later: Gillies received nine games and Martin got four, and the Islanders were fined $100,000; Godard got an automatic 10-game suspension for leaving the bench.

"It was painful to watch the game I love turn into a sideshow like that," Lemieux wrote in his statement. "The NHL had a chance to send a clear and strong message that those kinds of actions are unacceptable and embarrassing to the sport. It failed. We must make it clear that those kinds of actions will not be tolerated and will be met with meaningful disciplinary action. If the events relating to Friday night reflect the state of the league, I need to rethink whether I want to be a part of it."

Konopka spoke up in Ottawa the next night when asked about Lemieux's statement. "TSN shoves a mic in my face: 'What did you think of Lemieux's comments?'" he said. "I said, 'Mario Lemieux should think about the guys who protected him.' I said, which was true, 'I've got a Mario poster on my bedroom door, and I'm going to rip it down because I've lost respect for him.'

"Sure enough, it was the slowest day in Canadian sports ever—they lead with me taking my poster down. I was getting death threats on Facebook! 'No respect for Lemieux. You don't understand.' I think I know him pretty well since I had his poster on my wall! It was more about him needing to think back about how he had plenty of guys to protect him."

It was yet another chapter in the Islanders-Penguins rivalry, one that may not have had the excitement of the 1975 or 1993 playoffs but meant a lot to a generation of success-starved fans.

57 Al Arbour's Lessons

When the Islanders were on the rise but not all the way there, from 1975 to 1979, each playoff disappointment was met with a year-end question from Al Arbour. "He'd always say, 'What did you learn this year?'" Bryan Trottier said. "He didn't just want you to head off without thinking about what you'd done, what the team had done. I'd try to come up with something and he would give his view—a very honest, direct one. Sometimes you didn't appreciate it.

"He was such a strong presence for me, and I really liked that. He was like my dad in that way—if you think your dad is wrong, he's still your dad. If I thought Al was wrong, he's still Al, and I had faith in him."

Arbour was ahead of his time as a coach in many ways. With the help of medical trainer Ron Waske, Arbour insisted on conditioning being as big a part of training camp as any other part of the Islanders' system. "'I don't care if the roof falls in! You keep skating until I say stop!' That was Al," Denis Potvin said. "We learned long before we won our first Stanley Cup that if we did the things Al wanted us to do, we could be successful. And conditioning was a big part of that. We could skate all night."

There was also Arbour being one of the early adopters of video scouting—with some off-the-books help breaking down the tape. "Claire [Al's wife] would record the games, and Jay, Al's son, would break them down," Jiggs McDonald said. "Jay's job went to Butch Goring later on when Butch was a player-assistant. And there was so much credit to Al for being a kind of sports psychologist, which a lot of coaches nowadays need to be. His biggest asset there was Claire—at that time coaches' wives were welcome in the family room. If there was a colicky kid, relatives visiting from out of town, any distractions, Al knew because Claire knew. She was the mother hen to the wives and Al was the father figure to the guys."

Brent Sutter was a 19-year-old rookie during the 1982 play-offs, part of a team going for its third Stanley Cup. He learned the hard way about Arbour's tougher side. "We were playing the Rangers, Game 1 of the [Patrick Division finals] at home," Sutter said. "I was coming out of our zone, last one up the ice, and Rob McClanahan took the puck off me, went down, and scored. The Rangers won that game, and I didn't see a regular shift for the rest of the playoffs. I played, but I wasn't a regular, maybe three to four shifts. Al never said a word to me.

"Then in Game 2 of the final against Vancouver, we're up late, he sends me over the boards for a power play. Games 3 and 4 he played me till I dropped. I hurt the team—he was sending a message to me that that can't happen."

In the joyous aftermath of the third Cup, equipment manager Jim Pickard pulled Sutter aside. "He said, 'Pup, Radar [Arbour] wants to see you outside,'" Sutter said. "So I go out in the hallway and he's there. He's a big guy with broad shoulders. He twists my T-shirt around—he's not exactly choking me, but I don't really know what to think. He gets six inches from my face and says, 'What did you learn through all this?' I'm stunned. He says, 'I'll tell you what you learned: You're going to be the mentally strongest player in the league and you're going to play a long time.' Then he turned around and walked off. And he was right."

Even in his later years behind the bench, Arbour never lost the ability to connect with his players and make them understand what he was looking for.

Tom Fitzgerald split his time between the minors and the Islanders during his first three seasons in the pros, not quite able to establish himself on Arbour's Islanders teams of the early 1990s. After the 1990–91 season, his sit-down with Arbour was the most important conversation Fitzgerald had about his burgeoning career. "He was the one who sat me down and told me what kind of career I could have if I wanted to," Fitzgerald said. "My first two years in the AHL, I scored close to 60 goals, put up some pretty good numbers, won a Calder Cup. I figured I could slide into a top-six role. He saw me differently. He kind of molded me into this role I played the rest of my career. He sat me down after year three and said, 'Did you notice the way I used you? I threw you out there as a second center, D-zone starts, played against some top lines.'

"He just said, 'If you want to play in this league—if you can be physical, be versatile, be trusted, win faceoffs—you can play a long time. If you think you're getting screwed, you're not going to play very long.' I left that office and I reinvented myself. Those are the greatest words of advice I was given as a player."

58 Pat LaFontaine and the 1990s Decline

As the dynasty years receded from view and the dynasty core players peeled off either through waivers or retirement, one star was left: Pat LaFontaine. His dramatic goal to win the Easter Epic in the 1987 playoffs stamped him as a prime-time player at age 22, and he carried it through the next four years, scoring 187 goals from 1987 to 1991. Only Mike Bossy had a better four-year run in franchise history. "That was a moment that helped push me," he said of the four-overtime winner against the Caps. "It gives you confidence to go through something like that."

But the franchise was starting to find itself in a different place. The Islanders won the Patrick Division in 1987–88—the last division title they've won—but fell in six games to an upstart Devils team in the opening round. Al Arbour returned to the bench midway through 1988–89, but the Isles managed just one playoff appearance the next three years, and it was an incredible downer.

The hated Rangers picked off the Isles in five games in the 1990 playoffs, and LaFontaine suffered a scary concussion in Game 1, his head bouncing off the Madison Square Garden ice. Then an insane Rangers fans rocked the ambulance that was trying to take LaFontaine to a New York City hospital for examination.

The next season revealed to the hockey world what Bill Torrey and Al Arbour had been trying to stave off: John Pickett, who saved the Islanders in 1978 and helped support the dynasty, had moved to Florida five years earlier and begun closing the open wallet that allowed Torrey to keep his team intact and happy.

Torrey bought out the final two years of Bryan Trottier's contract, leaving captain Brent Sutter as the last link to the Stanley Cup era.

LaFontaine, the team's unquestioned star, had been approached by Torrey—seemingly at Pickett's behest—to discuss an extension on a contract that had one year (and an option) left at $425,000 per season. Red Wings captain Steve Yzerman had just inked a deal worth $1.5 million per season, and LaFontaine's camp saw that as a good comparison; Torrey, showing a bit of his old-school mentality, did not.

LaFontaine walked out the week before the 1990–91 season began, returning four days later. He still led the Islanders in scoring that year, but the impasse made him understand that things were not what they once were with an Islanders team that was also in disarray on the ice. "I've come to the great realization that there is a business side to this job I love, and in the past seven months I've come to see where I stand in the view of those two people," LaFontaine said of Torrey and Pickett in a *New York Times* interview in December 1990. "Let's just say our views are different: Now I'm playing for my coach, my teammates, and the fans, but that's it. The obligation ends there."

Torrey called it "Bad Bill vs. Nice Patty," an allusion to LaFontaine's all-American good looks and eager personality. But Torrey was basically covering for his owner, who would be revealed in the spring of 1991 to be looking for a buyer for the Islanders. Pickett wasn't able to go to as many games and wanted to put an expansion team closer to his Palm Beach home.

That didn't matter to LaFontaine, whose dissatisfaction grew through the ugly 1990–91 season. His agent, Don Meehan, revealed months later that LaFontaine had requested a trade right before Pickett announced he was selling the team. "Pat did not want them to construe the request for a trade as a means of eliciting a contract offer with more money from the Islanders," Meehan said. "He simply does not want any of their money anymore. There is no offer they could make that would interest him…. Pat won't accept any contract if the ownership hasn't changed."

A too-late offer of four years at $1.5 million per came in, but LaFontaine took a principled stand. He felt he was lied to by Pickett and Torrey, and there was no going back. "What Bill and Al built stands the test of time," LaFontaine says now. "There were difficult moments at the end, but they were difficult because I loved being an Islander, being part of what they built."

Torrey traded LaFontaine (and Sutter) on October 26, 1991. They were decent trades, considering the public animosity that had built up. Pierre Turgeon, Benoit Hogue, Dave McLlwain, and Uwe Krupp came from Buffalo for LaFontaine, Randy Hillier, and Randy Wood; and Steve Thomas came from Chicago for Sutter. All four of those new players would figure prominently in the Isles' brief 1993 revival.

"I took a stand for my principles, for being honest, for being treated the way [I] deserved to be treated," LaFontaine said after the trade. "Promises were made that were broken by this ownership, and they knew it got to the point where money was no longer the issue with me and mistrust was; I've come out of this a lot wiser, and I'm just excited to be going to a new team for the second half of my career."

It marked the beginning of a new chapter in Islanders history—one many fans would just as soon forget.

59 10/26/91: Severing the Last Dynasty Tie

The headline deal from October 26, 1991, was Pat LaFontaine being traded to the Sabres in a multiplayer deal. LaFontaine was a true star in the league by that point and wanted to be paid like one. The Islanders' deteriorating ownership situation—with longtime principal owner John Pickett looking to sell at least a healthy interest in a team that was a far cry from what it had been a few years earlier—led to some broken promises between LaFontaine and Bill Torrey and severed bonds that could not be mended.

And yet, with a star holding out at the beginning of another disappointing season, Torrey managed to swing a deal that benefited both teams, bringing in first-line players in Pierre Turgeon and Benoit Hogue as well as defenseman Uwe Krupp.

There was another longtime Islander dealt away that same day, and that one was more emotional for the parties involved and the Islanders fans who had grown to love their team during the dynasty years: Brent Sutter, captain for four-plus seasons, was sent to the Hawks. He was the last Cup winner on the roster, leaving only Torrey and Al Arbour as links to the past glory—and Torrey would be pushed out 10 months later.

"We were choked up, Bill and I," Sutter said. "It was a tough talk, even though I knew it was coming. That was it for the Cup years; I was the last one."

Sutter and Torrey had had numerous talks since the 1990–91 trade deadline. That season was the Isles' worst since their second year of existence, and Sutter, under no illusions about where the franchise was headed, put his Long Island house up for sale before he headed to the Canada Cup in Montreal that summer. While there, he and Torrey spoke again and Sutter reconsidered. "Bill flew in and met with me, sat and had a really good talk. He said 'Leave it be,'" Sutter said. "So I took the house off the market, thought, *Maybe this can get worked out, ownership [can] dig in a little bit, change some things here.* But I got back and Bill said, 'Things aren't going to change here.' I played six games. Two days before the trade, Bill asked me to give him a list of four teams I'd like to play for. I did that, and he came to me the next day—we were actually playing an exhibition against the U.S. Olympic team—and Bill said, 'We're not going to dress you here, just in case.'"

Between periods of that game, Torrey called Sutter down from a suite at the Coliseum to deliver the news: Sutter and Brad Lauer were going to Chicago for Adam Creighton and Steve Thomas. But the trade hadn't been approved yet by Hawks owner Rocky Wirtz, who was having a minor operation that night. "Then the next morning my wife brings in the paper, and there it is on the *Newsday* cover—I've been traded," Sutter said. "No going back then."

As hard as it was to get the official word from Torrey, who'd drafted Sutter 17th overall in the 1980 draft, the same round and slot as Torrey had drafted Brent's brother Duane a year earlier, the conversation with Arbour was torture for Sutter and his coach. "Al treated me like a son," Sutter said. "He knew when to push, when not to—there were mornings, days of games on the road, we'd have a coffee and we never talked about the game, the team; he just wanted to talk. It was a lot of stress for him too, to have gone from where we'd been to where we were.

"Al's office was a long, narrow office. I walk[ed] in and the room was completely black, all the lights were off except two right above his desk. He was facing his wall unit behind his desk; all I could see was the top of his head. I sat down, and he didn't turn his chair right away. Then he turned his chair and he was crying. And heck, I broke down too—that was a really tough conversation. We both knew that was it; the Cup years were officially done."

Sutter played six more years in Chicago then began a coaching career at the junior and NHL levels that has spanned two decades. He's also a GM of the Red Deer Rebels in the WHL. "Every day I think of something Bill or Al said to me, taught me," he said. "Until the days they both passed, I wanted nothing more than to hope I made them proud. They gave me the opportunity."

60 Ziggy Palffy and a New Low in the Late 1990s

John Pickett finally found a buyer for the Islanders. Seven years after he declared his intention to sell—after a failed deal with Cablevision founder Charles Dolan, after the Gang of Four nearly wrecked the brand and, of course, after the John Spano insanity—Pickett found an interested party.

The group, headed by onetime Arizona Coyotes co-owner Steven Gluckstern and the Milstein brothers, Howard and Ed, bought the Isles for $195 million, with the deal finalized in February 1998—during yet another aimless Isles season, though at least this one didn't feature the team wearing Fisherman jerseys.

Gluckstern and his group saw the most potential in the land around Nassau Coliseum, but they were eager to give GM Mike Milbury the money to turn things around—Milbury told reporters the team had operated during the 1996–97 season with a $20 million budget as the Spano mess unfolded.

Once the new owners got control, however, they quickly realized the political landscape in Nassau County was a nightmare. Developing the area around the Coliseum was no easy task, and things quickly devolved—the owners asked the county to declare the Coliseum unfit, moved the team's employees out of their Coliseum offices, and began a 26-month nightmare that, somehow, made Islanders fans feel even worse about their team.

"They gave Milbury no chance," Howie Rose said. "I remember being outside the locker room one night before a game, and David Seldin, the team president under those owners, stopped to talk. He told us, 'I could give you the team right now for nothing and it'd be a bad deal for you.' This wasn't even a year into them owning it! How'd they make such a bad deal? That regime is under-reported when it comes to all the stooges who dragged the Islanders down to the depths."

You'd think a con man trying to buy the team would be rock-bottom, especially since it happened just a couple years earlier. Spano, at least to Islanders fans' eyes, wanted badly to be the owner and had good ideas; Gluckstern and the Milsteins simply gave up and ordered Milbury to sell anything that wasn't nailed down.

So Mad Mike obliged, making dozens of trades in those two years. Including the selling off of one of the 10 most talented players ever to wear an Islanders uniform.

Ziggy Palffy was the 26th pick of the 1991 draft—another Bill Torrey selection—and worked his way up through the Islanders system. A dynamic offensive player, he was the type of skater and scorer the Isles lacked. "He didn't love the defensive side of the game," Rose said, "but he was a goal scorer. That's all he ever wanted to be."

Palffy had a tremendous run from 1995 to 1998, posting seasons of 87, 90, and 87 points on teams that, frankly, stunk. He and Milbury, who was coach and GM for the majority of those seasons, didn't always see eye to eye, but there was no doubt who was the brightest star on a dismal squad.

So Palffy's decision to stay in Slovakia without a new contract at the start of the 1998–99 season wasn't a surprise, given the tight-fisted attitude of ownership. Palffy wanted a contract akin to the Leafs' Mats Sundin ($6.8 million per year); Milbury was offering something closer to $4.5 million per year. Palffy settled in December for five years and $26 million.

The stalemate gave the Isles world two things. The first was one of Milbury's best-ever one-liners, delivered about Paul Kraus, Palffy's agent. "It's too bad he lives in the city. He's depriving some small village of a pretty good idiot," Milbury said.

Palffy and his mullet in 1997.

The second thing was a trade proposal so lopsided that the league had to step in. As we know now, Palffy was dealt to the Kings on June 20, 1999, a week before the draft. Bryan Smolinski also went to L.A. Olli Jokinen, Josh Green, Mathieu Biron, and the Kings' first-round pick, No. 8 overall, went to the Islanders. That's a bad trade. But it wasn't the original one. Milbury was under pressure from ownership to get out from under the contract almost immediately. And the Isles' next-door neighbors came calling.

The Islanders made a deal with the Rangers, then owned by Cablevision, to send Palffy and Rich Pilon to the big city for Todd Harvey, Niklas Sundstrom, Patrick Leahy, the 11th pick in the 1999 draft, and cash. That last part was the key—Gluckstern and Milstein wanted Cablevision to increase the annual payments to the Islanders for broadcasting the games as a way around the NHL's $2.5 million cap on cash changing hands in trades. There was also a proposal to partner with Cablevision on financing for a new Islanders arena, as Gluckstern's group had been feuding with SMG, owners of the onerous lease on the building.

Unsurprisingly the Rangers and the NHL washed their hands of that deal. So Milbury turned around and dealt Palffy to the Kings and took an unheard-of $12 million budget into the 1999–2000 season, which was (also unsurprisingly) another in a long string of awful Islanders seasons.

But at least by the end of it there was yet another ownership change.

61 The Maddest Mad Mike Moment of All

Mike Milbury's tenure could fill half the chapters in this book, and it still might not be enough words to describe his decade as Islanders GM and coach. Milbury came in as coach in 1995 under the aegis of the Gang of Four minority ownership partners and endured through the John Spano fiasco, the Gluckstern/Milstein era of penny-pinching, and right through the first half dozen years of the Charles Wang era.

There were many wisecracks, a few intense moments, and trades. Lots and lots of trades—88 of them to be exact, from the throwaways to blockbusters. But nothing defined Milbury's tenure like the events of June 24, 2000—a day that set the course for the next decade of the Islanders.

The Isles had won the draft lottery. In 2000 that meant they moved up four spots from No. 5 to No. 1, the first time the Islanders had the first overall pick since 1973, when Bill Torrey selected Denis Potvin and changed the course of the franchise.

Milbury always thought big. He'd had plenty of top picks in the previous four drafts for which he was GM but never No. 1. With a potential franchise goalie ready for the NHL in Roberto Luongo and several other good, young pieces, the top pick from among talented forwards Dany Heatley or Marian Gaborik could have put the Isles on a path out of the dark days of the 1990s. Wang had just purchased the team and was evaluating whether to spend big. Milbury decided his big move was to ditch his previous plans and build around the latest, hottest young thing: Rick DiPietro, a New Englander like Milbury, with a lot of confidence and goaltending skills to match. "I think Mike just fell in love with Ricky, plain and simple," Howie Rose said.

So that day in Calgary became a blur of moves ahead of selecting DiPietro. First, Milbury unloaded his other goalie, 25-year-old Kevin Weekes, who had played 36 games in the 1999–2000 season. Weekes and a second-rounder went to Tampa for the Lightning's first-round pick, which was fifth overall—Milbury gave himself

Five Other Mad Mike Moments

1. *Trading for Linden.* On February 6, 1998, Milbury traded his young captain, Bryan McCabe, and another young Islander with potential, Todd Bertuzzi, to the Canucks for their disgruntled captain, Trevor Linden. Milbury immediately had the *C* sewn on Linden's jersey and gave the 10-year NHL vet a $2.5 million contract, greenlit by incoming owners Steven Gluckstern and Howard and Ed Milstein.

   But the owners quickly soured on crazy ideas like spending more than the bare minimum, and Linden was an ex-Islander a year later. McCabe and Bertuzzi both went on to play more than 1,100 games.

2. *The Yashin deal.* At the time, on the 2001 NHL Draft floor in Florida, it was a boon to the Isles: Milbury swung a deal for unhappy Senators captain Alexei Yashin, one of the elite players in the league. The cost was a hulking young defenseman with some promise and the Isles' first-round pick, second overall.

   How was Milbury to know that the player he gave up and the player drafted with that pick would still be playing 20 years later? Zdeno Chara became a force in Ottawa, then a champion in Boston; Jason Spezza's distinguished career carried him through 1,100 games over 18 seasons.

3. *Calling Green a "gutless puke."* The day before Milbury traded McCabe and Bertuzzi, he swung a six-player deal with the Ducks, sending five-year Islanders vet Travis Green away for not much return. Green's first meeting with the Isles the next December resulted in a hit that left Kenny Jonsson concussed and Milbury seeing red.

   "He's a gutless puke, that's what Travis Green is," Milbury said. "That's why he doesn't wear an Islander uniform anymore. And he gets paid way too much, but that's my fault."

another chance to draft an impact forward, at the very least. "I actually got a call about an hour before to tell me they had traded Kevin Weekes, so I thought, *Oh, good, I'll have a chance to start this year,*" Luongo told the *Vancouver Sun* in 2013. But Luongo received a second call, this one to inform him that Milbury had traded him

Green retorted: "Oh, Mike. some things never change. He knows everything. Maybe he's right. Nothing surprises me at all that that guy says. I've seen it all, and I know everyone else has. I'll just leave it at that…. I'm not going to dip down to Mike's level."

4. *Let's go to the videotape!* During the epic 2002 first-round playoff series, Milbury corralled the reporters who cover the Islanders on the off-day between Games 2 and 3 and presented a video compilation of various uncalled offenses by the Leafs in the opening two games, both Toronto wins. In particular he singled out McCabe, his former captain, for the "can opener"—a defensive move where McCabe put his stick between an opponent's legs and shoved the player down.

"I have pretty much no comment on it. I'm not going to get into a pissing match with him," McCabe said. "All I can say is he didn't seem to mind when I played for him."

The late Pat Quinn, the Leafs coach in 2002, seemed to enjoy the back-and-forth. "There weren't a lot of people who liked or respected how he played," he said of Milbury's brawling style as a Bruin in the 1970s.

5. *Milbury's first training camp.* The Islanders brought Milbury on as coach prior to the 1995–96 season, and he made his mark—quite literally by jabbing his finger in the chest of the Isles' No. 2 overall pick, Wade Redden, after the teenager didn't follow Milbury's instructions. "It kind of shocked me," Redden said at the time. "But maybe that's what I needed. He's definitely the boss out there. I think maybe the other guys saw that and worked a little harder."

Eh, unlikely. And once Milbury was named GM three months later, he sent Redden packing while he was back in juniors. The trade to Ottawa brought in Bryan Berard, who won the Calder Trophy as an Islander in 1996–97.

to the Panthers, along with center Olli Jokinen, for forwards Mark Parrish and Oleg Kvasha.

Milbury made one more deal that draft day, a decent one—he picked up Roman Hamrlik from the Oilers for Eric Brewer, yet another under-23 defenseman with a high ceiling. Hamrlik would be a workhorse for the Isles for the next four years.

The total remake was a bit astonishing considering all the young talent Milbury had on hand. "As dangerous as this might be, maybe Mad Mike has something going for him," Milbury said. "We have not made the playoffs in far too long. We need to get there. It's a roll of the dice a little bit."

DiPietro himself was a bit prescient that day: "Obviously, there's going to be a lot of pressure. Roberto Luongo will probably end up being a franchise goaltender with Florida. I enjoy the pressure."

Milbury was gleeful that night. At No. 5 he selected Raffi Torres, a skilled winger with a bit of an edge—more than a bit as his post-Islanders career unfolded, but he was too raw to have an impact even as the Islanders improved drastically with all of Milbury's moves prior to the 2001–02 season.

That may be the lasting image of the Draft Night 2000 Mad Mike madness: He was so sure he'd turned things around, yet it took another wave of trades to really put the Islanders in position to succeed after the 2001–02 season got underway.

Milbury had full faith that night in Calgary, though. "'We've suffered slings and arrows of critics over the years," he said. "We're a lot closer to a playoff spot today than we were yesterday. We've pushed ourselves ahead a couple of years.... We filled the holes we wanted to fill. It's a win-win day for us. We're doing a little dance over at the Islanders table.

"This is it. This is my job. My job is squarely on the line. If we're not a better team immediately, if we're not a very good team over the long haul, then off with the head."

We know that didn't happen for a few more years. And without the big trades and big spending from his new owner in the next off-season, the lingering effects of 2000 would have been even greater.

62 Wearing the *C*

When it comes to the Islanders and captains, there's "B.P." and "A.P." That's "Before Potvin" and "After Potvin," in case you needed an explainer. Denis Potvin was the longest-serving of the Isles' 15 captains and, of course, the captain who meant the most—he's got four Stanley Cups in those eight years and the other 14 captains have zero.

We've looked at Eddie Westfall (1972–77), the first Islanders captain. He transferred the *C* to then-22-year-old Clark Gillies (1977–79), who won the popular vote to become captain but got headaches from the stress of having to confront his teammates.

Potvin (1979–87) was the gold standard: confident, strong-willed, the best possible leader for the best possible team. "In the playoffs I never had to say too much," he said. "I'd say, 'Who wants it tonight?' And there'd be 20 guys calling out in response."

Let's go through the post-Potvin captains:

Brent Sutter (1987–91): This one was a surprise. With Potvin surrendering the *C* in advance of retirement at the end of 1987–88, most assumed the captaincy would go to Bryan Trottier, still going strong into his 13th Islanders season. But Bill Torrey was already remaking his team younger and went with the 25-year-old Sutter instead. "I was named captain, and that was hard on Bryan—rightly so," Sutter said. "I still understand it. He'd been a leader for a long time. But all these young players were coming in, the

175

makeup of the team was younger; they felt [it would be good] if they had someone closer in age to be their captain."

Outside of winning the Patrick Division in 1988, there weren't many good times during Sutter's captaincy—which ended early in the 1991–92 season when he was traded to Chicago.

Pat Flatley (1991–96): Named captain the day Sutter was dealt, Flatley was never a star in his dozen seasons on the Island but was the definition of "lead by example." He was not a flashy player by any means, but he provided great stability during an era when there was almost none outside the rink.

Bryan McCabe (1997–98): Like Gillies, McCabe was 22 when Mike Milbury tabbed him as captain after the Isles went through the 1996–97 season without one. McCabe had all the tools to be a leader, but in retrospect, the *C* wasn't good for McCabe mentally. "I put it all on me," McCabe said. "Being captain at 22, it just messed with my head. I just put too much pressure on myself to be the guy."

McCabe's five-month run as captain, the shortest in team history, ended with a February 6 trade to the Canucks for the next man to wear the *C* for the Isles.

Trevor Linden (1998–99): Linden had been the captain in Vancouver for more than six years already at age 27 when new Islanders owners Steven Gluckstern and Howard and Ed Milstein greenlit a Milbury move to acquire the big center, who returned from the 1998 Olympics and was immediately named the new Isles captain.

After another failed year in 1998–99 and ownership selling everything that wasn't nailed down, Linden was shipped out to the Canadiens. The merry-go-round of the *C* continued.

Kenny Jonsson (1999–2001): It's easy to forget one of the most underrated Islanders in team history was also captain for two of the worst seasons in team history. Jonsson had already trudged through three and a half awful years on the Island before being named captain just prior to 1999–2000, mercifully Gluckstern/ Milstein's last year owning the team that they had stripped bare.

Jonsson would ultimately spend eight and a half years with the Isles, but he surrendered the *C* before the 2001–02 season to someone a bit more experienced.

Michael Peca (2001–04): "When Pecs came in," Mark Parrish said, "it was like instant credibility." At just 25 he had been captain of the Sabres team that reached the 1999 Finals, so there was a pedigree. After Peca sat out all of 2000–01 with Buffalo, the Islanders brought him in on the wave of positive Milbury moves ahead of the 2001–02 season and named him captain.

Peca won the Frank J. Selke Trophy that year as the top defensive forward in the league. The low hit he took from Darcy Tucker in Game 5 of the series against the Leafs kept Peca out into the 2002–03 season, and he wasn't the same after that. Neither were the Isles, of course.

"It was an incredible honor," Peca said in 2019. "I think it's an honor regardless of what organization you get the honor of wearing the *C*, but I think there are a handful of organizations, the New York Islanders being one of them, where I think it's even more of an honor because of your being on a list with Hall of Fame players and legends of the game."

Alexei Yashin (2005–07): Yashin was also not the same player he'd been when the Isles acquired him before that magical 2001–02 season, but he was one of the senior Islanders coming out of the 2004–05 lockout, and Milbury and Coach Steve Stirling bestowed the *C* on this highest-paid player.

Yashin wasn't a talkative leader; that was never his style. And when Milbury was let go and Garth Snow, a teammate of Yashin's for three years prior to the lockout, took over as GM, Yashin was bought out after five seasons.

Bill Guerin (2007–09): Guerin had worn an *A* in three of his previous NHL stops, but this was the first time for him as a captain—and the teams weren't very good, of course. "It was still fun," he said. "Having a relationship already with Snowy, we were very honest with each other. There were some good things starting to happen there."

Snow did Guerin a big favor at the 2008–09 trade deadline, sending his captain to the Penguins—where Guerin won his second Stanley Cup, 14 years after the first one.

Doug Weight (2009–11): He was diminished on the ice, able to play only 54 games those two seasons because of back problems. But Weight served his role well as John Tavares's first captain and landlord, with Tavares and Matt Moulson living in the Weights' guesthouse.

Those were struggling teams too, but the young guys learned a lot. "Dougie just knows how to be a leader," Frans Nielsen said. "I think a lot of us got better being able to watch him then."

Mark Streit (2011–13): Another veteran, though much quieter than his two predecessors. Streit was one of Snow's best free-agent signings, coming over in 2008 from the Canadiens to bring some calm to a defense that struggled all throughout his time there.

His influence on Tavares was strong too—Tavares went with Streit to Bern, Switzerland, to play during the 2012–13 lockout. Streit now owns the team in his hometown.

John Tavares (2013–18): Everything that the Leafs want him to be now as their captain, he learned on the job after getting the *C* from Snow at age 23. He took the role incredibly seriously, as Tavares does all things hockey-related. He was the voice of his teammates in all things, from meals on charter flights to asking to move morning skates from Brooklyn back to Long Island on Barclays Center game days. "He was always a quiet guy, but so focused," Jack Capuano said. "The guys didn't respect him just because he was the best player. They respected him because he worked as hard as anyone and cared about their concerns."

Anders Lee (2018–present): When Lou Lamoriello and Barry Trotz took over (and Tavares departed), it looked like the Islanders might start a new era without a captain. But they felt the team needed one, and the choice was obvious. "When we came in as a coaching staff, we talked to every player," Trotz said. "We asked them all, 'Who do you think should be the next captain?' And it was unanimous. It was clear as day to me that Anders would be the captain."

Lee said the team history came to the forefront when word spread he'd been named captain the night before the 2018–19 opener in Carolina. "[I was] getting texts from Michael Peca, Dougie [Weight]…Denis called me," he said. "When Barry announced it that night…it's still a special feeling. It's an honor."

63 Bill Torrey's Greatest Hits

They're sprinkled throughout this book, of course, since Bill Torrey's personnel decisions shaped the championship years. But a separate chapter breaking down the biggest moves he made is worth it.

10. **Jean Potvin from the Flyers for Terry Crisp, March 5, 1973:** Potvin wasn't necessarily the key piece of the expansion-season puzzle that Torrey sought. This deal had more to do with what lay ahead in the 1973 draft, where the Islanders had the No. 1 pick.

   The Islanders brought in Denis Potvin's big brother, which helped keep the WHA at bay and brought Denis to the Island. For that alone, this deal deserves top 10 status.

9. **Wayne Merrick and Darcy Regier from the Cleveland Barons for J.P. Parise and Jean Potvin, January 10, 1978:** Part of Torrey's genius was recognizing that his teams, even when they started to become consistently good, needed to change.

In this case, it was getting younger and faster up front. He already had young stars in Bryan Trottier, Mike Bossy, Clark Gillies, Bob Bourne, and Bob Nystrom. With this deal, he found a depth center in Merrick who had skill and fit the roster better than the 36-year-old Parise.

And as the Islanders would come to learn with many of their players, Merrick played to the moment. He never scored more than 20 goals in a regular season, which he did in 1978–79. But he had six playoff goals in the 1981 and 1982 Stanley Cup runs, including the Cup winner early in Game 5 of the 1981 Finals over the North Stars.

Jean Potvin returned as a free agent prior to the 1979–80 season, primarily as a spare defenseman.

8. **Mike McEwen from the Colorado Rockies for Chico Resch and Steve Tambellini, March 10, 1981:** Resch was a beloved figure in the Isles room, but he longed to play more and had planned on leaving as a free agent after the 1980–81 season. Tambellini, the Isles' first-round pick in 1978, was emerging as a reliable No. 3 center in 1980–81.

But the Islanders had just lost Gord Lane to a thumb injury, and Torrey needed a defenseman. McEwen, who'd been a hated Ranger and part of the 1979 squad that bounced the Isles, was still young at 24 and had some real offensive skill. He didn't do much after the trade in the regular season but was a force in the 1981 tournament, scoring six goals in the playoffs. He also had three points in the Isles' first-round win in 1982, when the Penguins had the champions on the ropes.

7. **J.P. Parise from the North Stars for Doug Rombough and Ernie Hicke. And Jude Drouin from the North Stars for Craig Cameron, January 5 and 7, 1975:** Two of Torrey's first great in-season trades, for a couple of seasoned veterans his young team needed in its first season above water.

Parise was 33; Drouin was 26. They'd been teammates in Minnesota, and Al Arbour had them on a line together for the remainder of the 1974–75 season, then into the playoffs, where Drouin-to-Parise produced the biggest goal of the young franchise's history.

6. **Ray Ferraro from the Whalers for Doug Crossman, November 13, 1990:** Even near the end of his two-decade run as GM, Torrey still had an eye for what his team needed. At the start of the 1990–91 season, coming off a blowout first-round exit at the hands of the Rangers, Torrey dealt away Crossman—whose 59 points in 1989–90 were the most by any defenseman since the dynasty era—for Ferraro, a 40-goal scorer in Hartford.

Ferraro had four solid seasons on the Island. The fifth, an injury-plagued 1992–93 in which he produced 27 points in 46 games, was quickly erased by one of the best individual playoff performances in team history: 13 goals in 18 playoff games on the miracle run to the 1993 Eastern Conference final.

5. **Gord Lane from the Capitals for Mike Kaszycki, December 7, 1979:** With Denis Potvin out long-term, Torrey needed a defenseman. He found one who wasn't even playing. Lane was just starting his fifth season for the hapless Caps when he walked away in late November, planning to retire. Washington GM Max McNab was able to get Kaszycki, a decent young center, in exchange for Lane, who figured he'd give it a shot with a team as good as the Islanders.

The extremely unflashy defenseman only scored nine goals over six seasons on the Island, but his steady, physical presence gave the Potvins and Stefan Perssons a breather.

4. **Pierre Turgeon, Benoit Hogue, Uwe Krupp, and Dave McLlwain from the Sabres for Pat LaFontaine, Randy Wood, Randy Hiller, and a 1992 fourth-round pick. And Steve Thomas and Adam Creighton from the Blackhawks for Brent Sutter and Brad Lauer, October 25, 1991:** These were gut-wrenching deals for Torrey and Arbour to make. Sending away the best player in the organization in LaFontaine and the captain and last link to the dynasty era in Sutter was not by choice; the Islanders' messy ownership situation, with John Pickett closing his wallet while he looked for a buyer, made both stars prepare to move on.

Which is what makes these deals all the more impressive. Torrey was able to work out an eight-player deal with the Sabres for LaFontaine, who was holding out at the time, and get back two top-six forwards in Turgeon and Hogue as well as a very capable defenseman in Krupp.

Thomas turned out to be another top-line winger who had some of his best career numbers on the Island.

Torrey was pushed out by the Gang of Four within 10 months of making this deal. By the end of the following season, the Isles were on a surprising run to the conference final, fueled in large part by these two trades as well as the Ferraro deal.

3. **A 1983 first-round pick from the Colorado Rockies for Bob Lorimer and Dave Cameron, October 1, 1981:** If you wanted to put this one at the top, feel free. There's an obvious choice sitting at No. 1, and that deal makes the most sense—it helped put the Islanders on track for four Stanley Cups.

But for sheer general-managing cleverness, none really top this one. The Rockies were about to begin their last of six lousy seasons in Denver; the Islanders were embarking on the road to Stanley Cup No. 3 and had a rookie defenseman, Tomas Jonsson, in the fold, which made Lorimer expendable.

Torrey convinced Colorado GM Billy MacMillan to give up not his next first-round pick but the one after that—far enough down the road, apparently, that it may not have occurred to MacMillan that his franchise would still be at the bottom of the league once it moved to New Jersey.

Torrey was disappointed to see the Devils finish 19th overall in 1982–83, not 21st and last as he had hoped. "We're very disappointed that we didn't get that first pick," Torrey said at the end of the 1982–83 regular season. "We don't like finishing third to anyone. But we still think we'll be getting a pretty good player."

He never dreamed LaFontaine would fall to the Isles at No. 3. The North Stars took Brian Lawton first and the Whalers, in a surprise, went for Sylvain Turgeon at No. 2. So perhaps the player the Isles wanted all along if they had picked first was still there, making this trade as lopsided as any in team history.

2. **Bob Bourne from the Kansas City Scouts for the rights to Larry Hornung and future considerations (Bart Crashley), September 10, 1974:** As Bourne tells it, Kansas City didn't see much of a future for him just a couple months after the Scouts selected Bourne in the third round of the 1974 draft.

They asked where he wanted to go. He knew a few players on the Islanders, so he asked about going there; Torrey sent the rights to two players in the WHA, and Bourne arrived for his first camp at age 20 and stayed for 12 terrific seasons.

All the other core dynasty stars were homegrown. Bourne basically was, except for this thievery before the team got good.

1. **Butch Goring from the Kings for Dave Lewis and Billy Harris, March 10, 1980:** The granddaddy of them all. Torrey had the ingredients of a team that could do what the previous three playoff teams hadn't; all he needed was another veteran up the middle to strengthen his forward group.

Lewis had been a regular defenseman since 1973, but with Ken Morrow's arrival nine days earlier and Potvin's return from injury, he was expendable. Harris, the first-ever draft pick, had been a solid contributor, but the Islanders needed a center behind Trottier and in front of Lorne Henning and Merrick.

There were hard feelings all around. Goring wasn't happy to leave L.A. after a decade and the longtime Islanders were unhappy at seeing two of their core go. Those feelings were dispelled pretty quickly. The Islanders didn't lose a regular-season game after Goring arrived, going 8–0–4 into the playoffs.

As with all these deals, Torrey knew best.

64 The House on Weyford Terrace

There are lots of little stories you've read here so far about how close a lot of the Islanders teams have been over the years. Not just the dynasty guys who were together for a decade in some cases but the recent clubs of the 2010s that formed close bonds as they grew together through some rough times.

And then there's just a time when four guys who've played together a little bit pile into a house together for a season and it becomes the centerpiece of the team. That's what happened in 2001. Mark Parrish had been an Islander for a year, coming over in *that* trade in June 2000, and Parrish suffered through his first year as an Islander living by himself in a house on Weyford Terrace in Garden City.

Toward the end of that 2000–01 season—the worst full season since the 1972–73 expansion debacle, mind you—Parrish had a teammate come up to him. It was Steve Webb, not a guy to be messed with. "Webby just announced we'd be living together next season," Parrish said. "I mean, you're gonna tell him no? But it was a little lonely there that year, so it was fun to look forward to having someone to talk to."

As the summer went on, Parrish heard from Eric Cairns, who wanted in on the house share. And as training camp approached for the 2001–02 season through a summer of some incredible changes, newcomer Shawn Bates needed a place to stay, so the five-bedroom house became his home too.

Four 20-something guys, all single and four of the younger guys on what had rapidly transformed into a veteran team. The house became a magnet for hanging out during that memorable season. "That was my NFL Sunday spot," Garth Snow said. "I'd bring bagels, coffee, just settle in if we weren't playing that night. Usually [I'd] just let myself in if they'd been out late."

The fact that Islanders team began the season 9–0–1–1 under first-year coach Peter Laviolette made the house even more high-energy. There were plenty of stories the guys who lived there didn't want to tell, especially since they're all middle-aged guys now with families—and, in Parrish's case, pursuing sobriety. Most of the juicy tales will stay with the four guys who lived there. "Let's just say we had a great time that year—on and off the ice," said Cairns, who has been the Islanders' director of player development for the last seven years. "And I think you can say we all had pretty great seasons too. We were young, we were part of a great team, and we enjoyed it. That house had a lot of traffic."

One off day after a night out, all four housemates had friends in town. "Cairnsy wanted Taco Bell—again, you're gonna say no?" Parrish said. He was dispatched to the drive-through. "And the orders kept coming as each guy chimed in. So I get to the window, and this poor girl… It's like $200 worth of tacos. You know how many tacos you need to hit $200 at Taco Bell 20 years ago? I was about halfway through the order, and she goes, 'Uh, could you just drive around?' She definitely thought it was a prank."

The house was so well-known as the hangout/pregaming spot—Dublin Pub in New Hyde Park was the group's favorite bar—that Laviolette pulled Parrish and Bates aside after a practice late in the season to ask a favor. "He basically wanted us to tone it down a little, not have as many guys over or going out with the playoffs coming up," Parrish said. "We said 'Sure, of course, no problem.' I'm not sure we followed through, but it was almost like, 'Wow, that's some respect if the coach wants us to keep it toned down!'"

And in that unforgettable playoff series with the Leafs, the housemates' bond shone through—for example, Cairns's pummeling of Shayne Corson late in Game 6 came after Corson and Darcy Tucker had a run at Bates.

All four guys were with the Islanders for a couple years after that season, but the house was never quite the same and they had scattered by the 2003–04 season. Still, a small part of the 2001–02 resurgence spilled over onto Weyford Terrace. "A great spot," Snow said. "And I'm glad I didn't live there. Always remember: You want a friend with a boat; you don't want to own the boat."

1976 and 1977: A Good Team Falls Short

After the surprise success of 1975, the Islanders were determined not to be a flash in the pan. With Bryan Trottier joining the 23-and-under core of Denis Potvin, Clark Gillies, Bob Nystrom, Lorne Henning, Garry Howatt, and Dave Lewis, plus full seasons from veterans J.P. Parise and Jude Drouin alongside the 30-something crowd of Ed Westfall, Bert Marshall, and Billy MacMillan, the Islanders were not content to roll along. They wanted to contend.

"After the '75 finals were over, I really thought we could have won the Cup," Potvin said. "We took Philly to seven games and we'd played Buffalo really tough that year. We were getting really, really close."

Arbour's belief in conditioning was starting to have an effect. They were a fast team, now armed with better skill; in Chico Resch and Billy Smith, the Islanders had two goalies who were equally strong and split the season almost evenly.

They took another step forward with a 101-point regular season, finishing fifth overall but still a ways behind the two dominant teams: the two-time defending Stanley Cup champion Flyers and the Canadiens, the gold standard of NHL success. So it felt inevitable that the Islanders would have to go through one of those two teams to get to their ultimate goal.

The Islanders dispatched the Canucks in a two-game sweep in the best-of-three preliminary round in the 1976 playoffs. Then came the Sabres, the No. 4 seed, in the quarterfinals.

Game 5 was the key. The series was 2–2 and the teams were tied 2–2 after a period, and the game got chippy—Dave Lewis laid out Sabres forward Craig Ramsay, inciting a scrum—and the Sabres pulled ahead on Jim Lorentz's goal past Smith with 9:44 left. But Potvin uncorked a blast by Desjardins with 4:28 to go to tie it. Then came a sighting as rare as a comet.

Marshall, the veteran defenseman scooped off the 1970s version of waivers by Torrey from the Rangers prior to the 1973–74 season, let one go from the point that found its way through a crowd with 19 seconds left. It was Marshall's first goal of the entire year. "I can't very well describe the goal," Marshall said, "because I don't score too many."

The Islanders closed out the Sabres at the Coliseum two nights later, a 3–2 win on Gillies's goal in the third. These weren't the dominating Islanders teams of a few years hence, but they were finding ways to win and had reached the semifinals once more.

The Canadiens were waiting. "They were the team we wanted to be," Trottier said. "We studied them. Great scorers, incredible defense, stingy goaltender—we wanted everything they had and we had to learn it." The hard way, especially in 1976. The Isles blew a 2–1 lead in the final seven minutes of Game 1, losing 3–2 in the Forum. Which was followed by a 4–3 Game 2 loss. Then a killer Game 3 loss at home, a 2–0 lead entering the third disappearing on Yvon Lambert's winner with 3:48 to go.

There was no rallying from 3–0 down to this Habs team. The Isles won Game 4, but they were spanked 5–2 in Game 5, ending the season. "I think at times our lack of experience showed against this club," Arbour said. "But we're gonna keep our heads up high. There is certainly nothing to be ashamed of."

The next season felt like Groundhog Day to the Isles. Their young core was a year older and better, the veterans were still going strong, and Torrey made hardly any changes. The biggest change came in February 1977, when Westfall told Torrey and Arbour it was time for a new captain. Westfall was still a solid contributor, but at 36, he felt it was time for one of the younger Islanders to represent the group. The team voted in Gillies, who was only 22 but had an easy way with the whole team.

So with a new captain, a seasoned group, and a 106-point season, the Islanders marched into the playoffs once more. Another preliminary round sweep, this one of the Blackhawks. Another quarterfinal meeting with the Sabres, but this one was an Islanders sweep. Gillies had the game winner in each of the first three games, Smith stood on his head in the two games in Buffalo, and Billy MacMillan, in his final season in the NHL, scored the series clincher in the third period of Game 4 for a 4–3 win to close it out.

And again the Canadiens were waiting. Arbour's squad had learned a few things, but the one area where they were lacking was goal scoring. They had their share in 1976–77, but they were a score-by-committee team with seven 20-goal scorers but no consistent game breaker.

The Canadiens had several. They also had Ken Dryden, who pitched shutouts on the Isles in Games 2 and 4, the latter giving Montreal a 3–1 series stranglehold. The Islanders pulled out Game 5 in overtime in Montreal on Harris's game winner, but Dryden slammed the door again in the Coliseum in Game 6, only allowing Potvin's goal with nine seconds left in a 2–1 Habs win.

They were on their way to the second of four-straight Cups themselves. The Islanders had now been left behind in the semis for a third-straight year.

"The improvement's there from last year. The hunger's still there," Gerry Hart said after the series ended. "And the determination too. If we started the series tomorrow, we'd win. We're better than Montreal now. It took this series to make us believe it."

"Look, we got our asses kicked two years in a row by them," Potvin said. "But we still felt good about ourselves."

66 1978 and 1979: Regular-Season Breakthroughs, Playoff Disappointments

Things took a decidedly upward turn in 1977–78. Mike Bossy's arrival had a lot to do with that; so did the arrival of Stefan Persson, who gave the Isles a second offensive scoring threat from the blue line behind Potvin.

Bill Torrey dealt J.P. Parise and Jean Potvin to Cleveland for Wayne Merrick, a young center who provided some depth behind Trottier and the otherworldly Trio Grande. Smith and Resch were old hands at rotating in goal.

And the scoring went up—way up. Bossy became the Isles' first 50-goal scorer; Trottier's 123 points were also a franchise best and second in the league. Six Islanders, including Denis Potvin, broke the 30-goal plateau; that was the same number of 30-goal scorers the Islanders had in their first five seasons combined.

The Islanders also captured their first Patrick Division title, finishing with 111 points. That marked six consecutive years of improvement in the regular season, and this time it meant something concrete: The Isles got one of the four playoff byes through the preliminary round and would await the winner of one of the best-of-three series they'd been through the three previous playoffs.

The Maple Leafs emerged as the Isles' opponents. Toronto had been the picture of NHL mediocrity for a decade—good enough to be one of 12 teams to make the playoffs but not good enough to advance, having won four-straight preliminary series and lost four-straight quarterfinals.

Toronto did have one wild card: first-year coach Roger Neilson. He was long an innovator in his 16 years behind seven different NHL benches, but no one knew back then, in his first time as an NHL coach, about his commitment to defensive hockey.

The Leafs knew they were inferior to the Islanders, so they worked twice as hard. Even at that, the Islanders pulled through to a 2–0 lead with a pair of wins at the Coliseum, Game 2 ended by Bossy on his third whack at a loose puck in front of Leafs goalie Mike Palmateer. Toronto allowed just one goal in the two games in Maple Leaf Gardens, and the series was even.

Bob Nystrom, the Isles' Mr. OT, scored a humdinger of a winner in Game 5. He steamed up the right side, put the puck through Toronto defenseman Brian Glennie's legs, and hammered a shot past Palmateer, sending the Coliseum crowd into a frenzy.

Another trip to the semifinals beckoned. Borje Salming, the Leafs' world-class defenseman, was out of the series with an eye injury suffered in Game 4. The Isles could taste this one, and they had the confidence to stare down any of their possible semifinal opponents. But the Leafs put on a clinic in Toronto in Game 6, forcing the Isles into a Game 7 at home for the first time in their history. It was another tight game, 1–1, and it went to overtime.

A busted play dashed their dreams. Lanny McDonald corralled a puck that skipped past both Potvin and Gillies. Resch, who started every game of the series, cheated a bit to his right, anticipating a backhand deke. McDonald shot it low where Resch had been and—at 4:13 of overtime—quieted the Coliseum crowd.

"The Leafs checked us very well," Arbour said, "and if you had to find any difference in this series, it might be that they outworked us. They put out 150 percent, each and every one of them. They were on top of us all the time. I guess it just wasn't meant to be."

Resch beat himself up pretty good after the game. "That must have been the worst goal I've given up in the whole series," he said. "I think they were hungrier than we were. Besides, they didn't have anything to lose and [had] a lot to gain. Not to take anything away from them, but they got the breaks too. We sacrificed offense for defense, and I have to hand it to our guys. They played super defense. But when it came to the one goal that counted, I panicked."

That was the takeaway from the upset loss: The Leafs were tougher. The Islanders had plenty of toughness in their lineup, from Gillies to Nystrom to Howatt to Hart, but this was more about tenacity. "We were ready to sail, and then it all came crashing down," Resch said.

Whatever confidence may have been lost with that defeat returned for the 1978–79 regular season. Another young, talented draft pick was added to the mix—a feisty winger named John Tonelli who'd spent three years in the WHA.

The Trio Grande soared to new heights. Bossy scored 69 goals, second-most in NHL history; Trottier posted 134 points and won the first Hart Trophy in team history. Potvin became the second defenseman in NHL history to break the 100-point barrier and won his third Norris Trophy.

Five Islanders made the two NHL All-Star teams. And on the last day of the season, a 5–2 win in the Garden over the Rangers (coupled with a 1–0 Canadiens loss in Detroit) made the Isles regular-season champions. "Everything just clicked," Trottier said. "Guys were jumping off the ice early to get me on so I could win the Art Ross [Trophy, for top scorer in the league]. Mike had 69 goals. Clarkie had a terrific year, Chico, Denis—we were clicking so well."

And so it went in the quarterfinal round, a sweep over the Blackhawks that was never close. Bossy had a hat trick in Game 1, the overtime winner in a 1–0 Game 2, and that was that. Chicago scored three goals total on Resch and Smith, who alternated games as they had during the regular season.

It was back to the semifinals for a date with the Rangers. The teams were meeting for the first time since the historic best-of-three in 1975, and their fortunes had changed drastically since then. The Islanders were kings of the league and the Rangers were on their fourth coach in the four seasons since the 1975 upset. Luckily for them, that coach was Fred Shero. He'd coached the Flyers to their two Stanley Cups, taking out the Islanders in the 1975 semis. He, like Neilson in Toronto, was a different sort of coach. And he knew for his Rangers team that finished 25 points in back of the Isles to win the series, they had to shut down Bossy and the top line as well as Potvin.

For Potvin, the strategy was simple: dump the puck into his corner, make him retrieve it, take a piece off him every time, and don't release until after the play is long gone. "They're staring into my eyes even after I give up the puck," Potvin said during the series.

For the Trio Grande, it was physical punishment. Everyone in the league felt Bossy could be thrown off his game by an extra bump or several whacks with a stick, even though he'd endured that much and worse since he was a kid in Montreal. But this was relentless and also involved a forward maintaining position on Bossy everywhere he went in the offensive zone—not exactly radical for the current hockey era but pretty radical back then.

And it worked. The Rangers surprised the Isles in Game 1, a 4–1 loss that showed the Rangers' gang of pluggers could score. Potvin's deflected slapper gave the Islanders a 4–3 overtime win in Game 2, and they split the games at the Garden, with Nystrom's OT winner tying the series in Game 4—it was a crazy play where John Davidson, the Rangers goalie, tried to beat Nystrom to a loose puck, but instead the puck caromed off both of them, into the air, and settled right at Nystrom's skates with an empty net. "I wanted to call a fair catch," Nystrom said. "Waiting for it to come down was the longest moment of my life."

Back at the Coliseum for Game 5, the Islanders felt confident. Why wouldn't they? They were the best team in the league, they'd lost four times all season at home, and their power play, which was a league-best 31.1 percent that year, still hadn't clicked against the Rangers. And the Trio Grande, which had just one goal in the first four games, was ready to break out.

But it didn't happen. A seesaw game had the Isles scrambling to tie it twice in the third, the last on a Nystrom goal to make it 3–3 with 10:27 to go. But the Islanders got beaten to pucks on a late shift and Anders Hedberg flipped a puck over a sprawled Smith with 2:13 left for a 4–3 Rangers win.

"You have to change your style of play during the playoffs," said Resch, who got the call for Game 6 at the Garden. "It becomes more of a physical game, with less finesse. It's tighter checking. If we can't blow the Rangers out, and we haven't, we'll have to grind them out. We didn't think they were going to be as tough as they are in the corners."

Bossy and the power play broke through to open the Game 6 scoring, but the Rangers scored twice in the second and simply held on. The vaunted Isles offense mustered just 21 shots on Davidson, and that was it.

The clip of Potvin slumped on the boards as the Rangers celebrated was a lasting image. Four years of growing success, four years of heartbreak in the playoffs. And worse now—this last indignity suffered at the hands of the big-city rivals. "No matter how much blame anybody wants to put on us, and it will be easy to say we choked, I think we lost because the Rangers stood up to us and played better than us," Bossy said after the loss. "I still don't think they have a better team.... We didn't expect to walk through the series, but we did expect to win."

"It just felt like things were going to change," Nystrom said. "We were a great team, but we hadn't delivered."

They were going to change—just not the way the players imagined.

67 1979–80: Change on the Bumpy Road to Glory

The first sign that things were changing came just before the start of the 1979–80 season. Clark Gillies, captain for the last three years, told Al Arbour and Bill Torrey he was giving up the C. "I'd get tension headaches from trying to lead and trying to play at the same time," he said in 1982.

Gillies's teammates had voted him captain at 22. The Islanders' failures in the playoffs during Gillies's tenure weighed on him. "It became too much for me," he said. "I was conscious of the older guys on the team, and it was hard for me to criticize. I didn't like being the middle man between the players and management."

This time around, Torrey and Arbour decided who should be captain. Denis Potvin was the choice. "Clarkie is one of my best friends," Bob Nystrom said, "but he wanted to be liked by everyone. He's a fun-loving guy. Denis was a little more above it all. He could handle the responsibilities of being captain."

What no one foresaw was Potvin struggling through the most injury-riddled season of his career. He missed the first eight games of 1979–80 with a collarbone injury, then tore ligaments in his thumb right after Thanksgiving and missed nearly three months. "It was one thing after another that year," he said.

Without him on the ice, the Islanders stumbled badly out of the gate. They were 6–9–4 at Thanksgiving, then got dumped in Denver 7–4 by the bottom-feeding Colorado Rockies. Things looked as bleak as they had in years. "It felt like we were scrambling," Bryan Trottier said. "Everyone was on us—the media, the coaches, Bill. Losing Denis right off the bat hurt, then when he went out for as long as he did, it was a huge blow. We just couldn't find our footing after all the good seasons we'd had the years before."

Torrey had done his usual off-season tinkering, adding 27-year-old Swedish pro Anders Kallur and Steve Tambellini, the 1978 first-round pick, to the forward mix. But nothing clicked the first two months, and then Potvin was sidelined.

So Torrey went to work. He brought in another recent first-rounder, a talkative 19-year-old winger named Duane Sutter, from his junior team in Lethbridge. Sutter's first game was the one where Potvin hurt his thumb, but the kid from the hockey-mad family fit right in. "Here was this squawking, yapping kid, never stopped talking or sticking his nose in," Trottier said. "It brought a real different element to our room right at the time we needed it."

A week later Torrey pulled off one of his best under-the-radar deals, picking up physical defenseman Gord Lane from the Caps for Mike Kaszycki. Lane had been toiling away with Washington for three years and got so fed up with Caps management he'd left the team two weeks earlier, planning to retire at age 25. Instead he came to the Island and added a snarl that invigorated a listless team. "That move was almost as important as the ones that came later in the year," Potvin said. "Nobody messed with Gord."

A seven-game winning streak in January helped ease the tension and get the Islanders at least into a consistent playoff spot. But they were trading wins and losses the next six weeks before an eventful 10 days in March that changed the team for good.

68 Listen to Ricky on the Radio

The way it ended for Rick DiPietro as an Islander, you could forgive him if he decided to go literally anywhere else but the Island once his NHL career was over. Instead he dug in and reinvented himself as one of the more unlikely sports talk radio hosts around.

The cocky kid who came to New York as a talented teenager with a *Good Will Hunting*–esque Boston accent is now into his seventh year as a host on New York's ESPN Radio station, holding forth on every sport in a crowded scene. As Islanders fans have learned over the years in the boom of sports talk radio, hockey doesn't get much love on the air. But DiPietro makes sure to talk hockey in addition to all the other New York sports teams he's become well versed in.

"I love it here," DiPietro said. "From the second I established myself as a player, this is where I wanted to be. I stayed here during the off-seasons; I became a huge New York sports fan."

DiPietro (left) with former broadcast partner Alan Hahn in 2015.

DiPietro's career started inauspiciously when Mike Milbury, after learning the Islanders had won the draft lottery to move up four spots and select first in the 2000 draft, traded Roberto Luongo to the Panthers and selected DiPietro, then a freshman at Boston University, first overall.

When the Islanders had their revival in 2001, DiPietro was in the minors—leading the Sound Tigers to the AHL Finals in Bridgeport's first season of existence. He got the call up to the Isles for good in 2003; in the 2006–07 season, he was an All-Star and became the proud owner of a 15-year contract courtesy of Charles Wang and new GM Garth Snow, who'd shared the Isles net with DiPietro for a couple years.

The deal was ridiculed at the time—Wang was seemingly fond of such deals, having signed Alexei Yashin to a 10-year, $90 million deal that would be bought out following the 2006–07 season—but it was actually for a somewhat reasonable $4.5 million per season, straight salary with no bonuses. "There'd be years you'd be underpaid and years you'd be overpaid," DiPietro said, "but it wasn't a crazy amount of money for a No. 1 goalie."

But the injuries started that season and never stopped: Hip problems. A knee that seemed like a minor thing at the time but was ultimately what ended his career. Concussions. Broken bones in his face from a 2011 fight with Penguins goalie Brent Johnson. "When you're not stopping the puck and you're frustrated about your health, you look for other ways to feel part of the team," DiPietro said. "Like going in for a fight and not realizing how big Brent Johnson is."

After a loss in Ottawa on February 19, 2013, the Islanders waived DiPietro and sent him to the AHL, back where it all began. He didn't fuss, played 18 games for Bridgeport, and was then bought out of his lengthy contract on July 3, 2013. At age 30 his tumultuous Islanders career was over.

A little over a year later, he started his next chapter. Alan Hahn, the onetime Islanders beat writer for *Newsday* who moved over to radio and television, invited DiPietro on his show, and the bosses at ESPN heard something they liked. "It started off as fun with me and Alan when he covered the team. He'd say, 'You love to talk. You should do some TV or radio,'" DiPietro said. "He invited me in to do it when things were over. It came natural to us. I was nervous at first, but once we got going, get some phone calls—I used to love the 'I'm a huge Ranger fan but I love listening to you.'"

And seven years later he's still going strong. He wasn't the most popular Islander when his 13-year Isles career ended, but he's found Islanders fans are among his biggest supporters now. "It was one of the reasons I was hesitant to do the radio show—I didn't know how people would respond," he said. "But it's the best thing I've ever done."

69 The Brooklyn Detour

Frans Nielsen can say it now, since the Islanders are done with Barclays Center and Nielsen's been an ex-Islander for several years. "We hated it," Nielsen said of the Isles' move to Brooklyn in 2015. "It got a little better once we moved the morning skates back to Syosset, but before then every day felt like a road game. Leave the house early, get back late, hotel in between skates and the game—we got to, like, 30 games in that season and it felt like 70."

The move, of course, was borne of desperation. Charles Wang had struck out on his Lighthouse Project several years earlier, stymied by the town of Hempstead's desire not to have major traffic in the area. The Nassau County referendum went down hard in 2011. That left Wang holding the bag with a team that lost $20 million annually and had no avenues to change that.

Until Barclays Center came along, that is. Nets owner Bruce Ratner built the arena in downtown Brooklyn to house his team, and Wang—looking to get out from the Isles but without the possibility of moving them out of the area—saw Barclays Center as an exit ramp. The 2012 announcement that the Isles would move to Brooklyn for the 2015–16 season, when the onerous Coliseum lease finally ended, was met with some excitement and a bit of trepidation.

Islanders fans come from all over the Island—even the part that belongs to New York City. Those fans were thrilled. So were the ones who worked in the city who could never get to a weeknight game at the Coliseum due to its famous lack of public transportation nearby. But the Isles fans who loved to drive 15 to 20 minutes and tailgate outside the Coli were very unhappy.

And so too were the players, especially once 2015 rolled around and they discovered that the Long Island Rail Road was the only "quick" way to Brooklyn from their homes near the Coliseum. "When we found that out," Johnny Boychuk said, "it wasn't a very popular situation with the guys, let's just say that."

So the Islanders players and coaches turned into commuters in the morning. Jack Capuano started that season having the players get hotel rooms near Barclays Center for the day rather than trying to get back and forth from the Island again closer to the afternoon rush hour.

And the problems inside the building were apparent early on: The arena's original design was for basketball and hockey, but the developers scrapped the hockey footprint for cost reasons. So the building's ice-making capacity was inadequate—it was the only building in the league with PVC piping for ice-making rather than steel pipes, and the rink extended so far at one end of the building that several thousand seats were obstructed-view. "The ice was awful most of the time," Nielsen said. "We tried to make the best of it, but we had a pretty skilled team that first year. It wasn't easy."

John Tavares took players' complaints to Capuano midway through that season, and the Islanders moved their morning skates back to Iceworks. The players would take the train to Brooklyn in the afternoon.

Between the players' gripes and the fans' unhappiness at having to trek to the city to watch their team, you'd think the 2015–16 Islanders were a disaster. Quite the opposite: A second-consecutive 100-point season preceded the first playoff series win in 23 years, capped by Tavares's iconic double-OT goal in that very building.

But in the bigger picture, the commute had a negative effect. Nielsen said he would never have considered leaving in free agency after that year without Brooklyn being in the mix. Tavares's decision to leave two years later had far less to do with the move, since he knew UBS Arena was on the horizon, but the uncertainty around the home buildings didn't help.

"I give the fans a lot of credit," Nielsen said. "They turned out for us that year. I can't imagine what it would have been like if we'd had a bad team."

70 Mick Vukota and Rich Pilon

Tough guys have long been revered in Islanders history. Garry Howatt and Gerry Hart were probably more popular than they were productive during the 1970s and early 1980s; the dynasty teams had more grit than you might remember, with Clark Gillies,

Denis Potvin, and Bob Nystrom all key members of those teams who could throw down when the time called for it. And Billy Smith's battlin' ways will live on as long as his amazing saves too.

But once the leaner Islanders years came along, enforcers took on a bigger part of the Isles' appeal. The team didn't win much at all from 1987 to 2001, but they had some legendary toughness then. And character.

Nobody embodied those traits more than Mick Vukota and Rich Pilon, who happen to sit at No. 1 and 2 in team history for penalty minutes. With fighting almost extinct now and the enforcer role basically gone with it, Vukota's 1,879 penalty minutes over 10 seasons is a record that will surely stand. And no one's probably going to challenge Pilon's 1,525 PIMs either. They came from the same hometown, Saskatoon. They faced off against one another in the Western League. And they finished their Isles careers with exactly 509 games apiece.

Vukota was a free agent when he signed on prior to the 1987–88 season. He got a taste of the NHL with 17 games but spent most of that season in Springfield of the AHL, where he racked up seven goals and 372 penalty minutes. He earned a regular spot with the Isles the next season, which was also Pilon's rookie year.

Pilon played for Terry Simpson in juniors and came to the Isles with Simpson as their coach. But 27 games into that year, Al Arbour returned to replace Simpson, and Pilon—who'd been getting solid minutes as a 20-year-old—found himself barely playing. "Al told me, 'I don't see you being an offensive defenseman in this league. Your goal is not to please me,'" Pilon told the PTIsles podcast in 2014. "He said, 'Your goal is to be the best teammate you can be. It's all about you and your teammates. You've got to be mentally tough and zone me out. If you want to play in the league, you're going to be a defensive defenseman, a shutdown guy, and if you're willing to do it, you'll play in the league a long time.'"

Pilon was obviously no slouch with his fists either. He and Vukota combined for 479 PIMs that 1988–89 season; those two own 7 of the top 10 slots for PIMs in an Islanders season all-time. And they also had a "secret" plan to get revenge on Dale Hunter minutes after his horrific blindside hit on Pierre Turgeon in Game 6 of the 1993 Patrick Division semifinal at the Coliseum.

"The Capitals had to walk by our room to get to the bus, and I was going to hide in the stick room," Vukota told the PTIsles podcast in 2019. "Rich was going to cause a disturbance, and when everyone went to him, I would come out of the stick room and I would jump Dale Hunter. I guess security found out. They ended up escorting him all the way around the building, not by our room. I guess we thought we were pretty clever, pretty discreet. Al was like, 'I appreciate what you're trying to do, but knock it off.' I was like, 'What? I'm just taping a stick.' He said, 'Knock it off, go get dressed, go home.'"

Pilon had only three goals at that point in his Islanders career, so he took Arbour's words to heart. Vukota had 16 goals—three of them on a memorable night early in the 1989–90 season. The Islanders were on their way to Washington for a game on October 20. Vukota had his role—few shifts and make them count, usually with his big body or his fists. But it was eating at him. "Early in my career, I would get bummed out if I didn't get to play," Vukota said. "If I didn't get ice time, I felt—'I'm willing to do anything. Can I just get a regular shift?' I was basically feeling sorry for myself. Pat LaFontaine sat next to me on the bus; he could see I was down. He said to me, 'What you do for us isn't measured in ice time. When you're there, I'm bigger. I feel better.'

"So like, Pat LaFontaine's got nothing better to do than cheer me up? That meant a lot to me, that a teammate of his stature would take the time to tell me that. My teammates always made me feel appreciated."

In a span of five minutes in the first period of that October 20 game, Vukota became a legend. He scored his first goal of the season to open the scoring off a nice feed from Don Maloney, his future general manager; 4:32 later he deposited a feed from his other linemate that night, Gilles Thibaudeau, for a 2–0 lead. The line stayed on for the faceoff, and Vukota tapped in a rebound for a natural hat trick. He'd have one more goal the rest of the season and never scored more than three in any of his remaining eight NHL seasons. After that three-goal game, his teammates presented him with a puck that had been sawed into a square.

Pilon's legend is a bit different. In 2012 he got a call from former Isles teammate Dean Chynoweth asking him if Pilon had seen "the statue." "He said, 'There's a statue of you,'" Pilon said in 2014. "I was like, 'Yeah, whatever.' I thought he was pulling my chain. Then my house phone rings and it's [TSN reporter] Bob McKenzie asking me if I've seen this statue."

The Penguins had unveiled a full-size statue of Mario Lemieux outside their new arena—but it wasn't just Lemieux. It was Mario squeezing between two defenders, taken from a *Sports Illustrated* photo. The defensemen were Islanders: Jeff Norton and Pilon.

"I did a lot of interviews, and it's fine," Pilon said. "I guess I'm going to be above ground for the rest of my life, so that's cool. The Penguins called to apologize for not telling me beforehand, and there's nothing to apologize for."

71 Bill Torrey's Legacy

To gauge Bill Torrey's impact on the NHL beyond what he did in two decades with the Islanders—building them up from quite literally nothing to the greatest team of the last 50 years—look at the people around him.

One of his first hires was a young scout who had recently been let go by the Blues, Jim Devellano. Devellano worked his way up from scouting eastern Canada to head scout to assistant general manager under Torrey, leaving in 1982 to become GM of the Red Wings.

Devellano is associated more now with helping build the foundation in Detroit from the dismal 1980s there to the Wings' status as one of the best teams of the last 25 years. But he cut his teeth under Torrey and carried that style over to Detroit. "Torrey was the kind of man, as I've said, who let people do their jobs," Devellano wrote in his autobiography, *The Road to Hockeytown.* "He was the boss, there was never any question about that, but he allowed the people under him to do their own thing and do their jobs the way they saw fit, which is not an easy thing for some people in the hockey business to do.

"He did what the really great leaders in any business are not afraid to do—he delegated authority, provided support and consultation, and gave final approval to the decision that you were allowed to make. That made him the perfect boss and the perfect mentor. No wonder the Islanders were one of the greatest dynasties in the history of the NHL under his direction."

Don Maloney became Torrey's assistant GM after retiring as a player with the Islanders in 1991. He may not have anticipated replacing Torrey within a year, as that was hardly his goal. "He helped show me the business," Maloney said of Torrey. Maloney went on to become the Coyotes' GM from 2007 to 2016, part of three decades in NHL front offices.

The Torrey influence even extended to players he drafted. Four of them became NHL general managers; two of them, Kevin Cheveldayoff and Tom Fitzgerald, are on the job currently with the Jets and Devils, respectively. "I consider Bill a mentor, weird as that may sound since I only played for him," Fitzgerald said. "I always kept in touch. If I was at a game in Florida, I'd hunt him down. He was a big part of the AHL summer meetings. I admired him so much, I considered him like a dad—so positive, so incredibly encouraging. He drafted me at 17, you've got two years of non-pro, then five years in the organization. He goes to Florida in 1993, takes me in the expansion draft, and I spend another five years with him. I was fortunate to be around him, just to have him be a sounding board as I finished playing."

Another protégé of sorts went on to be the architect of a very sour moment for any Islanders fan. Neil Smith was a lanky defenseman that Torrey selected in the 13th round of the 1974 draft. He never made it beyond the minors, but when he retired after the 1979–80 season, Torrey and Al Arbour made Smith an advance scout. He went on to work with Devellano in Detroit and then run his own team when the Rangers made him GM in 1989. Five years later Smith and the Rangers ended all those Coliseum "1940!" chants by winning the Cup. Smith did get to be Islanders' GM, of course, but for only 40 chaotic days under Charles Wang in 2006.

There's a long line of former Islanders who played for or were drafted by Torrey who got into coaching and front-office work: Lorne Henning went from assisting on Bob Nystrom's Cup winner in 1980 to assisting Arbour, part of nearly 15 years as an Islanders assistant over three different stints. Dave Lewis, Bryan Trottier, both Sutter brothers, Dave Cameron, Greg Gilbert, Todd

McLellan, and Travis Green have all been or currently are NHL head coaches.

"You couldn't help but learn from Bill and Al," Brent Sutter said. "When you're part of a successful team, you watch how the leaders carry themselves. Even now—I've been a coach and a GM for 20 years, and I'll think back: *Is this what Bill would do? What he would say?*"

72 Charles Wang

Charles Wang's legacy as Islanders owner is a complicated one for fans. No owner held control of the team longer; John Pickett had a majority interest in the Isles from 1978 to 1997, but he ceded operation of the team years before he sold.

Wang's way was different over his 16 years owning and operating the Islanders. Like every owner since Pickett, he was desperate to find a way out of the onerous Coliseum lease that restricted revenue; unlike all the misfits between Pickett's sale follies that began in 1991 and Wang buying the team (with fellow Computer Associates International executive Sanjay Kumar) in 2000, Wang had enough money to withstand the losses and, at times, spend to make the team competitive.

Inside the world of the Islanders, Wang was also a different sort of owner. Billy Smith once noted about original owner Roy Boe: "You better be standing at your locker when he comes in. I remember him asking Ralph Stewart how the family was, and Ralph doesn't even have kids."

With Wang the team was family. "I didn't know anything about Charles when I signed here," Garth Snow said. "We were up in Lake Placid for training camp before the [2001–02] season. We had a barbecue to kind of kick things off, and Charles flew up to be there. My brother Glenn had had a bone marrow transplant the year prior, and he wasn't doing well. Charles pulled me aside and talked to me, listened to me, and that was the first time we'd met. He showed the human side, and it wasn't something I'd seen from an owner before."

And it was that way from Wang's early years as owner to his final ones. "He came up to me at the team dinner before the season, I think I'd gotten traded maybe a couple days before," Johnny Boychuk said. "He wanted to make sure I was OK with the move, asked if he could help get my family settled when it was time for them to come down. It was different. I'd never talked to an owner like that before."

"There's not many owners before or after Charles who'd rather give hugs in the locker room instead of handshakes," Mark Parrish said.

It's hard to square that view of Wang with how the fans saw his tenure at times. The unique outlook—Wang once brought the *Hockey News* draft preview magazine to a Mike Milbury–run pre-draft meeting and wondered aloud why he was bankrolling so many scouts when the magazine's rankings were just fine; then there was his infamous sumo wrestler–goalie theory that was more in jest than serious—stemmed from a curious man who knew very little about the sport even after he'd bought the team.

And there was also a stubbornness born of his Computer Associates International success, some of which was certainly tarnished by investor lawsuits that made it easier for Wang to step away from the company he built in 2002—several years before Kumar, his business partner with the company and the Islanders (the latter until 2004), was indicted and convicted for securities fraud in 2006.

Wang, announcing the Isles' new lease agreement, in 2011.

On the day Wang hired Snow as general manager in 2006, he said: "I think it's unorthodox. But a lot of things we do in life, sometimes we do unorthodox things with the idea that maybe this is a better way, a different way."

Fans already knew how Wang viewed his hockey team by then, with Wang having signed Alexei Yashin to a 10-year deal and Michael Peca to a 5-year deal (Milbury talked Wang down from 10 years) upon greenlighting Milbury's trades for the two big-name players in the summer of 2001. Then came Rick DiPietro's 15-year contract in 2007. None of the three players finished their contracts with the Isles, with Snow buying out Yashin and DiPietro and Peca being traded in 2005.

Wang's biggest idea was the Lighthouse Project, his and developer Scott Rechler's vision to reimagine the area around the Coliseum with almost exclusively private financing. Town of Hempstead executive Kate Murray balked at the project's scale; Wang's refusal to play local Long Island politics by hiring longtime area politico Al D'Amato's brother as a "consultant" also didn't help.

Wang turned to Nassau County for a referendum in 2011 for a $400 million bond to renovate the arena and the surrounding area. Where Murray, a Republican, had thwarted Wang's Lighthouse ambitions, this time it was Democrats in the county legislature who opposed the 4 percent property tax increase. The referendum failed, and Wang looked for a way out after losing more than $200 million in a decade. "I got it from both sides," he said with a rueful laugh a few years later. "Not too many people can say that."

Wang announced the move to Brooklyn soon after the referendum defeat, saying the team would leave the Coliseum after its lease was up in 2015. Two years later, in the summer of 2014, he announced the Islanders would be sold to Scott Malkin and Jon Ledecky in the summer of 2016.

He was done after 16 years. Wang remained friends with Yashin, with Milbury, with Snow—that was his favorite part of owning the team. "Lifelong friends, all because of hockey," he said on his last day owning the team.

73 40 Years, Three Voices on TV

The Islanders haven't been a model of consistency since the Stanley Cup years ended. Changing owners, jerseys, arenas, GMs, coaches, players—they were all shuffled around more than the average NHL team during a long period without much success.

But the broadcast booth has been a remarkable bastion of consistency over the last 40 years. Only three men have worn the headset of the team's television play-by-play announcer, part of broadcasts that in recent years on the MSG Network have broken ground for hockey and pro sports in general.

That's the way most of the fans get their Isles fix (and media too, at least in 2020 and 2021), so the TV broadcast has never been more important. And as it was when Ken McDonald left the Atlanta Flames television booth to join Ed Westfall in the Isles booth for the 1980–81 season, you know what you're in for when you turn on an Islanders game. "I had been in Atlanta for eight years, and it was definitely more of a laid-back attitude," said McDonald, who is, of course, better known as Jiggs. "When I came to the Islanders, it was all business with Bill [Torrey] and Al [Arbour]. Great fun getting to know them and the team, but they were about one thing: winning."

For 15 years Jiggs and Eddie were the soundtrack to Islanders games. Three more Stanley Cups those first three seasons behind the mic for McDonald and then some other huge moments over the years: David Volek's OT winner in 1993, emceeing a number of jersey retirements for the dynasty core.

And there were the personalities. "Clarkie [Gillies] was as outgoing and funny as anyone you could meet," McDonald said.

Ed Westfall is in the Islanders Hall of Fame.

"And the singing—he could do 'The Gambler' as well as Kenny Rogers. Bobby Nystrom has a great personality too. Denis [Potvin] was more serious, more competitive. Boss and Trots were more to themselves. And Butchie always had a one-liner for everyone; he could take a joke too, always kidded about how light he traveled. He had a way of loosening up that room."

When the changes came in the 1990s, Torrey was pushed aside by the minority ownership's Gang of Four and Arbour retired after the 1993–94 season. And the broadcast booth wasn't exempt. After the lockout-shortened 1994–95 season, the Isles' controlling group looked to make a change in the booth. In came Howie Rose, the guy famous for the "Matteau! Matteau! Matteau!" call on Rangers radio during the 1994 Cup run.

Rose had a long history with the Islanders. As a student at Queens College, he'd gotten a press credential to cover the first season of the Islanders' existence, doing tape-recorded interviews with players after games. "I learned so much about the job thanks to the Islanders," Rose said. So even though he had been a Rangers radio guy and he was replacing a legend who was a couple years away from going into the Hockey Hall of Fame, Rose was up to the task as far as Islanders fans were concerned.

And what a task it became. Rose's first season was 1995–96—the Fisherman jersey year. His second season was John Spano's time in the spotlight. The thought of winning anything seemed awfully remote, though Rose was able to form some good relationships.

"I really enjoyed dealing with Mike [Milbury], even as the place seemed to be crumbling down around us," Rose said. "He's a very funny, sharp guy. You could have a fight, a disagreement with him, and the next day it's forgotten.

"I remember we were down playing the Capitals my first year out in Landover, Maryland. They had a longtime bus driver for the visiting teams, a real character named Joe. And Joe was used to seeing fans waiting for the teams at the hotel, even at one or two in the morning. So we pull in, and there's no one there.

"Joe just blurts out, 'You guys must really suck! There's nobody here!' Mike just laughed it off."

Rose survived the ownership merry-go-round as well. "The Gang of Four brought me in, and two of those guys went to jail," he said. "Then Spano: con man, jail. Sanjay Kumar, jail. I had a hell of a track record."

Rose took over as the radio play-by-play voice of the New York Mets in 2004 and worked splitting his duties between the two New York teams for a dozen years. In total Rose manned the Isles booth for 21 years, and it took until some of the very last words he spoke on an Islanders broadcast for him to see a winning playoff series. The last game he called was Game 6 of the 2016 first round, when John Tavares gave the Isles their first series victory since 1993.

Rose had considered stepping away from the Isles telecasts to focus on his Mets radio duties and his family, but that Game 6 goal cemented it for him. "I still rage at what Jiggs got to call during his time in the booth," Rose said with a laugh. "It was a wonderful way to wrap it up. I couldn't fathom going 0-for-21 as a broadcaster, so that really helped."

The torch was passed immediately to a young up-and-comer who grew up in New Jersey, the son of a baseball writer. Brendan Burke fit the Isles mold immediately, and his 5 seasons on the mic have been just as smooth as the 35 before them.

"When I got the job over the summer, Jiggs was one of the first to offer his congratulations," Burke wrote on the MSG Network website in 2017, the night before McDonald was honored at Barclays Center for 50 years of hockey broadcasting. "I was upset that day because I hadn't been able to answer the phone when he called. Now I am actually happy that I will have that voice mail forever."

Add in the all-female studio team, with host Shannon Hogan and analyst A.J. Mleczko, and the Islanders broadcasts continue to be a step ahead.

74 Mathew Barzal

You can count on one hand the number of Islanders over the last 35 years who were as talented as Mathew Barzal. For sheer creativity and high-end skill, you're looking at Ziggy Palffy. Maybe Pat LaFontaine. Maybe John Tavares. That's it.

The Islanders play a tight style these days under Lou Lamoriello and Barry Trotz, so Barzal's wizardry that was fully on display his rookie season of 2017–18 isn't quite as apparent anymore. But much more apparent to Barzal: All those playoff games the last three years. "Sure, it'd be nice to have 30 or 40 more points," Barzal told the *Athletic* during the 2018–19 season. "We're in the hunt for a division. It's different. Playing last year at this time, you're floating around, just trying to get a couple points. Now it's 1–0 in the first period, all right, let's hold on to it.

"I could go out there and play similar to what I did last year and have 90 points. And finish 10th. You never know when you're going to be in this stage. I could go 10 years without making the playoffs. This is a chance we have. It's exciting."

The "finish 10th" remark was no accident—the Oilers were sitting around 10th in the Western Conference right then, and the Sabres were also fighting for 10th in the East. Connor McDavid and Jack Eichel went at No. 1 and 2 in the 2015 draft, the best collection of talent in one draft for the last 20 years; Barzal went 16th that year, even though he felt he should have gone higher.

Barzal's electric rookie season, when he was the runaway Calder Trophy winner, came during a tumultuous time in the franchise. Tavares was in his final season, as were Garth Snow, the GM who drafted Barzal, and Doug Weight, his second coach.

Trotz has taken a longer view of Barzal's development, one that isn't always employed for the high-end skill players who are younger than 25 in today's NHL. The mantra from day one between Trotz and Barzal: "When you have the puck, do what you do," Trotz said. "When you don't have the puck, do what we want you to do, and you'll get it back a lot quicker."

So Barzal's individual totals fell in 2018–19 and 2019–20. He still led the team but with 62 points in 2018–19, down from 85 in his rookie season, and then an improvement to 60 in the 68-game 2019–20 season.

In his first two playoffs, Barzal raised his game. His ridiculous rush in overtime of his first playoff game, against the Penguins at the Coliseum, didn't result in a goal. He faked Brian Dumoulin out of the camera frame, paused, and flipped a backhand off the post as Kris Letang drove Barzal into Penguins goalie Matt Murray. Josh Bailey followed up and deposited the OT winner. Barzal celebrated just as big as if he'd done it himself.

In 2020 Barzal did get the highlight-reel OT goal, scoring past Braden Holtby to give the Isles a 3–0 series lead over the Capitals. By the end of the run to the Eastern Conference final, Barzal looked every bit the playoff warrior: black eye and stitches from an errant high stick, bumps and bruises, and 17 points in 22 games. "He looked like a guy that had been through the wars," Trotz said. "I think he appreciated it. You don't always know how hard you have to work in the playoffs until you've been there a few times."

There were plenty of rumors around Barzal in 2019 and 2020 that his feelings for playing the Islanders' style were less than enthusiastic—that he'd rather be free to play offense and half-heartedly do the other things asked of him on another team, perhaps one closer to his Vancouver hometown. He laughed at that during 2019–20: "I did see one thing about [me going to] Seattle," he said of the expansion team that didn't even have a roster until this past summer. "That was pretty funny."

Barzal and the Islanders didn't come to an agreement on his second contract until four days into the 2021 training camp, but there was never much worry about a split on either end. Barzal wants to be the one who leads the Islanders to that fifth Stanley Cup, and if he has to do it with fewer points than some of his equally (or less-) talented peers, so be it.

75 Two Trades in Two Hours

Six days before the start of the 2014–15 season, Garth Snow remade the near future of the franchise in a matter of hours. Two hours, to be exact—it was in that short window that Snow achieved a position of strength.

First Snow grabbed veteran Johnny Boychuk from the Bruins for a pair of second-round picks. Then, before the excitement had cooled on that deal, Snow picked up Nick Leddy from the Hawks for a couple of prospects. They didn't turn out to be the Butch Goring–level deals the Islanders had hoped, but Leddy and Boychuk became an instant first defense pair on a team desperately in need of stronger defense.

And Boychuk, the voluble 2011 Stanley Cup champ with the Bruins, did compare to Goring in one way. "He was a huge, huge part of the success we had those couple years," Frans Nielsen said. "He always did it in a positive way, but he would just remind us all how good we were and how, if we kept doing the right things, the rest would take care of itself. The group of guys we had that was there a long time wasn't always the best at speaking out. JB encouraged that."

It was pretty apparent right away that they could have an impact. Both Leddy and Boychuk left teams they'd won Stanley Cups with, so neither was, shall we say, immediately thrilled at changing teams. "I was devastated," Boychuk said. "The Bruins were all I knew."

But once they arrived, they both saw what the Isles were working with as well as the opportunity. Even before that, really. "I was driving down from Boston with my stuff and I figured I'd give Nick a call," Boychuk said. "We were in the same boat, so I figured it'd be nice to get to know him."

They were a pair on the ice for part or all of their six seasons together after that, and close off it too. Boychuk, who had twin toddler girls when he was acquired and now has three kids, is an ever-smiling, ever-loud presence; Leddy, who's single, is as reserved as they come. But they lived near one another in Garden City almost immediately and drove together to the rink or the airport virtually every day. And Leddy was a fixture at the Boychuks' for Christmas. "Our house gets pretty crazy at Christmas," Boychuk said. "He's part of the family now."

Boychuk had the first goal of the 2014–15 season. Leddy scored his first two games later as the Isles got off to a 4–0–0 start. "They gave us that much more credibility," Snow said.

And it all began with a two-hour window on October 4. "You're sitting in the locker room after practice, regular day, and you hear about the first trade," Nielsen said. "It's like, 'Wow, that's big.' Then the next one comes down, and we were all pretty stunned. Snowy made a big commitment to improve the team, and we felt like we needed to respond."

76 Arbour's 1,500th Game

Ted Nolan used to do his morning media scrum before games in the 2007–08 season next to the Islanders' Hall of Fame plaques that lined the hallway outside the dressing room. It was Nolan's second season coaching the Isles, and he'd noticed many times what it said on Al Arbour's plaque: 1,499 GAMES COACHED. That was the germ of an idea.

"I remember getting a call from Charles Wang, the Islanders' owner," Arbour remembered a few years later. "He said to me, 'Do you know how many games you coached for the Islanders?' I said, 'No, I don't have a clue.' He said, 'Fourteen ninety-nine. You've gotta coach one more game so you can get 1,500 with the Islanders.'"

So Arbour ventured up from his retirement home in Florida back to the old stomping grounds he'd left 13 years earlier to join Nolan behind the bench for one last game. Arbour was 75, but being around the team for a couple of days seemed to energize him. "As the game went on, you could tell the fire started burning a little," said Bill Guerin, the Islanders' captain at the time. "It was just cool to have him back there and have him get more and more into it."

It was barely a month into the 2007–08 season, but it was very apparent that the Islanders hadn't been able to maintain momentum and carry over the dramatic run to the 2007 playoffs from a season earlier. They were 6–4–0 heading into a November 3 date with the Penguins, but the Isles had already given up eight goals twice. "We weren't the strongest team that year," Guerin said. "It was early, but it felt like we needed something to hang our hats on a little. That night was a fun one to have."

Over nearly two decades behind the Islanders bench, Arbour prided himself on knowing everything about his players. "He knew your parents' names, your wife's name, your kids," Pat Flatley said. "He knew how to treat every person as an individual. That's what made him so special."

He told Nolan before the game he was concerned he didn't know enough of the guys. "I told him, 'Just say "line one, line two," and go from there,'" Nolan said.

The Penguins took a 2–0 lead early in the second. Arbour was worried then too. "I thought, *Oh no, we're going to lose 10–0*," he said a few years later. But the Isles pushed their way back. Trent Hunter got them within a goal heading to the third and Miroslav Satan scored twice, the winner with 2:41 to play, and the sold-out crowd—one of a very few sellouts that season—roared as the final seconds ticked down. Arbour's smile was huge as Nolan shook his hand on the bench. "Things haven't changed at all," Nolan told Arbour.

It made the new banner-raising after the game to change Arbour's number from 1,499 to 1,500 all the more enjoyable. A parade of former players joined Arbour, his wife Claire, and their children and grandchildren for a photo in front of the new banner, along with the group of Islanders Arbour had just helped lead to yet another win, No. 740 in his career.

"It feels very good, but I really didn't do that much," Arbour said.

77 Josh Bailey, Always under the Radar

Like a lot of things about Josh Bailey, it probably escaped notice around the league that Bailey passed the 900-game mark during the shortened 2021 season. Bailey himself noticed it, but that's about all he'd like to do. It's significant, though, because Bailey is only the fourth Islander to hit that mark with the franchise, behind only Bob Nystrom, Bryan Trottier, and Denis Potvin in terms of longevity. Playing in the salary-cap era and for an Islanders franchise that's undergone heavy change during his 14 years here, it's even more remarkable.

"Josh could play another 15 years if he wanted," Frans Nielsen said. "He's that smart. I've never played with someone who has his hockey IQ. There were times I didn't see what he was trying to do on the ice, and maybe only he knew what he was doing. But he sees so much out there."

Bailey has been a lightning rod for Islanders fans, who split into "Bailey stinks" and "Bailey is elite" camps soon after Garth Snow traded down twice at the 2008 draft and took Bailey ninth overall. That Bailey remained with the Isles in his post-draft year, a season that was among the worst in franchise history with 61 points, probably hurt his stock a bit since he was never pegged as the type of talent who could put the team on his shoulders. "Bails took a ton of heat early in his career from the people on Long Island," Kyle Okposo said. "We lived together that first year. It was just a situation where he was happy to be in the NHL, but we were going through some growing pains. All his buddies were playing world juniors. He went through some periods where he wasn't producing, wasn't playing a lot, but he never lost faith. He does so many little things well that don't get appreciated by the fans."

After half a dozen solid but unspectacular seasons—mostly playing second and third line—when the Islanders started to turn things around in 2014, Bailey played most frequently with Nielsen and Okposo, two of the most popular Islanders of the last couple decades. Bailey got his chance to show off his skills when Jack Capuano put him with John Tavares in 2016–17, a line that led Bailey to his first NHL All-Star Game the next season at age 28.

There was barely any social media when Bailey broke into the league, but that changed quickly. Bailey didn't—he rarely pays attention to what's being said or written about him. Chris and Donna Bailey—Josh's parents, who have been to nearly every

Bailey gets fired up after scoring a goal during the 2021 Stanley Cup playoffs.

NHL city to watch their son play—have definitely seen some of the nastier stuff posted about him. But Josh takes it all in stride.

Bailey and his wife, Meg, are among the small group of Islanders who stay the majority of the year on the Island, where all three of their kids were born. "It's home now," he said. "It has been for a while, and we love it. There ares so many passionate fans here, but you also get a little of the anonymity; you can go out to eat pretty much anywhere, and if someone recognizes you, it's only to say something nice."

He's got three years left on his contract, which could mean 200-plus more games. That would bring him to right around Trottier's franchise record of 1,123, a mark that would be incredible for a current Islander to own.

There have been a handful of other Islanders who passed decent careers on the Island mostly in NHL obscurity. Derek King is among the top 15 players of all time in every offensive category, but he did it from 1986 to 1997, perhaps the worst stretch in team history. Hardworking center Claude Lapointe played more than 500 games as an Islander from 1997 to 2003, some very lean years.

Bailey may qualify as the most under-the-radar Islander, partly for the team and era he's played in and partly for what he does on the ice. "He's a bit of a Swiss Army Knife," Barry Trotz said. And it's not far-fetched to think that when he's done, Bailey's No. 12 could be up in the rafters for all he's accomplished.

"The way his career has progressed has been awesome to watch," Okposo said. "He's playing well, has kids; [I've seen] him grow up, become a man, become a father—it's special to me."

78 Inside the Isles' Trophy Case

Befitting a franchise that was a top NHL team for nearly a decade—and one that, despite the ups and downs of the last 35 years, still drafted a big crop of high-end NHL talent—the Islanders have won a bunch of the big NHL awards, starting with Denis Potvin's Calder Trophy in 1973–74.

That one began a long run of Islanders winning Rookie of the Year, the trophy Islanders players have won most. Perhaps it shouldn't be a surprise, given Bill Torrey's commitment to building from within in the 1970s and the frugal ways of owners from the 1990s on up. Both scenarios mean a reliance on younger (and cheaper) players who get more playing time.

It's telling that the kids who came up to the Islanders once they were champions—the Sutter brothers, Pat LaFontaine, Pat Flatley—never got much love in Calder Trophy voting.

But the list is impressive:

Denis Potvin, 1973–74. The heralded first overall pick came in as advertised, putting up 54 points and nosing out Atlanta Flames center Tom Lysiak for the award, the first in the two-year Isles history. It would not be Potvin's last piece of hardware.

Bryan Trottier, 1975–76. As the Islanders took a big step forward following their run to the 1975 semifinals, Trottier stepped in at the right time. His 95 points were an NHL rookie record, and he ran away with the award, leaving teammate Chico Resch as a distant second.

Mike Bossy, 1977–78. The first 50-goal rookie scorer, Bossy was pretty much fully formed as a dominant player his first year. It wasn't a close vote, with Colorado Rockies defenseman Barry Beck outvoted 232–113 for the award.

Bryan Berard, 1996–97. In the midst of the darkest timeline in Isles history—wearing Fisherman jerseys, going through the John Spano saga—Berard emerged as a bright spot, posting 48 points as a 19-year-old to garner 43 of 54 first-place votes and beat out Jarome Iginla for the trophy. A year and a half later, he was traded, which was par for the course back then.

Mathew Barzal, 2017–18. In the best rookie season since Trottier's Calder win, Barzal showed himself to be an amazing talent and got 160 of 164 first-place votes, dominating a good rookie field. Too bad the Isles were a mess, but that got solved at season's end.

There's only been one Islander to win the Hart Memorial Trophy, despite lots of good candidates. Trottier had an incredible 1978–79, leading the league with 134 points—the only Art Ross Trophy winner in Isles history as well as the league's top scorer. Trottier, Bossy, and Potvin routinely cannibalized each other's MVP votes, with Trottier finishing second to Guy Lafleur in 1977–78.

Once Wayne Gretzky got into the league, it was always a battle for runner-up. "That's why it felt so good to win it in '79," Trottier said. "My teammates really helped me there. And when Gretzky came along, it was hopeless. We were concerned with other things too."

Billy Smith long felt disrespected as the Islanders became one of the league's best teams in the 1970s—observers and Vezina Trophy voters seemed to feel the Isles were such a good team they didn't need great goaltending. Smith finally won one in 1981–82, beating out a host of contenders who all got first-place votes—including Resch, his old teammate. It's the only Vezina in team history.

Potvin owns three Norris Trophies, won in a four-season span from 1975 to 1979. Bobby Orr had won the previous eight before Potvin earned the award in 1975–76. Like a lot of these others, they're the only Norris Trophies in team history.

Bossy is still one of the greatest scorers in the history of the league, but his awards case is filled with mostly consolation prizes—three Lady Byng Memorial Trophies, given to the most gentlemanly player in the NHL. Pierre Turgeon won that one too, in 1992–93.

The Selke Trophy for best defensive forward is always a difficult one to judge. The Islanders had plenty of dynasty-era forwards who were skilled at both ends of the ice, but only Michael Peca took one home as an Islander, for the 2001–02 season.

Three Islanders have won the Masterton Trophy for perseverance and dedication to the game. Ed Westfall won it back in 1976–77 when it was more about service to the NHL; being captain of that motley 1972–73 squad, he deserved something. Mark Fitzpatrick battled back from a blood disorder to win the Masterton in 1991–92, able to resume his playing career after missing nearly all of the previous year with his illness. And Robin Lehner won it in 2018–19 after battling through and publicly detailing his mental illness and addiction troubles.

The Jack Adams Award for top coach has only been won twice by Islanders coaches. Al Arbour somehow only garnered one of those, in 1978–79, but it's a famously fickle award—Scotty Bowman has two and so does Jacques Demers. Barry Trotz also has two, the second of which he earned in 2018–19 with the Islanders.

And of course, four different Islanders—Trottier, Butch Goring, Bossy, and Smith—have Conn Smythe Trophies as playoff MVPs. Of course, there are also those four trophies they hoisted as a team from 1980 to 1983. "I think we'll all take those over any of the other ones," Trottier said.

79 The Underappreciated Jack Capuano

He was the second-longest-tenured Islanders coach—second to Al Arbour, which is a little like being second to Secretariat in the Belmont Stakes—and he will have the second-most wins and games coached behind the Islanders bench for a while, even with Barry Trotz's success these first three seasons.

It's time to give a little respect to Jack Capuano's nearly seven years as coach. "He doesn't get enough credit," Anders Lee said. "I think you look at most of the guys who have been here a while—they all learned something from Cappy. He got the most out of what we had."

When Garth Snow hired Capuano on an interim basis in November 2010, it was seen as another frugal move by a team that spent very little on its front office. The Islanders had hired one coach with previous NHL experience since 2001 in Ted Nolan, but he wasn't the right person for Snow's rebuild; Scott Gordon came in for two-plus seasons, but the few veterans bristled at his demands.

Capuano, meanwhile, had been around the organization for a long time. He came on as an assistant to Steve Stirling in 2005–06, moved over to being an assistant to Dan Marshall in Bridgeport the next year, and took over as Sound Tigers head coach in 2007–08. "I liked that he'd already coached a bunch of guys who came up through the system," said Snow. "He knew how to relate to these guys."

Capuano and Snow both went to the University of Maine but didn't know each other there—Capuano's brother, Dave, played briefly with Snow in college—so this was no insider hire, either.

Capuano looks on against the Washington Capitals on December 29, 2014.

And Capuano's main goal with a still-developing team in 2010–11—one that was in the midst of a 14-game winless streak when he took over—was to develop accountability in the room. Not by yelling and screaming but by making the Isles accountable to one another. "It wasn't easy," Frans Nielsen said. "We were a tight group and we were still young. You're used to making a mistake, coming to the bench, and having the coach yell at you, or give it to you during the video session the next day. Cappy would tell Kyle [Okposo] to say something to one of the guys, or me, or someone else. He wanted us to be able to say that to anyone in the room."

It took time. With a core of Okposo, Nielsen, John Tavares, Josh Bailey, Travis Hamonic, and Andrew MacDonald, along with veterans such as Mark Streit, it was not an in-your-face team. Capuano knew it would be a process, and 2011–12 looked a lot like 2010–11.

But Capuano's Islanders got to the playoffs in the lockout-shortened 2012–13 season and gave the Penguins all they could handle. After a dud the next year, the Isles posted back-to-back 100-point seasons for the first time in 30 years. Capuano had five full seasons as coach and the Islanders made the playoffs in three of them—not the greatest completion percentage but a damn sight better than any of his predecessors since Al Arbour. "You look at how it was when I came in, to get to where we got, those guys should be proud," Capuano said.

Snow fired Capuano midway through 2016–17 after the disastrous off-season, when the Isles saw Nielsen, Okposo, and Matt Martin leave in free agency and the team never quite recovered.

Capuano has been an associate coach with two teams since and interviewed for a couple of open head coach slots. His legacy through 483 games and 227 wins holds up, though. "They still have Cappy's DNA in that room," Nielsen said. "You can see it with how hard they work even now."

80 The Best Fourth Line in Hockey

Back in the 2013–14 season, Jack Capuano had an idea for a couple of his young forwards, plus one veteran the Isles had just traded for. Identity means different things to different teams, but he knew not only what he felt his Islanders team needed then but also what that identity had meant all the way through the franchise's history. "In the Cup years, they had so much talent, but I used to talk to Mr. Arbour from time to time, and he always mentioned how many hardworking guys they had on those teams," Capuano said. "The Kenny Morrows, the Garry Howatts. You have to have those guys for the big names to succeed."

So the Isles' Identity Line was born. Matt Martin, who'd been growing his game from being an enforcer in his early years with the team, joined Casey Cizikas, then a third-year center, and Cal Clutterbuck, who'd been brought in from the Wild at the 2013 draft.

Martin and Clutterbuck were prolific body-checkers. Cizikas had the wheels to be a tenacious forechecker and penalty killer. Capuano saw them as the line to put on the ice when the team needed a jolt—after an Islanders goal, after an opposing goal, or just when his team was drifting.

"We knew what Casey was going to be even before he got up there—a kid with maybe the best motor on the team," Capuano said. "Clutter was that guy you weren't sure—the way he shoots, skates, he can go up and down the lineup at that time. Cizikas is an engine, Cal's got a lot more skill than people think. And Matty is reliable, always going to play position, block shots, be smart.

"That was contagious—that line set an example, and it was contagious among our group. If you get your skill players to have that same fourth-line mentality, you're going to win."

From 2013 to 2016, that line played 204 games together—basically every night they were all healthy. After the disappointing 2013–14 season, the next two seasons were the best back-to-back years the Isles had had since the mid-1980s. They had lots of skill and they had that fourth line to back it all up.

Martin left, of course, in the summer of 2016. He had one good year in Toronto and then one enormously frustrating year when he was scratched over half of the 2017–18 season. Back on the Island, Cizikas and Clutterbuck had a solid replacement in Nikolay Kulemin, but it wasn't the same. When Lou Lamoriello took over the Islanders, one of his first moves was bringing Martin back.

And Barry Trotz wasted no time putting his Identity Line back together, but with a different purpose: Don't just crash and bang. Skate, forecheck, and create. "We're a little more grown-up as a line than we were—I was still in my mid-20s, Marty and Casey were young guys," Clutterbuck said. "The game has evolved too. The three of us can skate, think the game, and you need those things to be on the right side of the best players in the game. We create offense and defend well by handling the puck for longer periods of time in the opposing zone."

That led to another 100-plus games together the last three seasons, weaving through injuries. Cizikas had a 20-goal season in 2018–19 and Martin scored five in the 2020 playoffs. "They are definitely more than the sum of their parts," Trotz said. "They have some of the best chemistry as a line I've seen."

During the 2014–15 season, now-deposed Canadian hockey commentator Don Cherry anointed the Martin-Cizikas-Clutterbuck line "maybe the best fourth line ever in hockey, as far as I'm concerned."

It doesn't exactly roll off the tongue like Trio Grande or the Commotion Line, the original Isles fourth line of Howatt, Andre

St. Laurent, and Bob Nystrom four decades earlier. But Trotz called them his Identity Line, and that one fits for these guys.

81 Retiring Potvin's No. 5

Denis Potvin had accomplished everything there was to do as an NHL player and a defenseman. When he retired after the 1988–89 season, he owned every scoring record for defensemen: most goals (310), most assists (742), most points (1,052, the first-ever defenseman to cross the 1,000-point plateau), most playoff games (185), most playoff goals (56). He had four Stanley Cup rings and three Norris Trophies, and he had captained the greatest dynasty of any U.S.-based team.

Within two years, he was giving a speech at the Hockey Hall of Fame in Toronto, going in with his longtime teammate Mike Bossy as part of the 1991 class, which also included Scotty Bowman.

But it was seeing his No. 5 go to the Coliseum rafters that was perhaps the most poignant moment. On February 1, 1992, Potvin became the first Islander so honored. It was fitting: He was the first big piece of the puzzle when Bill Torrey drafted him No. 1 in 1973, and John Pickett saving the team from financial ruin in 1978 allowed the dynasty to happen.

Pickett's reign as owner was ending as he sought a buyer during that 1991–92 season. Torrey had been rumored to be headed out the door, and he was let go in August; Al Arbour was in his return stint as coach but would be retired for good two years later. So the timing was right. And so was the honor. "I can only think of one thing that would add to this evening, and that's if I had my skates

Other Banner Nights

- **March 3, 1992:** A month after No. 5 went to the Coliseum rafters, No. 22 followed. Similar to the 1991 Hockey Hall of Fame induction, when Denis Potvin and Mike Bossy went in together, it was fitting that Potvin and Bossy were No. 1 and 2 on number retirements.

    "I always said we went into games one or two goals ahead," Bossy said. "The game was ours to lose. You could see it in the other team's faces. Once we won the first Stanley Cup, we knew how to win."

- **February 20, 1993:** Billy Smith's No. 31 went to the rafters. He had retired four seasons earlier and went into the Hall of Fame the same year. A no-brainer decision for the gruff old goat.

- **April 1, 1995:** Eric Nystrom, future NHLer, asked his dad, Bob, once whether his No. 23 would ever be up there at the Coli. "I was a journeyman," Bob Nystrom told his then-12-year-old son. "They'll never retire my number."

    Oh, how wrong he was. Nystrom was the embodiment of Al Arbour's Islanders ethos, even if he wasn't as skilled as some of his teammates.

- **December 7, 1996:** Clark Gillies's No. 9 was retired. It was a great night that seemed even greater, as it fell during the honeymoon phase with John Spano; at least we still have the No. 9 banner to look at.

- **January 25, 1997:** Al Arbour's banner night. His was emblazoned with the No. 739, for the number of coaching wins he had behind the Islanders bench; when he returned a decade later to get to his 1,500ᵗʰ game coached with the team, the 739 banner came down and a 1,500 banner went up.

- **January 13, 2001:** There aren't too many teams in the NHL with a banner to honor a general manager, but having Bill Torrey's signature bow tie on his Coliseum banner was the perfect touch. For all he did for the franchise from its inception, Torrey's banner with the words THE ARCHITECT on it makes sense.

- **October 20, 2001:** After a long delay, Bryan Trottier's No. 19 joined his compatriots above the Coliseum ice. The Isles reportedly had reached out to Trottier for years to have a

(continued)

ceremony for their longest-serving player, and it finally came to pass early in the 2001–02 revival season.

- **February 20, 2020:** John Tonelli's No. 27 went to the rafters. It was a long-overdue honor for one of the hardest-working members of the dynasty.
- **February 29, 2020:** Butch Goring's No. 91 went to the rafters. He was only an Islander for five-plus seasons, but they were the five best in team history, and Goring played a major role. Retiring his number also helped get the fans past the most recent No. 91.

on," Potvin told the Coliseum crowd that night. "That would take away some of the stress I'm feeling."

Potvin welcomed the call to the Hockey Hall of Fame, a deserving honor that came so quickly after his retirement. "That's something you never really think about until later in your career," he said. "Then people start to talk about it and you realize you might be able to get there."

In his speech on the Coliseum ice that night in 1992, he expressed his feelings to the fans and some of his old teammates in a truly heartfelt way. Potvin was a good captain because he wasn't always one of the boys—Bossy and Bryan Trottier were tight because they loved to live quietly, Clark Gillies was the fun-loving center of the crew, Billy Smith and Butch Goring were older and a little more off-kilter. Potvin was the rare Islander who liked going to New York to socialize. After retirement he got straight into broadcasting, leaving the Island almost immediately to work Panthers broadcasts for 16 years, then Senators broadcasts in his hometown.

But he told the fans and the old Islanders assembled that night three decades ago what it meant to have that No. 5 go up. "The Hockey Hall of Fame will have some of my memorabilia, maybe a bust of me," he said, "but that's in Toronto.... This is where my playground was. This was my battlefield. If I'm going to be immortalized, it should be here.

"These were the very best years of my life."

82 The Rivalry

The Islanders were born in the Rangers' shadow, quickly surpassed the big-city rivals in success, and have been jockeying for position to return to glory for many years now. They've played 282 times in the regular season and in eight playoff series. There have been bench-clearing brawls, goalie fights, and too many fights in the stands at the Coliseum and Madison Square Garden to count.

So let's hear from a few Islanders about their favorite games against the Rangers:

Brent Sutter—Islanders 4, Rangers 3 (OT), April 18, 1982
"That was my rookie year, and you got a real taste of how it was against the Rangers from the exhibition games—line brawls, guys coming off the bench. They didn't prevent that stuff from happening like they do now, and it was just intense. I remember Billy Smith had to hide in the net during the anthem at the Garden because people would be throwing stuff.

"This game stands out to me because it was the first one in the city of that series. We won it in overtime [on a Bryan Trottier goal to take a 2–1 series lead in the quarterfinals], and we're getting on the bus, coming out of the tunnel underneath MSG to go back to the Island. We've got a police car in front, a police car in back, and police on horseback on either side of the bus. I never saw anything like it.

235

"And I'm hearing a policeman yelling at people, 'You come near the bus and you'll die in the hooves!' Can you believe it? I'll never forget that. 'You'll die in the hooves!' Just crazy.

"I've seen some intense rivalries in the NHL, been part of Hawks-Blues, Flames-Oilers. But it's hard to compare with how Islanders-Rangers was when we always had to go through them in the playoffs and we ended up winning all the Cups."

Mark Parrish—Islanders 6, Rangers 3, January 30, 2002

"Now, I had two goals in that one at the Garden. It was right before the All-Star break, but that's not why it stands out. [Alexei] Yashin had a hat trick, I think all in the first period, and then all hell broke loose later on. I think Yash had a fight [against Tomas Kloucek], [Mariusz] Czerkawski was mixing it up; it was just one of those wild Islanders-Rangers games, and we had a few of those that year.

"At the end of the game, every line of ours had a guy missing, either in the box or tossed, except my line, with me, [Michael] Peca, and [Shawn] Bates. And Pecs turns to us and goes, 'Does this mean we're wimps?'

"But that was a memorable year. We played them in the preseason at the Coliseum a few weeks after September 11, and I remember both teams on the ice wearing NYPD and fire department hats during the anthem. That was a special moment. Then the season started and you've got Theo Fleury doing the chicken dance at [Eric] Cairns and then this night at the Garden. At least we won this one."

Jaroslav Halak—Islanders 3, Rangers 0, January 13, 2015

"That was my first year [with the Islanders], and I remember that one really well. I made a couple saves early, they hit maybe two posts, and then we got out in front in the second period and I ended up with a shutout. It was always such a great atmosphere on the Island and at MSG, but especially at MSG. I don't really know why I was able to have good success against them [Halak was 11–3–0 against the Rangers as an Islander]; it's just one of those things.

"You know, I always felt like Islanders fans had a little chip on their shoulder compared to the Rangers, and we felt it too. That kind of thing can give you a little extra feeling when you play that team. They were always fun to be a part of."

Mike Bossy—Islanders 3, Rangers 2 (OT), April 10, 1984

"It was the first time we played them in the first round during our great run, and it was a real fight. We wanted to keep our streak alive and they wanted to be the ones to end it, of course, and that probably would have been very sweet for them to be the team that stopped our run. It came down to that Game 5 at the Coliseum and they tied it late [on Don Maloney's disputed goal with 39 seconds left in the third], and we went to overtime.

"They had a couple good chances to win it [Dave Maloney noted that Mikko Leinonen had the puck come to him in OT with no one around, and "it just hopped over his stick, like some Coliseum ghost was out there"], and then Kenny Morrow, who rarely scored goals, won it and got us through.

"We certainly had some battles with them, and I can still remember the painful feeling from 1979, when I didn't have a great series against them. But it was always so intense, and some guys really got into it—more the physical guys like Clarkie and Bobby Ny. That really wasn't my thing, so I never treated those games as something more special, but when you look back, they were always there when we needed to get somewhere in the playoffs."

Ryan Strome—Rangers 6, Islanders 5, February 16, 2015

"Funny to pick one when I was with the Islanders and we lost, but that one definitely sticks out. I had two goals, they came back in the third and won it, and the fans were really into it with all the goals and it going back and forth like that. A game that kind of had it all—probably a few fights during the tailgate or in the stands too. That's what I remember most about playing there with the Isles in those Rangers games—the fans were charged up pretty much from the minute they parked their cars. You can't beat that."

Matt Martin—Islanders 4, Rangers 3 (SO), February 14, 2013

"This is an obvious one for me. It was the lockout year, and we didn't start off that well. I think we came to the Garden on a [five-game] losing streak, and it felt like if we didn't get out of there with a couple points, we were headed back to the lottery even though it was still early in that season.

"They scored a couple goals and took a [2–0] lead into the first intermission. Dougie Weight [then an assistant coach] came in and really laid into us, reminding us how close we were to letting another year slip away. We rallied, won in a shootout, and that kind of set us up to go on the run we needed to make the playoffs. First time for a lot of us young guys then."

Butch Goring—Islanders 4, Rangers 1, April 8, 1984

"They had us down 2–1 in that series, and it was a significant one for me personally. I was on the fourth line, Al [Arbour] had Pat LaFontaine, Trottier, and Brent Sutter getting most of the ice time that series, and the Rangers kicked our butts pretty good in Game 2 and Game 3.

"After all the Cups, we had a lot of pride still in that room; I had a lot of pride in my own play. And we were down 1–0 going into the third period of that game at Madison Square Garden, on the brink of having it all end against our rivals. I remember saying a few things in the room after the second period, and Al put me back in the rotation a bit more, we got a couple goals, and I set up Clarkie for one late that kind of sealed it.

"Kenny Morrow's goal in Game 5 is the big one from that series, but we needed that comeback in Game 4 to even get there."

83 The Commotion Line

There's a reason Bob Nystrom is Mr. Islander, one of the earliest members of the franchise who scored a ton of big goals. But he never had the flash of some of his fellow dynasty members. He was a lunch-pail guy at heart. And that's why Al Arbour, in his coaching wisdom, put together the first fourth line in franchise history, with Nystrom as the top dog.

When Arbour took over after the 1972–73 expansion ugliness, his first goal was to cut down on the team's goals against. He wanted to improve everything, but building from the defensive zone out was his radical idea nearly 50 years ago, and in Arbour's first year, the Isles reduced their goals allowed by 100.

In 1974–75 Arbour got three of his young, energetic forwards together. There was Nystrom, who'd established himself with 21 goals in 1973–74, his first full season. He was 22. There was Garry Howatt, who was maybe 175 pounds soaking wet but as feisty as they come. "The Toy Tiger," Nystrom said. "Howie was tougher than anyone."

Howatt was also 22 and had made his bones as a rookie in 1973–74, but more with his toughness than his skill—he was fifth in the league that season with 204 penalty minutes.

And centering those two was a 20-year-old, Andre St. Laurent. Another undersized but tenacious player, Bill Torrey and Jim Devellano drafted St. Laurent in the fourth round in 1973 not necessarily projecting a prolific scorer but one who could help play a strong defensive role up front. "Everybody would like to score goals," St. Laurent said at the end of his 10-year NHL career, "but through my career I've had trouble scoring. When that happens, you find other ways to contribute."

They were hardly deficient in goal scoring in 1974–75, certainly by today's standards. Nystrom led the Islanders with 27 goals, Howatt had 18, and St. Laurent had 14. Probably making Arbour happier was their ability to keep opposing teams off the scoresheet while they were on the ice—plus/minus wasn't a statistic back then, and it's certainly been laughed at plenty these days, but Howatt [plus-32] and St. Laurent [plus-22] were the highest-rated Isles forwards that season.

And Howatt learned to control his temper, posting a career-low 121 PIMs. "This is a guy who, when we first got called up in 1973, tried to pick a fight with Bobby Orr," Nystrom said, laughing. "Bobby Orr! Can you imagine? And when games would get out of hand, he'd always be on the bench next to me going, 'C'mon, Bobby. The fur's gotta fly.' But he could play, and I think a lot of people don't remember that about him."

The line hit its peak in the 1975 playoff comeback against the Penguins. They hadn't done enough defensively as the Isles fell into a 3–0 series hole, but they produced at key times later in the series. St. Laurent scored the opening goal in a 3–1 Game 4 win and Howatt scored twice in a 4–1 Game 6 win, including the eventual winner in the second period.

Much like their fourth-line counterparts on today's Islanders, that line was able to set a tone without scoring. "You had the Flyers back then who were getting away with things that just shouldn't have been allowed," Chico Resch said. "You'd stand up to one of them, and then you had a whole mob on you.

"So now we have these three young guys who are just fearless. The glass at the Coliseum was really low back then, and the boards would just rock back and forth—they'd get those boards rocking.

Nobody messed with Howie, and Bobby Ny was always one of the toughest guys we had. They brought something, a team toughness, that we hadn't had before."

84 July 1, 2016

The Islanders had a good thing going in 2014–15 and 2015–16, their first back-to-back 100-point seasons since 1980–81 and 1981–82. John Tavares led a cast of talented, homegrown forwards, and Nick Leddy and Johnny Boychuk anchored the defense.

But as the 2015–16 season unfolded, a few different threads were coming together in a potentially unpleasant way for Garth Snow's team. Not on the ice—that first season in Barclays Center, despite the unhappy situation for fans and players traveling to Brooklyn, was a success even before Tavares sent the Isles beyond the first round of the playoffs for the first time since 1993.

Kyle Okposo, Tavares's sometime linemate, close friend, and fellow Islander for eight years, was pretty obviously headed out the door. Snow had quietly gauged trade interest in Okposo at the 2015 draft, clearly sensing that a contract either wasn't financially feasible or not a top Islanders priority. Okposo, just 28, was finishing a five-year deal worth $2.8 million per season—he would easily double that in free agency, and the Islanders had other plans right from the start of 2015–16.

There were two other pending free agents after 2015–16. Frans Nielsen, the longest-tenured Islander and the one who most deserved the "underrated" label among a team that was still lightly regarded around the league, was also ready to cash in after making just $2.75 million in the prior four seasons. And Matt Martin, who had emerged as one of the most popular players on the team in his sixth season, was due a big raise as well.

The other factor: Scott Malkin and Jon Ledecky were preparing to take over majority ownership from Charles Wang on July 1, 2016. To show they meant business, the new owners wanted Snow to make a free-agency splash.

The splashiest free-agent possibility in the run up to July 1 was Steven Stamkos. The Lightning captain was about to hit the market, and the week leading up to free-agency day had been marked as a contact window to allow potential UFAs to gauge interest from teams before the doors opened for real on July 1.

Ownership wanted the Islanders to get in line to talk to Stamkos. They also pushed Snow to recruit Andrew Ladd, former Jets captain and an old Stanley Cup teammate of assistant coach/GM Doug Weight. Those orders kept Nielsen, the player the Islanders could least afford to lose, on pause as the off-season got underway. Snow and Nielsen had known each other for a decade, and Snow hoped his No. 2 center could wait for a final pitch. "Snowy's one of my good friends; he always will be," Nielsen said. "It was just a tough spot to be in."

Nielsen and Martin started to have teams reach out to show their interest. Nielsen thought about the awful Brooklyn commute—"I never would have even considered leaving if we were still at the Coli," he said—and Martin, the ultimate lunch-pail player, knew he was unlikely to have another shot at cashing in.

Within minutes of noon on July 1, all three Islanders—with a combined 1,573 Islanders games between them—were gone: Okposo to the Sabres for seven years at $6 million per, Nielsen to the Red Wings for six years at $5.25 million each, and Martin to the Leafs for four years and $2.5 million per. Snow bagged Ladd for seven years at $5.5 million and another over-30 veteran, Jason Chimera, for two years and $2.25 million.

Nielsen has remained with the Red Wings since his trade.

"As a coach, you're proud that you had a hand in helping those guys go on and make the big paydays they got," Jack Capuano said. "But selfishly you want them around. They were a huge presence in our room."

The team simply didn't have the same feel the next season. Ladd and Chimera both scored 20 or more goals, but Ladd in particular was never a good fit—he was assumed to be a vocal leader but was more like Tavares, a quieter player who tried to lead by example. Outside of Boychuk and Cal Clutterbuck, there weren't really commanding voices in that 2016–17 room.

Okposo, Nielsen, and Martin had come up through the lean years and, with Capuano's urging, took on leadership roles; Okposo and Nielsen were Tavares's alternate captains. "It's hard to say because I obviously wasn't there, but all three leaving the same day must have been tough," Nielsen said. "We all gave a lot to that organization. It was all we knew."

The other hard part was watching all three former Islanders fail to have success in their new homes. Martin had a solid first season in Toronto but was benched often by Mike Babcock his second year and ended up back on the Island when Lou Lamoriello, who'd signed Martin for the Leafs as GM, traded for his fourth-line winger on July 3, 2018—bringing Martin back where he belonged.

Nielsen's Red Wings have been among the worst teams in the league during his years there. Okposo suffered through a hellish bout with concussion effects that took a toll on his mental health and now fills a bottom-six role.

None of the free agents signed on July 1, 2016, really panned out anywhere around the league. But no team took a bigger hit that day than the Isles.

85 Torrey and the Swedes

Of all the decisions big and small that defined Bill Torrey's genius over two decades with the Islanders, the one that perhaps gets overlooked is his ability to find talent anywhere. Even Europe, which in the 1970s was the great unknown.

Borje Salming and Inge Hammarstrom came from Sweden to join the Leafs in 1973 and met with mixed success—Salming was an amazing talent who thrived and Hammarstrom had a few good years but will mostly be remembered for a demeaning quote from wacky Toronto owner Harold Ballard, who declared: "Hammarstrom could go into the corner with two eggs in his pants and never break them."

Ulf Nilsson and Anders Hedberg came from Sweden next, in 1974, joining Bobby Hull for four dynamic years with the Winnipeg Jets in the World Hockey Association. They signed with the Rangers in tandem in 1978, helping turn the Rangers into a perennial playoff team that usually met its fate against the Isles.

Torrey was already on the case. He said a friend of Al Arbour's had moved to Sweden to teach and provided scouting reports on the Swedish pro teams. Torrey and Jim Devellano selected Stefan Persson, a defenseman from Umea, 214th overall in 1974. Persson made it over and into the Islanders lineup for the 1977–78 season and promptly scored 56 points in 66 games as a rookie. The Calder Trophy that year went to some kid named Mike Bossy, but true to the jingoistic nature of hockey in North America then, Persson didn't even get a single vote for Rookie of the Year.

Arbour's friend drifted away, but Torrey found another insider in Sweden to hunt for talent. "He has other duties in Swedish hockey," Torrey said during the 1983 Cup run. "He prefers to do it on the quiet. I talk to him on the phone maybe two or three times during the season."

And there was simply a commitment from Torrey to do whatever it took to find the right pieces for his team. That led him to perhaps the best free-agent signing in team history, a 26-year-old named Anders Kallur.

Torrey knew Eddie Westfall was retiring after the 1978–79 season and needed a similarly defense-minded forward to supplement the incredible high-end talent he had up front. Kallur, who'd been on the Bruins roster the season before but left for Sweden without playing a game, chose the Islanders over the Whalers for the 1979–80 season.

Kallur had played for seven years at the highest level of Swedish hockey but also worked as a gym teacher. "I knew what I could do," he told the *New York Times* in 1981. "I wanted to try something new." He talked to Persson, who convinced Kallur the Islanders were the right organization for him to jump to.

He paid instant dividends, scoring 22 goals that year playing mostly with Butch Goring and Bob Bourne. A shoulder injury kept him out of the entire playoff run to the first Stanley Cup, but Kallur scored 36 in 1980–81 and was a key member of the next three Cup teams.

And he did it while taking plenty of abuse from players in the NHL who didn't give Europeans much respect. "Andy has taken more shots than I did when I came into the league," Bossy said back in 1981. "He has responded to this treatment by scoring goals. In our league, people respect that. I think sometimes Swedish players do change their styles. It seems to me that Hedberg felt if he was going to stay, he'd have to change his style a little, be more aggressive. It might have taken a little from his offense."

Kallur also helped another Swedish Islanders draft pick, Tomas Jonsson, acclimate to North America for the 1981–82 season (Kallur had coached Jonsson in Sweden).

Kallur only played 383 games in the NHL, all with the Islanders, but he had a huge impact. His 19 shorthanded goals are still tops in franchise history, one more than Goring and Lorne Henning. Persson and Kallur were the first European-born players with their names on the Cup, joined by Jonsson in 1982 and Mats Hallin in 1983.

"The big knock against the European guys was that they were timid," said Bob Nystrom, who was born in Stockholm but grew up in western Canada. "Our guys would never fight, but they were tough. Like Bossy was. And them even coming here really showed what Bill was all about: He only cared if you fit on the team, not where you were from. And Stef, Andy, Tommy, those guys played huge roles for us."

86 Arbour Steps Down, Simpson Steps In

When Al Arbour made the decision to retire from coaching after the 1985–86 season, Bill Torrey thought he'd found the right man for the job. No matter who it was—in this case, it was a career junior coach named Terry Simpson—replacing Arbour was going to be a monumental task. "It's like taking over Berkshire Hathaway from Warren Buffett," Pat Flatley said. "Good luck to you!"

Simpson had a lot of attributes that Arbour had—he was relatively quiet, direct, and unassuming—but he was not Al. And even though several of the players from the Cup years had already departed, there was still so much history hanging over the team that was just two years removed from five consecutive Finals appearances that the task was simply daunting. "I'm coming into the job as a realist," Simpson said. "I'm certainly apprehensive about the situation, but that might work in my favor."

It was what Torrey was looking for. "He [came] in clean, with no preconceived notions," Torrey said. "One key factor in hiring Terry was that our championship teams have had their time, and what we have to do now is look to the future."

Arbour had brought on Brian Kilrea, also a successful junior coach, as his assistant prior to the 1984–85 season, clearly with the thought that Kilrea could take over when Arbour decided to step away. But Torrey wanted no ties to anything Islanders. "[Kilrea] was groomed to be Al's replacement," Jiggs McDonald said. "The guys loved Brian; he was a friend to the players. They wouldn't keep him on because he was too close to the players—we were in a changing era, but we weren't totally ready to change. Brian would have been the ideal guy. Terry Simpson was a good hockey man, but he couldn't communicate, couldn't get things going with those guys."

The Islanders in 1986–87 were much the same team they had been the previous two years: decent in the regular season but a clear third to the dominating Flyers and the slightly better Capitals, whom it seemed the Isles were locked into meeting in every division semifinal.

The Isles rallied from 2–0 down to win the best-of-five in 1985 before the Flyers dismantled them; the Caps finally defeated the Isles in 1986, a three-game sweep that told Arbour it was time for a new voice behind the bench.

Bryan Trottier at 30 still led them in scoring in 1986–87, followed closely by a hobbled Mike Bossy, who posted his only sub-50-goal season with 38 in 63 games as he struggled with back and knee problems. Denis Potvin at 32 was also slowing, with injuries in what would be his final season as captain and second-to-last NHL season. Aside from those guys and Ken Morrow and Billy Smith, every other Islanders regular was 26 or younger at the completion of the season. "We were trying to make some new memories for the fans distinct from the Cup years," Trottier said. "It was a hard break. Terry tried; he was a good man. But there were still a lot of expectations around a team that didn't exist in the same way anymore."

And yet the Islanders managed to succeed. The Easter Epic got them past the Caps and made a star out of Pat LaFontaine; they pushed the Flyers to seven games the next round. In 1987–88 the Isles won the Patrick Division, their last division title—that they did it with 88 points in a division in which seven points separated first from sixth didn't matter.

Torrey seemed vindicated in a sense, thinking he'd found the right coach to shepherd the club into a new era. But the upstart Devils took care of the Isles in six games, and then 1988–89 was a mess, with the team—now with only Trottier, Morrow, and Smith from the old core—completely out of whack from the start. In the midst of an eight-game losing streak that dropped them to 7–18–2 in December, Torrey fired Simpson—and succeeded in cajoling Arbour, who'd been around the whole time as VP of player development, back to the bench. "I think a person like Al has a chance to turn things around," said Simpson after his firing. "I didn't feel a lot of the players resented me, but there were a few."

Arbour coached five more full seasons after that, ending up as the last true link to the dynasty.

87 Mike Bossy Hangs 'Em Up

Of all the exits of the core dynasty players, none hurt as much as Mike Bossy's. Because everyone knew that he could have had—and deserved—more years to show his greatness.

Bossy was never injury-free, even during his best years. He took a ton of abuse from an early age in hockey because he wasn't a traditional tough guy in 1970s junior hockey, where bench-clearing brawls were as common as hat tricks.

As he wrote in a *Players' Tribune* article in 2017: "For whatever reason, some people will resent you for being a goal scorer. Other teams are going to target you, big time. You'll get jumped from behind. Sucker punched. Completely knocked out by blindside hits. (In the future, there's a serious injury called a concussion. You don't know what this is yet, but unfortunately you're going to have quite a few.)

"Some nights, you'll be sitting on the *bench* just trying to catch your wind when you'll look up and see the other team—literally the whole team—rushing your bench for a brawl. The slashing and cross-checking will be so common that it's barely worth mentioning. This is just the reality of junior hockey in the 1970s.

"The abuse will leave a mark on you forever. Your nose will be broken. Your ribs will be cracked. But it will leave a mark on your soul, too. Psychologically, just riding on the bus to games knowing the violence that awaits you is something that you're going to have a hard time with. There are going to be so many long bus rides when you'll think, *Why am I even doing this? What's the point?*"

When the Islanders drafted him 15th overall, the knock was that Bossy wasn't tough enough to withstand the NHL. His 53-goal rookie season in 1977–78 dispelled that; so did the next eight seasons, when he scored between 51 and 69 goals apiece, a record for consecutive 50-goal seasons that no one's going to break.

But the toll all that scoring took—the attention and the attendant abuse on his slight frame—wore him down over the years. The failures of the Isles in the 1978 and 1979 playoffs stemmed from the Leafs and Rangers getting physical and dirty with the Islanders, but with Bossy most of all. The Flyers tried the same thing in the 1980 Cup Finals and Bossy stood up to Philly center Mel Bridgman in Game 1, helping to set the tone.

And it freed Bossy in a way. His tear through the next three postseasons, when he scored 17 goals in each and won a Conn Smythe Trophy, is the greatest playoff run by any goal scorer in NHL history. "He was unstoppable at times during those years," Bryan Trottier said. "If I got him the puck, it felt like it was in the net. That's a great feeling."

His knee became an issue, then his back—the latter hampering him throughout the 1986–87 season. "No way am I playing anywhere near to what I have in the past," he said after a win over the Penguins just before Christmas.

Once it became clear toward the end of that season that he wasn't going to finish a 10th straight year with 50 goals—he "only" had 38, which would still be great for anyone playing in the last 25 years or so—Bossy's spirit waned along with his physical state. "Teams have never liked me to score against them," Bossy told the *New York Times* in March 1987, "but now that they know I have a sore back, and that I was having a hard time going for the record, I've taken more illegal hits than ever before. In the heat of the action, there are players who don't care what they do to you, and I guess there are some kids in the league who don't give two hoots if they injure you."

He missed the final three weeks of the regular season and played barely half of the playoff games, missing the Easter Epic against the

Caps. And his back just never healed; the greatest scorer in the game sat out all of 1987–88, and then on October 24, 1988—after a brief dalliance with the Kings, who inquired with Bossy about whether he'd want to join Wayne Gretzky for a comeback—Bossy announced his retirement at age 30.

Oddly enough that was the age at which he predicted he'd hang up his skates and stick seven years earlier if he felt the game was taking him away from his family. "There's not a hole in my life," Bossy said at a teary-eyed press conference. "But until the day I die, I think I'll always be a little disappointed that my career came to an end because of this injury and not because it was the right time for it to come to an end."

With 573 goals and 10 brilliant seasons as an Islander, Bossy stepped away. His No. 22 went to the Coliseum rafters on March 3, 1992, a year after his induction into the Hockey Hall of Fame.

88 Pat LaFontaine, the Unlikely Islander Who Stayed on the Island

There's a long list of Islanders who have made the Island home after retirement. Bob Nystrom was one of the first, having met his wife there. In more recent years you're likely to find Radek Martinek or Arron Asham coaching kids at Northwell Health Ice Center. When Matt Martin hangs 'em up, he'll surely be a fixture on the Island for years to come.

And then there's Pat LaFontaine—you know, the star player who felt betrayed by ownership in the late 1980s, held out, and forced a trade. The retired player who rejoined the organization as a senior advisor to GM Neil Smith in 2006 only to promptly resign when Smith was fired 40 days later.

A young LaFontaine skates against the Maple Leafs in 1985.

And what he's done with his life on the Island means a lot to the people of the area beyond what he did as the best American-born player ever to play for the Isles and one of the best ever in the league. "I talk now in life about scoring goals when you're young, because life now is all about assists," he said. LaFontaine founded the Companions in Courage Foundation—a charity that provides playrooms and support for children in hospitals in the New York area and elsewhere—in 1997, just after concussions forced his retirement.

And there was no place he considered retiring to other than the Island. Mostly because it's where he got the biggest assist of his life, thanks to the Islanders. "I came to the team in 1984, after the Olympics, and Al [Arbour]—right off the bat, he dangled the carrot out there for me," LaFontaine said. "He threw me out there in every situation: 'Let's see what you can do, kid.' And I ate it up; me and Flats [Pat Flatley], we were charged up right from the start.

"And we get past the Rangers, then Washington and the Canadiens to get to the Finals, trying for the fifth Cup. We had a little bit of a break before the Finals started, and I remember one day at practice, Lornie Henning, our assistant coach, puts his arm around me and says, 'Kathy [Lorne's wife] and I really think the girl next door to us would just be great for you.'

"I was like, 'OK, Lornie. I trust your judgment and all, but can we try to win a Stanley Cup first?'"

The Islanders fell short, of course. And the 19-year-old LaFontaine did take Henning's advice and called up the next-door neighbor's daughter, Mary Beth Hoey. They went to a club that allowed teenagers in—she was 18.

"We dated for three years and we've been married for 34," Pat LaFontaine said last year. "We got married at St. Patrick's in Huntington, and my son just got married there too. It's amazing how it all came full circle."

The acrimony from 30 years ago is long gone, of course. Long Island is home and the Islanders have welcomed LaFontaine back into the fold, even after the quick reunion in the front office and split with Charles Wang 15 years ago.

There are plenty in the Isles fan base who feel LaFontaine's No. 16 belongs up in the rafters with the dynasty greats—and that it's not his fault John Pickett pulled away from the team as the 1980s went on. There may be time for that.

Right now LaFontaine is doing what he's been doing for more than 20 years—giving back to what the Island gave him. "I had to look up on a map where Long Island was when the Isles drafted me in 1983," he said. "I wouldn't have all the things I have in life without having come here."

89 Robin Lehner's One Special Season

There have been a few one-and-done types in Islanders history, mostly since the mid-1990s when stability and success went out the window for a while. Wendel Clark, a hero in Toronto, was an Islander for 58 games in the 1996–97 season; Roberto Luongo was an Islander for part of the 1999–2000 season, but you probably already knew that.

We'll likely never see a one-season wonder like Robin Lehner again, though. How he came in and how he became a fan favorite in such a short time will endure beyond his special 2018–19 season in the same way his tattoo of Long Island will endure. "Forever imprinted a place that means the world to me and Where I started my new journey," Lehner wrote on Twitter in February 2020 after getting the outline of the Island tattooed on his neck. "Tribute to a great place filled with great people. Will forever love the island."

Lehner's arrival was basically a marriage of desperation. Lou Lamoriello took over the president's job (and then the general manager's job) in the spring of 2018 with a couple of goals in mind: Keep John Tavares, of course, but also try to find a top-notch goaltender.

Well into free agency, the Isles were still sitting with just Thomas Greiss and no plan B. Lehner, meanwhile, was just trying to put his life back together, having left the Sabres at the end of March to go into rehab in Arizona, where he not only got treatment for alcohol and substance addictions but was diagnosed with bipolar disorder.

Lehner and Lamoriello met twice. "We talked about family and life," Lehner wrote in his first-person account of his mental-health and substance-abuse struggles in the *Athletic* in 2018. "I had two great meetings with him and, looking back now, those meetings became some of the best moments in my life."

On the eve of training camp, with Lehner having signed a one-year, $1.5 million deal, the *Athletic* published Lehner's harrowing account of his off-season—thoughts of suicide, heavy drinking, and finally some peace and a new professional home. His candor endeared him to his new teammates and Islanders fans. "It's incredibly brave," Josh Bailey said that first day of camp.

And then his play said even more. After a slow start while trying to fix technical elements of his game under the tutelage of goalie coaches Mitch Korn and Piero Greco, Lehner reeled off eight consecutive wins from December 18 to January 10 and posted five shutouts over his final 26 starts. He was even better in the first round of the playoffs, allowing just six goals to Sidney Crosby, Evgeni Malkin, and the Penguins in a four-game sweep.

Just after that series ended, Lehner was announced as a finalist for both the Bill Masterton Memorial Trophy, awarded for "perseverance and dedication" to the sport, as well as the Vezina Trophy as the top goalie. He was the first Islander named a Vezina finalist since Kelly Hrudey 32 years earlier.

"I'm happy with the recognition the issues have gotten," Lehner said. "To be honest, I've been living my life pretty much day to day this year. I've really locked myself away. So for me personally, it's nice, especially with the support of the fans here. But that's not the end goal."

After the season ended with a second-round sweep by the Hurricanes, Lehner was hopeful to lock in a long-term deal with the Islanders. They had other ideas, however, offering only a two-year deal that was initially rebuffed.

Lamoriello decided to look elsewhere for long-term solutions in goal, signing Semyon Varlamov to a four-year deal on July 1. Lehner took a one-year, $5 million deal from the Hawks, was a deadline acquisition by Vegas, and nearly carried the Golden Knights to the 2020 Finals, falling short in the Western Conference final as the Isles did in the East.

Lehner has a long-term home now in Vegas, having signed a five-year deal. The temptations of Sin City haven't affected him. He was certainly upset the Islanders didn't try harder to keep him, but he also will never forget the fans for supporting him in his first steps toward a sober life as he coped publicly and honestly with his mental health.

90 Butch Goring, the Unlikely Islanders Lifer

Funny that the last piece of the dynasty puzzle has ended up being the Islander who stuck around the longest. "It's definitely not what I would have imagined, no," Butch Goring said. Bill Torrey made trade-deadline history when he acquired Goring from the Kings on March 10, 1980, putting the right veteran into the mix at the exact right time. Four Cups and one Conn Smythe Trophy later, Goring was also the first of the four-time champion players to leave, claimed on waivers by the Bruins midway through the 1984–85 season.

He retired after that season and was immediately named Bruins head coach, having gained experience as Al Arbour's player-assistant for the last three of his Islanders seasons. Goring didn't last long in Boston, and he made it back to the Islanders organization within a few seasons, coaching the team's IHL affiliate in Denver and then Salt Lake City to back-to-back IHL championships in 1994–95 and 1995–96.

Before the 1999–2000 season, Mike Milbury brought him back to the Island, this time as head coach. A couple of Islanders Cup winners had been behind the bench before—Lorne Henning, who had been Arbour's assistant for several years, coached the lock-out-shortened 1994–95 season before being replaced by Milbury, and Bob Nystrom had been an assistant after he retired.

But this was different. Goring had worked his way up for his chance. Unfortunately it was the final year of the disastrous Steven Gluckstern/Howard Milstein ownership, which took cheap to a whole new level. The 1999–2000 team was destined to be bad, and they wanted Goring, a successful minor league coach, to build it up. "I remember [Howard] Milstein telling me, 'We want you to teach them how to win,'" Goring said. "I thought, *That makes sense.* But I didn't want to be fired after a year—things hadn't exactly been stable with coaching there under Mike."

Those Islanders won 2 of their first 10 games and 6 of their first 29, finishing with 58 points. Goring was ready to keep teaching a young crew that included future stars Roberto Luongo and Zdeno Chara, but Charles Wang stepped in to buy the team at the end of the season. "I knew going in this was not an overnight job, but I believed Mr. Milstein that he brought me in for the right reasons," Goring said. "It changed because Charles wanted to win right away. I told him that wasn't happening—I knew exactly who we had. I thought I was in a good situation."

Milbury's major moves before the 2000–01 season should have given Goring more to work with, but that team was so much worse—the 52 points that season were the fewest since the expansion year, and Goring was fired at season's end. "I really enjoyed Mike. Away from the rink, I had a lot of fun with him; we talked a lot about hockey," Goring said. "I don't know what happened when the ownership changed. We were picked dead last and we finished fifth from the bottom. Everybody was happy we were headed in the right direction. Mike doesn't have a lot of patience— the troubles started when we moved Luongo and [Olli] Jokinen. It really got away from the game plan. Taking Rick [DiPietro]—I have no criticism of Rick, but we had Lu and we had a chance at [Marian] Gaborik after we got lucky and won the lottery.

"I don't know what changed with Mike and his philosophy. But we weren't going in the same direction. He brought in some vets who weren't that good, changed the whole dynamic of the team."

So he'd been a player, then a coach. What was left for Goring with the Islanders? Well, how about a spin on TV? Goring had befriended the MSG Network crew that covered the Islanders during his two seasons behind the bench. He coached in Germany from 2002 to 2005, then returned to the New York area. The network brought in Goring as a studio analyst during the Isles' brief 2007 playoff run, then as a regular on a studio show with Dave Maloney and Ken Daneyko to talk about all three New York–area teams. "That really got me comfortable in front of the camera," Goring said.

When the Islanders were looking for a color analyst to pair with Howie Rose before the 2010–11 season, Goring was a natural fit. Now he's into his 11th season calling games. He worked with Rose and now Brendan Burke, but he also did some games with Jiggs McDonald, throwing back to the days when McDonald was on the mic and Goring was playing.

He was the last man in on the dynasty. Now he's the last one left. Goring was also the last of the dynasty champs to have his number retired, with No. 91 going to the Coliseum rafters on February 29, 2020.

"I had visions of retiring to Myrtle Beach after my Kings playing days were over," he said. "The Islanders, their fans—it's been great. I'm not going anywhere now."

91 Take Your Kids to the Matt Martin Hockey Camp

When Matt Martin returned to the Islanders before the 2018–19 season after two years with the Leafs, it brightened everyone's outlook on the Island. Martin will never be confused with Mathew Barzal, but there's a reason Casey Cizikas, one of Martin's closest friends, dubbed his pal the Mayor of Long Island.

Martin is from Windsor, Ontario, the Canadian city just across the Detroit River from Detroit. He's a Canadian kid who had the chance—when he signed a four-year, $10 million deal with the Leafs in 2016—to simply pick up and say goodbye to the Island.

Instead he not only returned to the Island those two summers he was a Leaf, he still held his youth hockey camp—right at Northwell Health Ice Center, where his old team practiced. Community means a lot to Martin, who married a Long Island girl—but not just any Long Island girl. Sydney Esiason is the closest thing the Island has to sports royalty, given her dad, Boomer, was one of the best football players from the area and is now on radio and TV talking sports most days of the week.

But it's more than just having local ties. The Matt Martin Foundation, started by Martin in 2015, started raising money for causes he cares about, such as the New York Police Department's Widows' and Children's Fund and ACDS, a Long Island–based group that provides support to families of children with Down syndrome.

Martin has a charity poker night before each season for the adults and rounds up just about every one of his teammates to participate. And in the summer, there's the hockey camp for kids ages 6 to 14, who get a chance to get real instruction from local players as well as Martin and some of his teammates.

Many Islanders have community initiatives, of course. Travis Hamonic's days with the Islanders and his commitment to helping kids who'd lost a parent, as he did at age 10, led to Hamonic winning the NHL Foundation Player Award in 2017. John Tavares, Josh Bailey, Anders Lee, and Andrew Ladd have all had community commitments that brought families to games and raised money for causes.

Martin is in it for the long haul on the Island. This will likely be home for him when his playing days are done. There's a reason why he's won the Bob Nystrom Award five times, more than any other player since the award was created in 1990 to honor the player who best exemplifies "leadership, hustle and dedication."

"I love it here, and that didn't change even after I signed in Toronto," Martin said. "To be able to do things like have the hockey camp here during that time, shows what a great organization this always was and is. And when Lou brought me back here, it felt just like coming home."

92 Go to the Hockey Hall of Fame

Just going to a local game at the Islanders' new arena feels like freedom these days, after the way COVID–19 shut down so many aspects of life and recreation through much of 2020 and into 2021.

If there's a road trip in your future and you're an eager Islanders fan, there's no better place than Toronto. Sure, you can let John Tavares know how you feel when the Leafs come to the Island, but the benefit of a trip north is getting to Toronto's best spot for Islanders fans: the Hockey Hall of Fame.

It's there you can see just how special the 1980 to 1983 run was. Not just from the five core players, coach Al Arbour, and general manager Bill Torrey—who are all enshrined there as individuals; there's also the Hall exhibit on Stanley Cup dynasties, replete with a jersey and a Prince of Wales conference trophy. There's also a reminder of the Isles' NHL record 19 consecutive playoff series wins, a record that will certainly stand the test of time.

In total there are eight members of the Hockey Hall of Fame with ties to the Island—nine if you count Lou Lamoriello, who went into the Hall in 2009 in the Builder category nearly a decade before beginning his tenure with the Islanders.

Starting with the dual enshrinement of Denis Potvin and Mike Bossy in 1991, the Hall had a dozen-year run of welcoming

Islanders-affiliated people from the team's heyday. "I don't think anybody really thinks about that until the later years of your career when people start talking about it," Potvin said. "It comes up in the media that your career accomplishments will lead you to the Hall of Fame. That's when you start realizing it. When I went in 1991, there were fewer than 200 people who were in the Hall of Fame, and I started to realize the magnitude of being chosen."

In 1993 Billy Smith went into the Hall. "It just tells you how well you played," Smith said. "It shows what you accomplished, especially when you're in there with all the great guys you played against and respected and now you're actually up there on the wall with them in a building where hundreds of thousands of people

NHL Top 100 players and Hall of Famers (from left to right) Denis Potvin, Billy Smith, Bryan Trottier, Mike Bossy and Pat LaFontaine pose for a portrait in 2017.

go through every year. It's a great feeling. It makes you realize you really accomplished something. It's the best thing that ever happened to me after hockey."

Two years later, in 1995, it was Torrey's turn. The Architect was an easy choice for the Hall committee. So was Arbour the next year. He had officially retired from coaching just two years prior with 739 wins, second all-time to Scotty Bowman (it would go to 740 a little more than a decade later), and there was no doubt he'd end up in the Hall.

In 1997 Bryan Trottier joined the group. The trio of inductees that year was incredible for the league: Trottier, Mario Lemieux, and Glen Sather. Trots was a no-doubter too; the Hall simply had to wait for his epic career—which included two more Cups with Lemieux and the Penguins after his four with the Isles—to end. "Damn, this feels good!" Trottier exclaimed at the end of his induction speech.

It felt good for Clark Gillies to get into the Hall in 2002, well after the core four of the Isles' glory days. That may mean Gillies was a questionable selection since his career numbers weren't what Bossy's or Trottier's were, but Gillies was no less important to that group. "When people would say, 'You've got a shot at getting in the Hall of Fame,' I would go, 'Uh, I don't know.' I never paid much attention to it," he said. "Then I got in. When I found out I just started bawling my eyes out. They were happy tears."

The last Islander to be inducted was Pat LaFontaine, who went into the Hall in 2003. His Islanders tenure was fraught, and he was not likely a Hall of Famer when he was dealt to the Sabres in 1991, but there's no ignoring his seven seasons on the Island as a huge part of his Hall worthiness.

Perhaps there will be more. Maybe Tavares will get in, provided he can win a Cup at some point in his post-Isles career. Barry Trotz, now third all-time in coaching wins, will definitely get his

Hall call someday. Maybe way down the road Mathew Barzal will have a résumé worthy of induction.

For now, provided a road trip is possible, take one to Toronto. Go see the Isles' glory for yourself and see how well it holds up compared to the history of the league.

93 Those Guys Were Islanders?

The Islanders had plenty of star power that they developed themselves, of course—players who became stars after the Isles acquired them. And then some were already stars, came to the Island, and... well, it just didn't work out.

Perhaps the best-known of this second category is Ron Hextall. The feisty goalie won just about every NHL award for a netminder in his rookie season with the Flyers in 1986–87, including the rare Conn Smythe Trophy as playoff MVP despite Philly losing the Stanley Cup Finals to the Oilers in seven games.

Hextall went to the Quebec Nordiques before the 1992–93 season as part of the whopping package for Eric Lindros. After one season there, Islanders GM Don Maloney thought he'd solved his team's goaltending situation by making the deal for Hextall, whom the Nordiques would have left exposed in the expansion draft. "There's no way we would have gotten him except for the unusual circumstances," Maloney said. "It was too good a deal to pass up."

That meant Glenn Healy, who'd stood on his head to get the Islanders past the Penguins to the Eastern Conference final a few months earlier, was a goner in that expansion draft. That didn't sit well with many Isles, even with Hextall's impressive résumé. "I

Five Players You Don't Remember Were Isles

Keith Acton, 1993–94: The 1988 Stanley Cup winner and 15-year NHLer spent season No. 15 with the Isles, picked up off waivers from the Caps in the first month of the season. It wasn't a banner year for Acton at 35; he had nine points and retired after the Isles were swept by the Rangers in the opening round.

Ruslan Fedotenko, 2007–08: The Islanders can't boast many players who won a Stanley Cup before *and* after being on the Island. He scored the Cup-winning goal for the Lightning in 2004, signed as a free agent with the Isles for one solid season for him and a dismal one for the team, then signed with the Penguins the next year—and won his second ring.

Thomas Vanek, 2013–14: He was probably the most productive one-year wonder for the Isles, with 44 points in 47 games after coming over in a deal with the Sabres. Vanek and John Tavares had great chemistry—but not great enough for Vanek, a pending free agent, to accept Garth Snow's seven-year, $50-million offer that February. The Isles dealt Vanek for peanuts at the deadline, and he went to the Eastern Conference final with Montreal before taking fewer years and less money to go to the Wild.

Wendel Clark, 1995–96: The Leafs legend already had a decade in the league and a season in Quebec when he was part of a three-team deal that landed Claude Lemieux in Colorado, Steve Thomas in New Jersey, and Clark on the Island. He spent 58 games in the Fisherman jersey before Mike Milbury put Clark out of his misery, trading him back to the Leafs for a first-round pick that would become Roberto Luongo.

Martin Straka, 1995–96: That same awful 1995–96 season saw the Isles make a major swap, sending Wade Redden to the Senators for Don Beaupre, Bryan Berard, and a 23-year-old wing, Straka, who had been a 30-goal scorer with the Penguins two years earlier. Straka lasted all of 22 games under Milbury before the Isles waived him—and the Panthers claimed Straka on their way to a Cup Finals appearance. Straka played a dozen more years, mostly with Mario Lemieux and Jaromir Jagr back in Pittsburgh, and probably wondered what the hell happened with those seven weeks on the Island.

don't think people understand how big a part of the team Glenn was," Pat Flatley said. "That move definitely hurt us."

Hextall was pretty solid in the regular season, with Al Arbour riding him to 60 starts—the first time in team history to that point a goalie had made so many starts. The Islanders were a .500 team most of the year, but Hextall battled, figuratively and literally—his 52 penalty minutes that season were a team record for goalies, even outdoing Billy Smith in his heyday.

Jamie McLennan, Hextall's rookie backup, told TSN a few years back about a day in St. Louis when Hextall, showing off a brand-new suit, had a waiter spill food on him at lunch. "All I remember is him leaning over and saying, 'You better be ready tonight because I'm going to kill somebody,'" McLennan said. Sure enough, Hextall gave up three goals in the first 10 minutes and chased Petr Nedved around the ice on his way to the bench.

Hextall's downfall was the playoffs, which the Islanders managed to squeak into. They finished with 84 points, 28 behind the league-leading Rangers, their first-round opponent. And it was as bad as feared. Worse, maybe.

Hextall heard the derisive chants of his name in Madison Square Garden as he gave up six goals in fewer than two periods before being pulled. McLennan started Game 2, and the result was another 6–0 shelling. Hextall played Games 3 and 4, which were 5–2 and 5–1—a sweep with the sort of lopsided numbers the Isles used to hang on first-round opponents 15 years earlier.

Maloney ended the Hextall experiment the following September, sending the goalie back to his old home in Philadelphia for Tommy Soderstrom. And Hextall was reborn, leading the Flyers to a conference final in 1995 and the Stanley Cup Finals in 1997.

94 Gillies and Bourne, Together Forever

Clark Gillies marvels at his 50-year connection to Bob Bourne. "I can't shake the guy," Gillies joked last year. The remarkable connection between two of the four-time Islanders Cup champions has to be read to be believed.

Before either of them had ever heard of Long Island, they were already teammates. And not even in a hockey rink. Gillies was from Moose Jaw, Saskatchewan; Bourne was from tiny Kindersley, about a four-hour drive northwest. They played against each other in amateur hockey in Saskatchewan, but both were also good enough baseball players to be invited to Houston Astros training camp in 1972.

They ended up playing rookie ball in Covington, Virginia, two of the three Canadians on the squad. "We both played first base," Bourne said. "We basically platooned at first—I'm a lefty and Clarkie's a righty. And it pissed me off because I never got to hit against lefties; I was terrible at it. But we were a couple of kids from the farm down there and we became good friends."

Two years later both had returned to the rink and were drafted in the 1974 NHL Draft—Gillies went fourth overall to the Islanders and Bourne went No. 38 to the Kansas City Scouts, who turned right around and traded him to the Islanders two months later.

The old friends were together once more and became neighbors in Dix Hills. "We lived next door to each other all the years we were on the Island, in a little cul-de-sac," Gillies said. "Our house was first to the left and Bournie's was second. I'd just step out the back and yell over, 'Bournie, beers! Here or there?' Or I'd chip some golf balls down to his yard and he'd chip them back."

Gillies and his wife, Pam, were sources of support for Bourne and his then-wife, Janice, when the Bournes' first child, Jeffrey, was born with spina bifida in November 1979. Bob missed 10 days of that season while he and Janice switched off sleeping at the hospital. "There was a lot of stress for him and Janice," Gillies said. "Everyone has to make sacrifices with family when you're a pro athlete, but they dealt with more than their share."

Gillies and Bourne came into the NHL together, won four Cups together, and exited the Islanders on the same day: October 6, 1986. The preseason waiver draft arrived and Bill Torrey left both his longtime wingers exposed, with the Sabres claiming Gillies and the Kings claiming Bourne. Both of them lasted only two more seasons in the NHL before retiring—again, together.

Now we get to the best part of this lifelong friendship. When the Islanders inducted Bourne into the team Hall of Fame during the 2006–07 season, Bob had his son Justin with him. Justin was a senior at Alaska-Anchorage at the time, about to embark on a brief pro career that took him through Bridgeport for a couple months in 2007–08.

The Gillies were there, of course, with their three daughters. Brianna, their youngest, was there that night—she and Justin knew each other as toddlers when their dads were Islanders but hadn't seen one another since. Numbers were exchanged. And in 2011 Justin Bourne and Brianna Gillies were married—on Long Island, naturally—making Clark and Bob extended family after 40 years of friendship.

Justin and Brianna have two kids and live in Toronto. So the old friends, Gillies and Bourne, are now fellow granddads.

"It's a pretty crazy story," Gillies said.

95 First-Round Draft Misses

The Islanders' draft history has some amazing highs and some disappointing lows. There's Denis Potvin and then there's Dave Chyzowski. There's Pat LaFontaine and then there's Scott Sissons. For every John Tavares, there is a Branislav Mezei.

You can't hit on every draft, even the ones when the Islanders have picked in the top five—something that's happened often over some of the leaner years in recent memory. So we compiled some of the first-round misses, in case you were starting to feel good about your Islanders memories.

Duncan MacPherson, 20th overall, 1984: From the day in June 1972 when Bill Torrey made Billy Harris the first-ever Islanders draft pick, the draft hits just kept on coming in the first round: Potvin, Gillies, Bossy, the Sutters, Flatley, LaFontaine. It didn't matter where the Isles picked in the first round—usually at the end—Torrey and Jim Devellano, his first head scout, found gold almost every year.

MacPherson's selection ended that run, and it was simply a sad, tragic tale. The big defenseman out of Saskatoon wasn't taken over anyone particularly stunning at the end of the 1984 first round, and the Islanders did get productive defenseman Jeff Norton in the third round and future Game 7 OT legend David Volek in the 10th round, but MacPherson simply didn't pan out and was out of hockey by 1989 after four minor-league seasons.

Then tragedy: MacPherson was on his way to play in the newly formed English Hockey League for a team in Dundee, Scotland, when he detoured to the Austrian Alps to see an old friend and hike. He was never seen alive again. His body thawed out of the ice 14 years later, the apparent victim of an accident with a snowmaking machine and an unforgivable cover-up by the ski mountain operator.

Dean Chynoweth, 13ᵗʰ overall, 1987: Chynoweth was slowed by injuries throughout eight seasons in the organization. He's also one of a very few Islanders draft picks who played and coached for the team, as he was an assistant coach with Scott Gordon and Jack Capuano from 2009 to 2012.

Dave Chyzowski, 2ⁿᵈ overall, 1989: Probably the biggest draft miss of the Torrey era. Chyzowski had the right profile to be a No. 2 pick; he just never panned out after playing 34 games with the Isles as a 19-year-old. Future Isles captain Bill Guerin went fifth to the Devils.

Scott Sissons, 6ᵗʰ overall, 1990: The merciful end to a string of Torrey misfires. The Islanders took Sissons right after the Penguins took some Czech kid named Jaromir Jagr. Of the top eight picks in that talented draft, seven played more than 900 NHL games. Sissons played two.

Brett Lindros, 9ᵗʰ overall, 1994: In hindsight, this was a very *meh* first round; the best player to come out of it was Ryan Smyth—taken three picks earlier by the Oilers—a guy who'd end up an Islander 13 years later for a brief but compelling stretch.

GM Don Maloney doesn't have a lot of legendary quotes attached to his Islanders tenure, but the one that will always stay is Maloney, perhaps tongue-in-cheek, remarking that the Isles taking already-a-star Eric Lindros's kid brother gave the Isles "the better brother" between the two. The hard-hitting, light-scoring younger Lindros had concussion issues that ended his hockey career after two seasons. Eric went to the Hall of Fame.

Ryan O'Marra, 15ᵗʰ overall, 2005: One of Mike Milbury's final drafts was the least productive draft in team history that included a first-rounder. The Isles picks played a combined 66 NHL games, and O'Marra got none of his 33 with the Islanders, having been dealt away by Garth Snow in the Ryan Smyth deal in 2007.

Josh Ho-Sang, 28th overall, 2014: The talented but mercurial Ho-Sang was a lightning rod entering this draft, with some teams unwilling to take him at all. Snow traded the 35th and 57th picks to Tampa to move into the first round and select Ho-Sang, welcoming his new winger with these classic words to TSN on the draft floor: "He'll fit right in; they shit on me too."

Perhaps the best thing to come out of this pick was the T-shirt that fan site Lighthouse Hockey had printed up to commemorate Snow's words. Ho-Sang had so many ups and downs through two GMs and three coaches but never could catch on in the NHL despite world-class talent.

96 Two Great Seasons and Two Near Misses in 2015 and 2016

It's easy to look back at the 2014–15 and 2015–16 seasons now and be a little dismissive of those two Jack Capuano–coached teams' place in Isles history.

The Isles did make the playoffs both seasons, and that qualifies as an accomplishment in the last 30 years. They won a playoff round in 2016 for the first time in 23 years, another feather in those teams' caps. And they had at least 100 points both years, something that had happened only once since 1978–79. "Those were good teams," Johnny Boychuk said. "I'm not talking good relative to some other Islander teams. We were just good."

And so, so close to doing something *great* both years. Take the last day of the 2014–15 regular season: The Isles stumbled a bit, going 4–7–2 in the 13 games heading into the finale against the Blue Jackets at the Coliseum. A win would have given the Isles home ice against the Caps in their first-round playoff series. The

Isles opened up a 3–1 lead on the long-since-eliminated Jackets early in the third, saw Columbus come back and tie it, then took the lead back on Nikolay Kulemin's goal with 4:24 to play. Home ice, here we come!

But the Jackets tied it with 1:35 left, then tied up the shootout on the last attempt of the first round of three shots apiece. Columbus pulled out the shootout in the fourth round, dropping the Isles into a tie with Washington at 101 points, but the Isles lost the tiebreaker due to more regulation and overtime wins by the Caps. Oh, and John Tavares lost the Art Ross Trophy as the league's top scorer the same night after a late assist by Dallas's Jamie Benn.

The first-round series against the Caps was tight, but Game 7 was a lopsided affair in D.C. Only Jaroslav Halak's heroics kept it close into the third, when Evgeny Kuznetsov's goal with 7:18 left snapped a 1–1 tie and sent the Isles to defeat. They had lost defenseman Travis Hamonic to injury on the final weekend of the season, then Lubo Visnovsky and Calvin de Haan in the series; that Game 7 featured Matt Donovan and rookie Scott Mayfield.

It was also a real what-if: Had the Isles simply taken care of business in Game 6 that Game 7 would have been at the Coliseum, which was in its final season of existence (or so we all thought at the time). The outcome could have been much different.

Fast-forward a year and the Islanders had finally broken through to the second round on Tavares's Game 6 double-OT winner to defeat the Panthers. Next up was the Lightning, and the Isles split the first two games in Tampa, bringing it back to a raucous Barclays Center (no, really, it was) for Games 3 and 4.

In Game 3 the Islanders had a 4–3 lead inside of a minute to go. Nikita Kucherov found space in the slot and snapped one past Thomas Greiss to tie the game and send it to overtime; no worries there, as the Isles had won three of their four games over the Panthers in OT.

Tampa's Brian Boyle came up high on Thomas Hickey at the Islanders blue line early in overtime, catching Hickey in the head. Hickey was down and a bit dazed as the puck went into the Islanders zone. No whistle blew, and Boyle scooped up a loose puck at Greiss's left and tucked it in, standing in a spot Hickey would have occupied.

The Isles were livid, but nothing could be done. In Game 4 the Islanders again had a one-goal lead into the third period, and again Kucherov pulled the Lightning even, this time with 12:12 to play. Again it went to OT, and this one lasted just 1:34, with Jason Garrison blasting one by Greiss to quickly end it.

The Isles folded in Game 5, and that was that. Looking back now, it may have seemed like a lopsided series, but the Isles were 32 seconds away from a series lead and had another chance for a win in Game 4.

"I'm proud of how those teams played," Capuano said. "The playoffs, especially those close games, they can go either way. You need a little luck in the playoffs to go with good execution, and we fell a little short both times."

97 Check Out the Heals and Flats Show

You've made it this far in our list, so you know that the period from about 1987 to 2001 was pretty dark as far as Islanders success went. There were plenty of characters on every Islanders team, but the character side comes through a bit more when you're not winning and looking for ways to keep sane.

That's how the *Heals and Flats* show was born. Kevin Meininger was the producer of the Islanders telecasts on SportsChannel (MSG

Network's forerunner), and the broadcast crew traveled with the team. It was there, on flights and buses, where Meininger saw he could make some memorable television with a couple of the Islanders veterans. "I think Kevin just saw us chirping at each other all the time and thought we could get a few laughs on the game broadcasts," Patrick Flatley said.

Flatley was the Islanders' captain at the time, into his eighth season with the Isles. Glenn Healy had signed on prior to the 1989–90 season after three years with the Kings—he'd been pushed aside in Los Angeles by Kelly Hrudey, who went from the struggling Islanders to Wayne Gretzky's playhouse the season before.

Flatley and Healy are both from Toronto and loved cracking wise with one another and just about everyone else. There are a few of the brief between-periods episodes of *Heals and Flats* floating around YouTube, especially since the Islanders have brought them out during games in recent seasons. On the episodes, Flatley and Healy come across as not-so-distant cousins of Bob and Doug McKenzie, the very Canadian brothers portrayed by Rick Moranis and Dave Thomas in the 1980s on Toronto-based *SCTV*.

And Flatley and Healy tried to look the part. They didn't have the parkas and toques of the McKenzie brothers, but they looked a bit ridiculous wearing very fashionable (for the early 1990s, mind you) shirts with SportsChannel logos pinned quite awkwardly to their chests.

The topics were also very Canadian: A 1991 episode breaks down the inherent greatness of the Canadian Football League compared to the NFL—"or Not For Long," Flatley said, because the CFL was poised for an American takeover.

Another episode from 1992 shows Healy describing the geography of Canada, with Vancouver being "so beautiful it belongs in the east" and calling Alberta, Saskatchewan, and Manitoba "filler until you get to the king province, Ontario."

Their deadpan deliveries definitely hammer home that these two could be genuinely funny on camera. Healy went on to have a post-playing broadcast career before settling into his current role as director of the NHL Alumni Association. Flatley is back in Toronto, doing some day trading and enjoying retirement. And, as Flatley put it, trying to get people not to check out his brief TV comedy career. "Heals and I have been trying to keep 'em hidden—we don't want them out in public," he said. "We talked about it; it's just one of those weird things. People found some familiarity in two buddies sitting around talking and giving each other crap—it was a daily occurrence with us. Everybody watching the show had a friend like that, I guess."

98 Justin Johnson's Amazing Weekend

The Islanders have had more than their share of players who made a brief appearance for them—one or two or a handful of games—and then disappeared into the hockey ether. None of them can match what Justin Johnson accomplished in his only weekend in the NHL.

It was as if your average beer-leaguer got called up for the final two games of 2013–14—yet another dismal Islanders season—as long as that beer-leaguer was a nine-year pro who'd taken mixed martial arts lessons every off-season since he was in college.

Johnson was 32. He'd spent the year in Bridgeport doing what he'd done for his entire pro career—which had taken him from his hometown of Anchorage to Boise, Salt Lake City, Cincinnati, and Manchester, New Hampshire: protecting his teammates and fighting whenever called upon.

"Whether helping guys slow down a bit off the ice, speeding up a bit on the ice, recognizing how they can stick and get to the next level, that's a whole other education, and I got to be part of that for some guys," Johnson told the *Athletic* last year. "I feel like I got a chance to help people, and it wasn't always with my fists. I did more for guys not fighting than fighting. Fighting got me credibility; I'd stick up for people and do things some people wouldn't. But I got to affect guys because they knew I cared about them. I wasn't their coach, their dad, their agent. Maybe they felt they were competing with some of their younger teammates for ice time, for a call-up, and I don't think many guys felt that with me.

"I couldn't tell them how to be a world-class hockey player. But maybe I could help them get through the tribulations of trying to be one."

Doing that for his only season in the Islanders organization earned Johnson a call-up for the final weekend of 2013–14, his first taste of the NHL. A month shy of 33, there almost certainly wouldn't be another chance. So he had to make his mark the best way he knew how: fighting an NHL heavyweight.

His first game was in New Jersey. Garth Snow pulled Johnson aside before that NHL debut to offer some firm advice. "He told me, 'Just go play tonight, take it all in,'" Johnson said. "He had tremendous respect for Mr. [Lou] Lamoriello; the Devils had Marty Brodeur, Patrik Elias, Jaromir Jagr. Garth wanted no silliness that night. But in Buffalo, 'Do what you do.'"

In Buffalo, for Johnson that meant a fight with John Scott. The 6'8" Scott was the reigning NHL enforcer, a rangy guy with a funny personality who never lost fights. For the 6'1" Johnson, it was a must.

Johnson and Scott had a chat near the red line during warm-ups that night. Scott told Johnson, "My coach likes you too much for me to beat you up." Ted Nolan, the former Islanders coach whose son, Jordan, was a teammate of Johnson's in the Kings farm system, advised Johnson against fighting Scott too. "He didn't think it would be good for me," Johnson recalled.

That didn't deter him. On his first shift, Johnson saw Scott hop the boards and just called the big Sabre's name out. They dropped the gloves. Johnson tried to get in tight, fending off a couple of big swings. Then Johnson connected: A big left hand that sent Scott to the ice, laughing.

In his retirement piece for the *Players Tribune* in 2016, Scott acknowledged that one moment, his only lost fight in the NHL: "Congratulations, Justin Johnson. You caught me with the left hook. What can I say? Good job."

Travis Hamonic came up to Johnson as he skated to the penalty box. "You're a legend!" Hamonic yelled.

Johnson flew back with the Islanders after the game—he asked the flight attendant on the team charter to wrap up his postgame meal, earning a few chirps—and that was it for him in the organization. One more season in the ECHL and he was done, retiring back to Anchorage to work in medical sales.

But he made it to the show and made it count. It was a meaningless season for a lot of Islanders and their fans in 2013–14, but it meant everything to Justin Johnson.

"That was the culmination," Johnson said of his night in Buffalo. "I was lucky it got to see the light of day. I can say it worked out…. Growing up you get cut, don't make teams, you go through all the juvenile emotions—*Maybe I'm not good enough to be friends with my friends because they made the team*, things like that.

"There's the awkwardness at times of being a Black hockey player. I think I was treated differently but in a good way. I had the best of both worlds. The part of town I was from is very diverse, and then just how I evolved and matured and all the people I've been around…hockey brought these guys into my life, and I'm better for it. To send them a text now and get one back from guys who are in the NHL, the AHL, that makes me happy.

"When you get to do something and be appreciated for it, man, there isn't anything better in life. And I had that. Having that time in hockey, with the Islanders, it set me up for the rest of my life."

99 The Islanders Send the Coliseum Out in Style

Anthony Beauvillier was right in the middle of it all on the night of June 23, 2021.

Right there to pounce on a pass and snap a shot past Lightning goalie Andrey Vasilevskiy 68 seconds into overtime of Game 6 of the NHL semifinals.

Right there with an epic celebration on the Nassau Coliseum ice, mobbed by his teammates as the Islanders finished off a rally from 2–0 down to send the semifinal to a Game 7.

And right there as the Coliseum crowd, officially listed at 12,978—about 1,000 less than capacity due to COVID-19 protocols—went bonkers. Half-empty cans of beer littered the ice, the sort of celebration more fitting for an end-of-semester kegger when you know you're not renewing the lease on the off-campus house and don't care if you get the deposit back.

"Going into overtime the building smelled like cigarettes," Beauvillier said. "Now it smells like beers."

The 2021 season didn't end with the first Stanley Cup Final games in the Coliseum in 37 years, but it did close out the old place on an amazing high note. After the team's surprising run to the conference final in the 2020 playoff bubble, where the Isles fell to the Lightning in overtime of Game 6, the 2021 season started with a confident Islanders team playing in a difficult, makeshift division and in front of no fans, on the Island or elsewhere.

That the Isles under Barry Trotz did what they could to make the empty Coliseum a difficult place to play once more, going 21–4–3 at home in the shortened 56-game season, made the arrival of the playoffs and the welcoming of at least a few thousand fans for the postseason all the more thrilling.

"Just a genuine feeling of honesty in the building, it reflects the fan base and the population really well," Cal Clutterbuck said of the Coliseum crowd. "As a player, you can feel it."

The Islanders started strong in the pandemic-inflected 2021 season, as they've done now for three years running under Trotz. A nine-game win streak in early March vaulted them into a comfortable playoff spot in the one-year-only East Division, though the seventh win of that streak came at a huge cost: Anders Lee suffered a torn ACL against the Devils, ending his season halfway through.

Lou Lamoriello was aggressive again at the trade deadline, picking up Kyle Palmieri and Travis Zajac from the Devils for a first-round pick. Neither acquisition had much impact down the stretch, but that's not why the wily old GM got them.

Game 1 of the playoffs was against the Penguins. It was Palmieri, born in Smithtown and the first ever Long Islander to play a playoff game for the local pro team, who stepped to the fore, scoring twice—including the overtime winner to set the Isles off and running.

Ilya Sorokin, a 2014 Garth Snow draft pick who spent seven seasons as one of the top goalies in the world in his native Russia, finally got his chance to shine in 2021 and especially against the Penguins in the first round. Semyon Varlamov sat out Game 1 with a minor knee issue, then came back and lost Games 2 and 3.

Sorokin went back in net and stole Game 5, a double-OT affair ended by Josh Bailey. And back to the Coliseum for a clinching Game 6 in front of 9,000 fans, up from 6,800 at Game 4.

In the second round against the Bruins, more heroics from up and down the lineup: Casey Cizikas' first playoff goal in six years was the overtime winner in Game 2 in Boston before a packed house; Varlamov, back in net and back in command, helped steal Game 5 to give the Isles a series lead.

Game 6 of that series in the Coliseum was up to 12,000 fans and the building went wild in a 6–2 thumping, sending the Islanders back to the playoff final four in consecutive seasons for the first time since 1983–84.

And again it was Tampa waiting. The Lightning won the 2020 Stanley Cup after getting by the Islanders and they had to go through Trotz and the Isles once more, this time in front of fans.

The Coliseum crowd did its part. Down 2–1 in the series for Game 4 on the Island, a 3–2 win closed on one of the more jaw-dropping finishes to a playoff game in recent memory: Ryan Pulock down on one knee in the crease to stop Ryan McDonagh's backhand just seconds before the final horn, a save for the ages.

After an 8-0 thrashing by Tampa in Game 5, the Islanders had to dig deep again at home. Plenty of fans were in the Coliseum parking lot by noon for an 8:00 PM puck drop. From the years of trying and failing to upgrade the place to the move to Brooklyn and back, to the decades of mediocrity and to a pandemic that took so much from everyone, there was a nervous energy racing around the place that June night.

If it was the last game there, win or lose, the fans weren't going to let it pass quietly. Same with the Islanders. Mathew Barzal set up Jordan Eberle to make it 2–1, then Scott Mayfield deep in the third to tie it.

Then it was Beauvillier. And beers.

"This is one of those moments," Trotz said.

"It gives me chills just thinking about it all," Pulock said.

The Isles fell short, a 1–0 Game 7 loss in Tampa. The sting carried over into 2021–22, but the Coliseum closed on a raucous high note.

"There's a lot of buildings in this league that are loud, but this one has a different tone to it," Clutterbuck said. "We really love it and we're looking forward to that sound being transported a couple miles down the road next year."

100 The Unsung Heroes of the 2000s

If you're an Islanders fan, you can always remember some players who were outside the core who were either colorful characters who got you through the dark 1990s or mid-2000s or, in rare instances, players who had an impact on the few seasons of success.

The stars and mainstays can't be overlooked, of course. The 2001–02 Islanders would not have made the playoffs without Alexei Yashin, Michael Peca, Mark Parrish, Adrian Aucoin, or Chris Osgood. The 2015–16 Islanders wouldn't have achieved anything without John Tavares, Kyle Okposo, and Frans Nielsen, or Nick Leddy, Johnny Boychuk, and Thomas Greiss.

But every playoff run of the last 20 years has had one or two of those guys—journeymen, fringe players—who came through at just the right time. In the 2002 playoffs, it was Kip Miller. He was 32 and playing in the AHL in Grand Rapids when the Islanders signed him in January, midway through the 2001–02 season. He'd already had two previous stints with the Islanders organization, so Mike Milbury knew him well; he was also someone who had a decent track record in limited NHL time, having scored 19 goals with the Penguins just three years earlier.

"I came in with no expectations," Miller told *Newsday*. "[I would] Just play hard and see how it went. I didn't expect it to go this good. But then again, I didn't think it couldn't."

He had 7 goals and 17 assists in 37 regular-season games, filling a solid power-play role alongside the Yashins and Parrishes. But in that grueling, nasty, seven-game series against the Leafs, Miller was always in the right spot. He didn't do much the first three games, with only one shot on goal and no points. But he kick-started the furious Game 4 rally in the third with a power-play goal to tie that game 2–2 with 6:44 to play; Miller scored in each of the remaining three games, including the eventual Game 6 winner in the third and another third-period goal in Game 7 that brought the Isles within 3–2.

Miller led the Isles in goal scoring that series, a fact that's easy to forget. He tied Alex Mogilny for the series lead in goals. He played two more pro seasons after that, two full ones with the Caps, so he earned himself a regular NHL paycheck with that clutch performance.

In the 2016 playoffs, there was Tavares—scoring the biggest goal in 23 years of Islanders playoff disappointment. His double-overtime winner in the Barclays Center in Game 6 against the Panthers capped a dominating series. And don't forget his tying goal with just more than a minute left in regulation.

But the Islanders needed two other clutch moments in OT just to get there. Enter Thomas Hickey and Alan Quine. Hickey has a real track record with the Isles, having been claimed off waivers from the Kings before the start of the lockout-shortened 2013 season and quickly working his way into a mainstay role.

Only 11 defensemen have played more games for the Islanders than Hickey, who never could quite crack the Kings roster after being the fourth overall pick in 2007. He's had a knack for timely goals—5 of his 22 career regular-season goals are overtime winners. And in Game 3 against the Panthers, he came through in extra time again. Diving down the slot into an open space behind Jaromir Jagr to deposit a Brock Nelson feed that gave the Isles a 2–1 series lead, it's Hickey's only playoff goal in his career. "He's not the biggest guy in the world," Jack Capuano said, "but he plays big."

In Game 5 the Isles dug even deeper to find a hero. Quine had been toiling away in Bridgeport for three seasons when he got his first call-up on the final weekend of the 2015–16 season. Capuano rested most of his regulars for those two games—not just to save them for the playoffs but also to jockey the Isles into a wild-card spot so they could play the Panthers rather than the Penguins in the opening round.

Quine scored a goal and got to stick around. Next thing you know, Capuano has him in the lineup for Game 1 of the playoffs and on the second power-play unit. That unit produced the first of the Isles' two double-OT goals. Down in Florida in a wild Game 5 that was 1–1 entering OT, Greiss denied an overtime penalty shot by Aleksander Barkov to keep the game going. In the second overtime, the Isles got two power plays; on the second one, Hickey and Marek Zidlicky sent the puck along the blue line and over to Quine, who one-timed a blast behind Roberto Luongo to get the Isles to the brink of advancing.

Like Hickey, it's Quine's only playoff goal. "When you've got guys like Quiner scoring big goals for us, it's a great feeling," Calvin de Haan said after the winner. Quine earned himself a regular spot with the Isles the following season and has bounced between the NHL and AHL with a couple organizations since.

You can always remember the big names and their big moments. It's nice, though—especially in an organization that's become an underdog in the last couple decades—to remember the lunch-pail guys and the moments when they stood tall.

Acknowledgments

Bill Ames first reached out to me in September 2020 to ask about contributing an Islanders book to the *100 Things* series, and the result is here. Bill and the Triumph team put a lot of faith in me to put this together, and I hope I rewarded them well. I certainly appreciate Bill taking that first step.

Jeff Fedotin and Laine Morreau, my editors on this project, provided excellent guidance and a steady hand during the months of interviewing, researching, and writing. That this whole thing reads as well as it does owes a lot more to Jeff and Laine than you know, and I'm thankful, as always, to have great editors making me look good.

I wouldn't have even been able to start down the road with this book were it not for an amazing team at the *Athletic*. Adam Hansmann, Alex Mather, and Paul Fichtenbaum brought me on board back in 2018, and it's been the most fulfilling stretch of my career, not least of all because I have the freedom to work on a project such as this one. And I owe a huge debt to my direct editors for the majority of my time there—Chris Strauss and Hannah Witham are two of the best we have.

And of course, my home team means the world to me, and that was especially true during my work on this book. My wife, Beth, juggles her own work with our family time, and I had a little less of that to give during the months of putting this book together, even during the long stretch of pandemic time when we had to keep our kids entertained within the confines of our house.

Talking with many former Islanders for this project was a real delight. I'd talked to many of them before over the years, but hearing them share stories they hadn't told for a long time was such a pleasure. Denis Potvin, Bob Nystrom, Ken Morrow, Bryan

Trottier, Glenn Resch, Bob Bourne, Clark Gillies, Butch Goring, Brent Sutter, Pat LaFontaine, Pat Flatley, Kelly Hrudey, Tom Fitzgerald, Bryan McCabe, Scott Lachance, Eric Cairns, Steve Webb, Mark Parrish, Rick DiPietro, Frans Nielsen, Bill Guerin, Colin McDonald, Josh Bailey, Johnny Boychuk, and Anders Lee all gave their time and their insight from their Islanders days.

Special thanks to Potvin, who graciously agreed to write the foreword and give this project a true air of credibility with Islanders fans—the same way he did on the ice for 15 seasons, overseeing the transformation of the team from expansion mess to dynasty.

Peter Laviolette and Jack Capuano gave their time as well, two Islanders coaches who presided over very different tenures and had lots of great stories to tell. The same for Garth Snow, the former Islanders player and GM who never much liked speaking to the media when he was in charge but has great behind-the-scenes war stories to tell.

My thanks to Kimber Auerbach of the Islanders for facilitating many of those conversations.

I must be brutally honest here for a moment: I hated the sound of Jiggs McDonald's voice through my television as a kid, because as a young Rangers fan growing up 10 blocks from Madison Square Garden, hearing Jiggs meant hearing the sound of my team's doom most nights.

Hearing Jiggs's voice now and for the last decade of leaning on him for great stories and insight is so different and so wonderful. He's truly one of the best people I've met in this business and, as always, he gave of his time and his deep well of memories here.

The same is true for Howie Rose, who didn't get to call many of the great Islanders games but had so many stories to share about the insanity of the 1990s and 2000s. Islanders fans are lucky to have had two great men and great voices as the narrators for 36 years of broadcasts.

I owe a huge debt personally and professionally to my old friend Stan Fischler, who hired me as a high school intern at 17 and gave me a foundation in reporting I still lean on. He's the true Islanders historian, and so much of my research for this book brought me to Stan's work. The only time my name has appeared in a book before was in the acknowledgments of a few of Stan's hockey books that I was fortunate enough to work on, so I'm proud to return the favor here.

My research also allowed me to revisit articles from many familiar names and Islanders fans alike, reporters who covered the team faithfully through the good and not-so-good years: Gerry Eskenazi, Robin Finn, George Vecsey, Jason Diamos, my *Athletic* colleague Tarik El-Bashir, Alan Hahn, Peter Botte, Pat Calabria, Mark Herrmann, and Andrew Gross, to name a few whose pieces helped put this puzzle together.

And of course, you Islanders fans are the final piece of that puzzle. From all the interactions at various arenas over the years, the random encounters in airports or even upstate Pizza Huts, to countless emails and direct messages, you've shown how much you care about this team. I hope I was able to return that care with a work you'll enjoy reading. I know I had fun writing it. Thanks.